UNLIKELY PARTNERS

UNLIKELY
Partners

Philanthropic Foundations
and the Labor Movement

RICHARD MAGAT

WITHDRAWN

ILR Press *an imprint of*
Cornell University Press
Ithaca and London

First published 1999 by Cornell University Press.

Printed in the United States of America.

Library of Congress Cataloging-in-Publication Data

Magat, Richard.
Unlikely partners : philanthropic foundations and the labor movement / Richard Magat.
   p. cm.
Includes bibliographical references and index.
ISBN 0-8014-3552-8 (cloth : alk. paper)
1. Labor movement—Research—United States—Finance. 2. Endowment of research—
United States. 3. Labor movement—United States—History—20th century.
4. Endowments—United States—History—20th century. I. Title.
HD4824.5.U5M34 1998
361.7'6'0973—dc21   98-28132

Contents

Preface

A year or so after I began research on connections between philanthropic foundations and the labor movement, I bought at a flea market the twentieth edition of the D.A.R. *Manual for Citizenship* (published by the National Society, Daughters of the American Revolution, in 1941, two years after the D.A.R. refused to permit the black singer Marian Anderson to give a concert in Constitution Hall in Washington). In a chapter called "What the Constitution Does for the Citizen" is the following (pp. 17–18):

> The workingman enjoys the right of private property when he may own his tools and his savings . . . when he may put his earnings into a home and own it . . . when he may put his earnings into a little shop and own that . . . put the earnings of his shop into Government Bonds and own them. Thus the right of private property enables the workingman to become not only an employer, but also a bondholder—a capitalist with money to invest. In this way American industry has been built up. It is composed of workingmen who are on the different rungs of the ladder of prosperity. Those at the top are workingmen whom the Constitution enabled to climb by protecting them when they were at the bottom. . . . Those at the bottom . . . may go as high as their brains and hard work and good character will carry them. . . . [B]ut the Constitution does not supply an elevator to lift the lazy or incompetent to prosperity along with the industrious and skillful. . . . Without the workingman, without the employer, without those who have saved their earnings and so become capitalists, the nation could not be run,

nor could it protect its citizens from crime, riots or revolutions, nor carry
on war to defend itself from invasion and conquest, and all from irretriev-
able disaster.

This paean to the vistas of opportunity open to American workers seemed
to me a tragicomic backdrop to what I knew of the thousands of miners who
struck in 1913 against a Colorado coal company controlled by the Rockefeller family, a major event in the history of relations between foundations
and unions. The mineworkers were overwhelmingly the immigrant stock at
whom such encomiums of the American way have long been aimed.[1] They
lived under wretched conditions: primitive housing, safety and health hazards, the company store, pay in scrip, long hours. Their attempt to unionize
was met by state militia and federal troops. The bitter struggle led to the
killing of strikers and their families in what became known as the Ludlow
Massacre, and the employment of strikebreakers finally defeated the miners'
union. Into this dreadful affair stepped the Rockefeller Foundation.

The fact that I wrote a review of a book about this struggle led to my research.[2] By then I had retired from active service in the foundation community, where I had spent the greater part of my working life. My direct ac-
quaintance with the labor movement was more limited—brief membership
in two unions.[3]

When I remarked that a search through databases disclosed no studies of relations between organized labor and foundations, an academic friend replied,
"There's no research because there's no there there. Organized labor relations with foundations? An oxymoron." But there is a there there, and this
book provides the evidence.

In gathering that evidence as an independent scholar, I have been especially fortunate in obtaining the help of labor historians and other social scientists, colleagues in the foundation community, and representatives of organized labor. Some two hundred men and women kindly spent time in
interviews and correspondence with me.

My first encounter on this journey was with the distinguished labor historian David Montgomery. Although he was not familiar with the subject, he
raised important points of context. Montgomery provides an inspiration not
only as a scholar but also because he was an industrial worker before he became a historian (he holds a chair at Yale named after Henry Farnam, a distinguished Yale economist who, early in the century, was a key figure in the
American Association for Labor Legislation and an adviser to the first major
foundation-supported research on labor). Montgomery put me onto the
Garland Fund, a maverick radical foundation, one of the very few ever to
have directly funded unionism, by referring me to a doctoral dissertation

about the fund that I might never have found otherwise, since neither "union," "labor," nor "foundation" appears in the title. Written in 1987 at the University of Rochester and since revised for publication, it is an absorbing history of a forgotten corner of foundation history, and I was fortunate in developing a valued friendship with its author, Gloria Garrett Samson.[4]

While doing this research I was privileged to be a Visiting Fellow at Yale University in the Program on Non-Profit Organizations (PONPO), whose founder, John Simon, I had known for many years. I attended seminars there and gave two on this research, early on and at the end. I am grateful to Yale/PONPO for the intellectual stimulus these contacts provided and to Bradford Gray, former director, for initial financial support for my research. I also appreciate grants from the Aspen Institute Nonprofit Sector Research Fund, the Bauman Foundation, New World Foundation, and the German Marshall Fund of the United States, which enabled me to present a paper in Hungary at the first conference of the International Society for Third Sector Research.

I have drawn inspiration, to say nothing of wise advice, from a long-time friend and hero, Robert H. Bremner, the preeminent scholar of American philanthropy, a man of wisdom, grace, and modesty. I am deeply indebted to Peter Dobkin Hall of Yale for his encouragement and tough-love criticism. I am also pleased to acknowledge assistance from former colleagues at the Ford Foundation—Mitchell Sviridoff, Terrance Keenan, Robert Schrank, and Basil Whiting; from friends and colleagues from other foundations who responded to my questionnaire, especially Kirke Wilson, one of the few foundation officers to have worked in the labor movement; from labor officials such as Thomas Donahue, Andrew Stern, Richard Bensinger, and Joseph Uehlein and the union leaders who responded to another questionnaire; and from Guy Alchon, Ann Bastian, Heather Booth, Emmett Carson, Leslie Dunbar, David Farber, Martin Halpern, David Hammack, Richard Healey, Meg Jacobs, Craig Jenkins, Stanley Katz, Connie Kopelov, Lance Lindblom, Peter Martinez, Robert McKersie, William McKersie, Brigid O'Farrell, Ronald Schatz, Tripp Somerville, John H. Stanfield, Oona Sullivan, Tani Takagi, Emory Via, and Andrew Workman. Richard Mittenthal and Joseph Stillman were generous in allowing me facilities at the Conservation Company. Christopher Schoenberg and Stephanie Nicholas patiently rescued me from computer terrors and provided logistical support.

As always, librarians and archivists were the anonymous collaborators in research. In comparison with the dozens of labor history archives, organized foundation archives are few. Useful to me in this research were the Rockefeller and Russell Sage Foundation collections at the Rockefeller Archive

Center, Pocantico Hills, New York; the Ford Foundation Archive, New York City; the Field Foundation Archive, at the University of Texas at Austin; and the Carnegie Corporation Archive at Columbia University. The most valuable labor history archives were the Walter P. Reuther Library at Wayne State University, the George Meany Center for Labor Studies in Silver Spring, Maryland, and the Robert F. Wagner Labor Archive at the Tamiment Institute Library at New York University.[5] I found important material on black workers and organized labor at the Schomburg Center for Research in Black Culture (New York Public Library) and the Robert Woodruff Library Center at the Atlanta University Center. I am also indebted to the staffs of libraries in my neighborhood—the Mount Vernon and Yonkers public libraries and the Sarah Lawrence College Library.

Although they usually do not admit it, many authors act as though their book were the only one on the publisher's list. I made no such assumption, but my manuscript was treated not only with a high order of professional skill but also, I sometimes sensed, with a certain affection. That was clearly the case when Frances Benson, editor in chief, accepted the work—which did not prevent her from making several constructive criticisms. Her assistant, Laura Healy, was patient and helpful, and in their meticulous copy-editing Kay Scheuer and Barbara H. Salazar rescued me from any number of errors and enhanced the manuscript stylistically.

Let me go beyond the customary author's tribute to a patient spouse. What I acknowledge first of all is that the book could never have been completed without Gloria Magat's encouragement and tangible help. From the time we spent a long anniversary weekend at the Reuther Labor Archive in Detroit, she did almost all the library research and performed major editing tasks. So I owe her professional gratitude along with deep affection.

R.M.

Bronxville, New York

UNLIKELY PARTNERS

Introduction: An Untold Tale

In view of the antagonism toward unions expressed by the captains of industry who established the early foundations, coupled with unions' suspicion of anything fashioned from "robber baron" wealth, it might be assumed that philanthropic institutions and organized labor would keep their distance from one another. But until now this assumption had not been examined systematically or critically. It turns out that, in fact, a panoply of connections has existed through most of the twentieth century—from the indirect to the direct, from confrontational to supportive or collaborative. These connections have covered a wide variety of ventures—in the condition and status of black and female workers, the struggle of farmworkers, the state of workplace health and safety, the union democracy movement, and the stake of union members in such new economic phenomena as the global marketplace.

How, then, explain the absence of any account of the relationship between philanthropic foundations and the labor movement? One reason is simply that labor generally has been of minor interest to foundations and to unions even less. The subject lies hidden in the shadow of major subjects with which American foundations have been preoccupied in their century of existence—education, medicine and health, community affairs, the arts, and, more recently, race relations and the status of women. Even when connections occurred, foundations were often reluctant (or outright refused) to disclose their role, or to permit their beneficiaries to do so. None of them wanted to attract the sort of public excoriation visited upon the Rockefeller Foundation for its role in the aftermath of a disastrous Colorado miners' strike. And

1

some organizations and individuals that enjoy foundation funding fail to ac-knowledge the fact. Further, there are no data on union-related grants in the database of the Foundation Center (the major repository of information on the field) before the mid-1980s. Nor do records exist of some defunct foun-dations that played a role in union-related events.

A final reason lies in the time lag between the labor histories of the late nineteenth century and the development of philanthropic studies as an aca-demic field a half century later. Traditional historians having ignored labor history, the field was developed in the 1880s by young, radical economists re-belling against the orthodoxy of classical economics (e.g., the axiom that in demanding the right to bargain with employers, workers were attempting to violate the freedom of the market). Two of those who rallied to the cause of organized labor, Richard T. Ely and E. R. A. Seligman, founded the Ameri-can Economic Association in 1885.[1] The pioneering research center for labor-oriented intellectuals was the University of Wisconsin, where Ely, with $30,000 secured mostly from reform-minded philanthropists, established the American Bureau of Industrial Research in 1904 and placed it in the charge of John R. Commons, a former student. The materials the bureau collected from far and wide formed the basis of a pathbreaking scholarly work that marked the first significant foundation support for research on or-ganized labor: the eleven-volume *Documentary History of American Industrial Society*, financed by the Carnegie Institution of Washington.[2]

The Wisconsin school focused on skilled workers and their unions. The current generation of labor historians argues that far more attention should be devoted to the unorganized—the majority of working people. David Brody, David Montgomery, the late Herbert G. Gutman, and others have contended that the key to exploring the diverse nature of workers' attitudes lies in a study of their religious beliefs, community life, and family struc-tures.[3] New approaches to labor scholarship are evident in the journal *Labor History*, established in 1960 and underwritten by a foundation, the Tamiment Institute.[4]

Foundations' reticence, not to say secrecy, made research on their own community difficult for scholars.[5] Singularly, Frederick P. Keppel, president of Carnegie Corporation, as early as 1937 chastised foundations "that make no public record of their activities, thereby failing to recognize their re-sponsibility to the public as organizations enjoying exemption from taxa-tion." The issue, he said, is "public confidence in the foundation as a social instrument."[6]

Books on foundations, such as Eduard Lindeman's *Wealth and Culture* and Horace Coon's *Money to Burn*, began to appear in the 1930s. Not until the 1950s were foundations required to file information on their activities with the Internal Revenue Service. The Foundation Library Center, later renamed the Foundation Center, a valuable resource for research on organized philanthropy, was not established until 1955. Also in the 1950s the Ford and Carnegie foundations made grants to encourage scholarship on foundations, the former with support for Merle Curti of the University of Wisconsin, the latter by underwriting the Foundation Library Center. But as late as the 1990s only some fifty of the thousand largest foundations maintained archives or deposited their papers in libraries or other collections open to researchers.

A major stimulus to scholarly study of philanthropy was provided by the Commission on Private Philanthropy and Public Needs, which was promoted by John D. Rockefeller 3d in response to congressional investigations that led to the 1969 Tax Reform Act. Called the Filer Commission after its chairman, John H. Filer, chief executive officer of Aetna Insurance, the twenty-six-member commission included business and academic figures but no union representatives. Its staff commissioned and presented to Congress five volumes of studies between 1973 and 1975.[7]

In the wake of the Filer Commission, several new institutions appeared in the philanthropic community—the National Committee for Responsive Philanthropy, a watchdog group set up in 1976 supported by foundations; academic research centers on philanthropy (Yale, 1977; Case Western Reserve, 1984; Indiana, 1987; Duke, 1986; and the City University of New York, 1986); and Independent Sector, a coalition of foundations, corporate funders, and national nonprofit organizations (1980), which stimulated research and data collection. Harvard entered the lists late in the century (1997) with the establishment of the Hauser Center for Nonprofit Institutions in the John F. Kennedy School of Government, by means of a $10 million gift from Harvard Law School alumna Rita Hauser and Gustave Hauser. Several foundations joined forces to establish the Nonprofit Sector Research Fund, based at the Aspen Institute in Washington (1991). It makes grants to scholars, practitioners, and graduate students for studies of the voluntary sector. Other new elements in the nonprofit research infrastructure include the Association for Research on Nonprofit Organizations and Voluntary Research and the International Society for Third-Sector Research and their scholarly journals.

Notwithstanding this mushrooming of research on the nonprofit sector, organized labor has remained a marginal subject, though unions themselves are nonprofit organizations, in the category of "self-help organizations."[8] Still, as far back as 1956, a foundation-convened conference of historians listed "philanthropic programs with benefits to labor" and "trade unions and philanthropy" among some 150 research topics that might "contribute effectively toward an understanding of American philanthropy."[9]

This book is a belated response to that call. It begins with the industrial and social context in which the first great modern foundations were organized early in the twentieth century—turbulent labor relations, exploding urbanization, the social gospel, and Progressive reform movements. Early attention is given to the Russell Sage Foundation because it was the first to address labor conditions and the union movement, and set an example among foundations by attempting to ameliorate industrial strife. Related efforts are then taken up, including the National Civic Federation and the American Association for Labor Legislation, along with such manifestations of "enlightened" business practices as welfare capitalism and employee representation plans pursued by the same men whose foundations were contributing to designs for industrial peace.

Chapter 2 focuses on the general development of foundations, the extent of their involvement with the labor movement in relation to other fields, constraints against such ties, and, of critical importance, hypotheses about foundations' motivations for interest in organized labor at all. I then deal with reciprocal attitudes of unions and foundations, from the early period onward to my own surveys of labor officials and foundation officials.

Almost from the beginning, Congress has scrutinized connections between foundations and the labor movement—less for their own sake than in relation to other targets. These investigations are covered in Chapter 3, from the tumultuous hearings of the U.S. Commission on Industrial Relations (the Walsh Commission) on the Rockefeller Foundation's role in the aftermath of the bloody Colorado coal strike in 1914, to later investigations in which union officials testified about the behavior of foundations in activities ranging from plant closings to alleged subversion. I then deal extensively with research—the largest single area in which foundations have demonstrated an interest in organized labor. The discussion places labor research in the context of the development of the social sciences, in which foundations also played a major role.

The next eight chapters—about half of the book—examine in detail union-foundation connections in several major areas—the black experience, women and unions, farmworkers, general and labor education, health and safety, economic development, and public policy. These fields do not exhaust foundation-labor connections. They can also be found in the areas of housing, international relations, and civil liberties, for example, and I hope this work will encourage others to examine them.

Two chapters then deal with foundation activity related to internal union issues that, as it turns out, have greater salience now than they had when I began my research—organizing and the union democracy movement. The book concludes with a discussion of challenges posed by major changes in work and the workplace and by the heightened public visibility of a labor movement promising rejuvenation. These issues, finally, are framed in what may be a new structure of labor-foundation relations, new initiatives and growing curiosity, and labor's outreach to various constituencies, including the intellectual community.

The significance of this book lies, I believe, beyond the details of the interaction of organized philanthropy and organized labor in the larger framework of how important American institutions operate. In the swirl of increasingly rancorous discourse, the importance of these two sectors is easily overlooked. Millions of unionized men and women operate factories and farms, government agencies and hospitals, supermarkets and schools. They figure in debates over the place of free labor and equitable income in national and international labor markets. As to foundations, their record as pacesetters, as change agents in social and economic issues carries forward today, although since there are now thousands of them, legendary foundations do not obtrude as they did when they numbered in the dozens.

The reader should keep two definitional distinctions in mind. One concerns types of foundations. I discuss not only labor-related activities of private foundations, whose activities are financed by income from endowments, but also those of several "alternative" foundations—technically known as public charities in that they raise funds as well as grant them. These foundations, derived from the pooling of funds of young heirs with liberal philanthropic impulses, include the Vanguard Public Foundation (San Francisco), the Haymarket People's Fund (Boston), Bread and Roses Community Fund (Philadelphia), and North Star Fund (New York). Another type of alternative foundation reflects the interests of particular groups, such as the Ms. Foundation. I also report the union-related work of a few corporate foundations. Finally, I note the efforts of a few foundations that no longer exist— the Stern Family Fund, the Field Foundation, and the Shalan Fund, for example—insofar as they related to organized labor.

The second definitional boundary concerns unions. The labor community, contrary to such rigid views as the *Wall Street Journal*'s, is no monolith. In additional to the American Federation of Labor–Congress of Industrial Organizations (AFL-CIO), a holding company with substantial but far from infinite power and resources, American labor encompasses dozens of national unions (usually called international, because they include Canadian unions) and hundreds of local branches and regional and state federations. They often vary in outlook and degree of vigor. Further, the book deals not only with these unions and combinations of unions but also with the growing phenomenon of workers' organizations which are not unions but deal with labor issues such as compensation, benefits, and workplace conditions. Whether or not they resemble unions in form, they are part of organized labor, and their ties to foundations merit attention.

During the miners' strike in Harlan County, Kentucky, in 1931, Florence Reece wrote a song titled "Which Side Are You On?"—a rallying anthem on picket lines and union conclaves ever since.[10] My own reply is that I am on the side of closer contact, improved mutual understanding, and more common effort between organized labor and philanthropic foundations. This book is intended in large part to promote such ties by opening up a substantial record of relations between these two American institutions. But more paths remain to be explored if we are to cover the full terrain, and I hope that future researchers will pursue them.

1

Social Order, Social Progress

Heir to the industrial empire established by his father, Cyrus McCormick, "the reaper king," Cyrus McCormick Jr. was president of International Harvester from 1902 until 1919. He had been hostile to labor unions since a bitter strike at the McCormick Harvesting Machine Company prompted the violent Haymarket demonstration in 1886. Cyrus McCormick Sr. had blacklisted all workers who had anything to do with labor organizations.[1]

International Harvester workers struck again in 1916 and won wage and hour concessions, but McCormick refused to recognize the union. He was "unconvinced that any broad labor relations strategy, other than the simple one of firing workers with union sympathies, was called for," a scholar noted later. Prompted by walkouts and the increasing complexity of industrial relations after the expansion of his corporation and another strike in 1919, McCormick established an employee representation plan—the Industrial Council Plan. It had "one fundamental purpose: to maintain managerial control over the workforce." The plan persisted in various forms until 1938, when the CIO Farm Equipment Workers Organizing Committee won an election at Harvester.[2]

Neither the elder McCormick nor his son established a philanthropic foundation on the scale of those founded by their fellow industrial titans Andrew Carnegie and John D. Rockefeller. The family did, however, hew to a noblesse oblige tradition. In 1912 they endowed the Elizabeth McCormick Memorial Fund, which began a program of investigation and legislative reform that made it a leader in the child welfare field. Later Cyrus McCormick Jr. and his brother

Harold (who was married to John D. Rockefeller Sr.'s daughter Edith) established health-oriented foundations.[3]

These were safe areas for philanthropic ventures. But decades later, in 1954, a foundation based on the McCormick family fortune was established with a markedly different stance toward organized labor than that of International Harvester's founders. Named the New World Foundation, it was created under the will of Cyrus Jr.'s daughter, Anita McCormick Blaine. She had been raised in a tradition of philanthropic responsibility. Her mother had funded settlement houses and the McCormick Theological Seminary, and Mrs. Blaine herself financed education reform, supporting the renowned laboratory school at the University of Chicago. She was also a trustee of the Chicago School of Civics and Philanthropy. Among the areas Mrs. Blaine hoped the New World Foundation would support was "the relationship to life, and the ethics, of industry and commerce." Later managers of the foundation interpreted that aim as "the ethical duties to society of business and labor, with emphasis on public accountability of economic power and the need for partnership between business, industry and consumers."[4]

New World has maintained a consistent interest in union-related activities. Among its grant recipients have been 9 to 5, Homeworkers Organized for More Employment, the Movement for Economic Justice Education and Training Center, United Woodcutters Services, the Brown Lung Association, the Fresno Organizing Project, Southerners for Economic Justice, the Institute for Labor Education and Research, the United Auto Workers New Directions Fund, the National Institute for Labor Education, the Teamster Rank and File Education Fund, and the Comité de Apoyo a los Trabajadores.

From the foundation's inception to 1977, it was shaped and presided over by Mrs. Blaine's granddaughter, Ann Blaine (Nancy) Harrison. She had been a union organizer in the southern textile industry, and later a lobbyist for the CIO in Illinois. Whether New World's interest in organized labor arose from Anita Blaine's principles, her granddaughter's experience with unions, or both, it is an exception among American foundations in taking a direct interest in organized labor.

American labor unions and private philanthropic foundations both emerged from a maturing industrial capitalism after the Civil War. The union movement was fairly well developed by the turn of the century, when the earliest major foundations were established. The fortunes of unions have oscillated widely, hitting low points in the 1920s and 1980s, while (except during the Depression years) private foundations have grown steadily and flourished.[5]

Continuing industrialization, urbanization, and economic instability marked the post–Civil War period. Bloody strikes on the railroads, in coal mines, and in other industries reflected a grim antagonism between labor and capital. In 1903 Theodore Roosevelt wrote, "The two great fundamental internal prob-

Anita McCormick Blaine, heiress to the International Harvester Company fortune, established the New World Foundation in her will, in which she expressed hope for a labor-business reconciliation. Her father and grandfather had been bitterly antiunion. (The State Historical Society of Wisconsin, negative no. WHi [x3] 32220)

lems with which we have to deal . . . are the Negro problem in the South, and the relations of capital and labor. . . . The last is the greatest . . . and is the one which, in some of its phases, most immediately demands a solution."[6] Between 1885 and 1916, Congress authorized four major inquiries into labor-management relations.

But the dawn of the twentieth century was infused not only by a sense of uncertainty but also by an optimistic belief that great problems could be plumbed and solutions to the nation's social ills devised. Social critics such as Henry Demarest Lloyd invoked the democratic spirit of cooperation to counter rampant individualism, reflecting a sense that without concern for social justice, industrial capitalism's feverish pursuit of profit would generate further class conflict and social chaos.[7]

The Social Gospel and Progressivism

Foundations were an institutional innovation that mirrored two vital movements in American society: the social gospel and Progressivism. Both were committed to ameliorating turbulent social conditions.

From the Civil War onward, evangelists and other religionists were concerned about the labor movement.[8] The Reverend Washington Gladden, most famous of the social gospel leaders, was appalled by industrial conditions, sympathized with trade unions, but feared labor unrest and socialism. Warning that wars between capital and labor would be inevitable otherwise, he called on employers "to rediscover Christ's law and take their employees as brothers into a partnership, which shared both adversity and prosperity."[9] Richard Ely and other founders of the American Economic Association, critical of laissez-faire individualism, promulgated an economic theory "that placed man—not wealth—in the foreground, and gave proper attention to the 'social factor' in his nature."[10] Ely warned church leaders that they would fail to fulfill their responsibility to God if they neglected the opportunity to connect the church to the labor movement.[11]

Several economists sympathetic to the union movement followed Ely's lead and joined the Church Social Union and the Church Association for the Advancement of the Interests of Labor (CAIL). Both were led by the Episcopal Church, the first Protestant denomination in America to recognize the right of labor to organize.[12] CAIL's proposal for tripartite labor arbitration (business, labor, and the public) was later adopted by the business-dominated, reformist National Civic Federation.

One clergyman who did not share the vision of the social gospel was the Reverend Frederick Gates, Rockefeller's chief philanthropic adviser. "One may sympathize with the aim of trade unionism to secure higher wages for labor," he wrote, "without approving the wholly selfish spirit or methods—violence to enforce demands."[13]

Progressivism, which one historian has characterized as "the last full-blown articulation of that optimistic, republican, tolerant, and liberal Protestant view of the individual and society that had informed America for one hundred years,"[14] pressed for justice, order, and stability. Blending muckraking journalism with efforts to effect corporate and legislative reforms, and parting with the socialists, who viewed class conflict as the central element in the social system, Progressives were dedicated to bridging the gulf between the proletariat and the bourgeoisie. But they were of two minds about organized labor. While opposing the exploitation of labor, they viewed union power as antithetical to their goals, as another brand of corporate monopoly. To them, in Robert Wiebe's words, "the closed shop violated individual rights, the boycott the canon of decency, and violence during strikes the elementary principles of social order."[15] Yet more sophisticated Progressives did accept collective bargaining as a means of reducing social tensions and regulating the economy in the public interest. They also believed that partnership between the corporations and the government would rationalize the tumultuous process of social and political change. Many rising business leaders saw in the pragmatism of the Progressive movement a means of securing the existing social order. As James Weinstein has observed, corporate liberals allowed potential opponents to participate (even if not as equals) in a process of adjustment, concession, and amelioration that seemed to promise a gradual advance toward the good society for all citizens.[16] And the emerging new middle class of managers and those with professional aspirations in economics, administration, social philosophy, and social work were all infused with reformist tendencies.[17]

The new foundations, in which ran strands of Progressivism, charity organizations, and the emerging profession of social work, also reflected a spirit of optimism—a belief that orderly solutions could be devised if the roots of problems could be uncovered and understood. They followed a "scientific" approach to social ills—investigating causes, applying new scientific and economic theories, and seeking fundamental change rather than palliatives.

The founders were not motivated by tax considerations; neither federal estate nor income taxes existed when Carnegie, Rockefeller, Mrs. Russell Sage, and Jeremiah Milbank established their foundations. Altruism combined with a need to dispose efficiently of a mass of accumulating wealth and to respond rationally to a flood of charitable requests. Some of them regarded the rush to give away vast sums as a personal competition. In their lifetimes Carnegie and Rockefeller disbursed a total of $850 million; in supporting organized philanthropies, they ran neck and neck—Carnegie $304 million, Rockefeller $317 million.[18] Both established several philanthropies. The former included Carnegie Corporation of New York (his largest), the Carnegie Endowment for International Peace, and the Carnegie Institution of Washington. The latter included the Rockefeller Foundation, the General Education Board, and the Laura Spelman Rockefeller Memorial.

The establishment of a foundation, however, may also reflect self-interest (rehabilitating a questionable reputation, a desire for adulation, maintaining family control of a business, or, for most of the past century, avoidance of taxes) or a personal focus (an interest in the arts or in a particular disease, a desire to help certain groups). That the modern foundation should serve public needs was reinforced by Carnegie's essay "The Gospel of Wealth," in which he advanced the doctrine that millionaires, after providing for their own needs, "should consider all surplus revenues which come to [them] simply as trust funds which [they are] called upon to administer, and strictly bound as a matter of duty to administer in the manner best calculated to produce the most beneficial results for the community."[19] To Carnegie the social gospel was a higher form of charity. Through foundations, the very wealthy could share with the reformers an agenda of humanitarian, generally acceptable political and social goals.

Scientific Philanthropy: The Russell Sage Foundation

The Russell Sage Foundation (RSF), the first to epitomize scientific philanthropy, also recognized at the outset that the improvement of labor conditions was fundamental to its task. It was established in 1907 by Margaret Olivia Sage, the widow of an unsavory speculator and financier of railroad and industrial ventures. Enormously wealthy, a miser and a convicted usurer (he served a jail sentence), Sage himself was sanguine about the relations between labor and capital: "I fail to see the dangers arising from wealth that the demagogues make such a hue and cry about. If such danger does exist, education of the masses will destroy it; there never was a day when capital and labor were so near together as now."[20]

The foundation's charter, calling for the improvement of social and living conditions, authorized broad participation in social welfare. Robert de Forest, president of the Charity Organization Society, chief adviser to Mrs. Sage, and a trustee of the foundation, made clear its interest in research (on causes) as the alternative to charity (attacking symptoms). Under his influence, the foundation led the way in professionalizing social work, which radical critics termed "a nationwide ideology of efficient, systematic amelioration."[21] The RSF operated departments of its own, among them Recreation, Statistics, Child-Helping, and Remedial Loans, and also supported projects initiated by others. Thus it helped financed the Pittsburgh Survey, a trailblazing, comprehensive effort to encompass in a single study the various phases of social, economic, and working life in a modern industrial community. The picture that emerged in its six-volume report, according to Robert Bremner, "was one of appalling waste resulting from social timidity and disinclination to interfere with the rites of money-making. In Pittsburgh, lives, health, strength, education, even the industrial efficiency of workmen were treated as things of little worth. The important matters were output, time, cost, and profit. In comparison to these considerations human lives and happiness were relatively unimportant."[22]

Thus the foundation's interest in the labor movement was an outgrowth of its early focus on the effects of industrial conditions on families and communities—"the effects of unemployment . . . no assurance of work or wage tomorrow, long hours . . . industrial accidents, strikes, misunderstanding, and bitterness of conflict between wage-earners and employers; conditions with which the individual . . . finds himself powerless to cope alone."[23] Edward Devine, another RSF trustee, persuaded his colleague John Glenn (who became general director of the foundation in 1907) to share his interest in industrial relations, including connections with the National Civic Federation.

The RSF grasped the nettle and established an Industrial Studies Department. For forty years it was headed by a remarkable graduate of Smith College, Mary Van Kleeck, who embodied the social gospel. The daughter of a minister, a devout worker for the YWCA, and president of the Smith College Association for Christian Work, Van Kleeck "fused religious faith, technical hubris, and social vision into a career at the creative center of industrial society," says her biographer, Guy Alchon.[24]

She and her staff undertook a series of investigations of child labor and the conditions of women's work in various trades. These studies, Robert Bremner has noted, "conclusively proved the fallacy of the pin-money theory and demonstrated that in case after case wages adjusted to the supposedly meager needs of the girl who 'lived at home' were a major cause of poverty and an important factor in perpetuating it."[25] Van Kleeck's findings were cited by Louis Brandeis and Josephine Goldmark in a court case that upheld the constitutionality of a law prohibiting night work by women.[26]

Van Kleeck eventually turned away from such gender-specific work in favor of an increasingly class-specific research program embracing men's and children's labor as well as women's.[27] Beginning in 1916, the RSF began studies of the problems, operations, and results of trade unionism. In an extraordinary memorandum to Glenn, Van Kleeck wrote, "It is true that all Foundations must meet the criticism that, as they represent the benefactions of the rich, they are expected to be defenders of the present order and therefore cannot speak with the disinterestedness of an official public agency or

Mary Van Kleeck (second from right) with other members of the Russell Sage Foundation's Industrial Relations Department, which she headed for forty years. Van Kleeck, a leading authority on unions, was accused of membership in the Communist Party in a congressional investigation in 1952. (Rockefeller Archive Center)

the incisiveness of an organization supported by the workers only or by the employers." But that suspicion, she said, is overcome by the foundation's unprejudiced and skillful investigative process.[28]

In the foundation's first decennial report, Van Kleeck observed that despite significant progress in labor conditions (for example, compensation for accidents, minimum wage legislation, and the growth of public employment bureaus), industrial unrest had mounted. In this climate, she wrote, the foundation had a unique opportunity:

> The Foundation is concerned with the labor movement from the viewpoint neither of employers nor of workers, but as representing the public interest. . . . The public interest . . . sometimes may be in conflict with the immediate interests of both. [The] important thing is that employers, workers, and the public should understand the facts and know the tendencies involved in action. The Foundation's . . . investigations have sought

not to influence conclusions, but to help establish the habit of making fact, rather than prejudice or self-interest, the basis of conclusions.[29]

Van Kleeck had become, as Alchon puts it, "a champion of the labor movement." In the troubled industrial relations climate of the 1920s and 1930s, workers, employers, and government officials looked to Russell Sage to carry on unbiased studies of experiments in giving workers greater responsibility for the quality of their output.[30] The RSF studied employee representation plans in the steel, auto, and coal mining industries, including the plan Rockefeller and W. L. Mackenzie King devised for the Colorado Fuel & Iron Company in the wake of the Ludlow Massacre. The staff concluded that despite improvements, the plan had not yet established "true participation in management" of the mines; and three strikes had occurred since the plan was introduced. About five thousand miners were enrolled in the plan, the report noted, in contrast to more than a half million who belonged to the United Mine Workers. "Reciprocal antagonism between the Rockefeller Plan and trade unionism was the crucial feature of the situation," the RSF analysis concluded. John D. Rockefeller Jr. tried—unsuccessfully—to block its publication in 1925.[31] Colorado Fuel & Iron abandoned its company union in 1933 and recognized the United Mine Workers, which, strengthened by the National Recovery Act, now controlled a greater percentage of bituminous coal production than at any other time in its history.[32]

In 1924, at the request of the Association of Motion Picture Producers, the foundation conducted a study of employment in the motion picture industry that led to the establishment of a central casting office. Two decades later, in 1948, Russell Sage was again approached by the industry, this time for an advisory survey on labor relations. According to Van Kleeck, an industry official told her he had not turned to the universities "because [their] labor-management centers, in the view of both management and labor, tend to be biased either toward management or toward labor and they have been unable to find any one of these centers acceptable to both sides in the motion pictures industry."[33]

Van Kleeck's associate in the Industrial Studies Department was Edward Wieck, whose 1942 report, "Preventing Fatal Accidents in Coal Mines," included recommendations the foundation believed could reduce major explosion disasters by at least 75 percent and criticized industry for "a lack of concern for [safety] measures and even active opposition to legislative action in this direction."[34] The following year a "desperate call for assistance" came from the War Labor Board's Fact-Finding Panel for data on the coal industry that would help in efforts to settle its chronic wartime disputes.[35]

Van Kleeck was a major force in the effort to merge social reform and scientific management on an international scale through the International Industrial Relations Institute, despite a provision in the RSF's charter restricting its work to the United States. Increasingly an apologist for the Soviet Union, Van Kleeck was investigated by the FBI and called before Senator Joseph McCarthy's Permanent Subcommittee on Investigations in 1953. Her stature in the social sciences notwithstanding, her increasing radicalism had become an embarrassment to the foundation. By the late 1930s it had begun to place disclaimers on her published work, and it never published the massive study of union history on which she had labored for fifteen years. In 1948 the foundation eased her out and let the Industrial Relations Department expire.

In view of the fact that other foundations shied away from the controversies inherent in labor and industrial conditions, the RSF's work was courageous. Nonetheless, some critics argue that the preponderance of its activities in its first decades supported social service and ameliorative reform as an alternative to more basic structural changes: "Some consequences of the structural poverty generated by industrial capitalism were treated, while fundamental problematics even with that system (socially irresponsible wealth, industrial concentration, political corruption) remained unchallenged."[36] This is an echo, more than a half-century later, of the assertion, made during the clash of ideologies of the Progressive era, that foundations buttressed ideas that supported the status quo. An even older target was one of the first foundations, the Carnegie Institution of Washington (1903), funder of John Commons's great history of labor. That work, a detractor asserted, supported "the construction of a pragmatic ideology of ameliorative reform that justified the perpetuation of industrial capitalists."[37]

Motivations

The record of foundations' relations with organized labor suggests four primary motivations:

- A desire for social control, the paradigm for which is Antonio Gramsci's concept of cultural hegemony. That is, the dominant class, one of whose instruments is the private foundation, retains its power less through coercion than through ideological control of civil society, including education, religion, and the media. To preserve its hegemony, it consciously and unconsciously imposes its values and beliefs to win acceptance of the idea that its interests are those of society at large.

- Pursuit of strategies of social change. To the extent that foundations have dealt directly with unions, most have viewed them as a means rather than as an end in themselves. Foundations have enlisted organized labor as a collaborator in their efforts to carry out their own agendas, from community development to educational improvement. In the 1960s, for instance, the Ford Foundation joined with the United Auto Workers and other unions to support community development corporations in south-central and east Los Angeles after the Watts riots. More recently, the John D. and Catherine T. MacArthur Foundation granted more than $1 million to the Chicago Teachers Union for school-based teaching improvements, part of a school reform movement in which several Chicago-based foundations played principal roles.[38]
- A quest for economic stability. From the nineteenth century on, business reformers and political leaders have sought solutions to volatile economic cycles, which are so often accompanied by severe labor unrest. In a twenty-five-year period marked by the Haymarket Square demonstration, the Homestead and Pullman strikes, Coxey's marches of 1894 and 1914, massive immigration, and the radical appeals of the IWW, anarchists, and the Socialist Party, it is not surprising that union activities fanned public fears of subversive assaults against the established order (armories in several cities were built with public subscriptions).[39] So foundations that wanted to solve acute social ills also supported efforts to stabilize the economy. Foundation-sponsored research on ways and means to steady the economy increasingly developed an industrial relations cast. Barry Karl and Stanley Katz theorize that "the original foundation donors' . . . view of unions was only in the process of reformation, from total hostility to some form of association they could govern in what the more enlightened among them believed to be their mutual interest."[40]
- A desire to strengthen labor unions. This is the least usual motivation for foundations' connections to organized labor. Among instances of *direct* philanthropic assistance to the labor movement is the support of a handful of foundations for the "union democracy" movement, an effort by dissidents to revitalize corrupt or ineffectual unions. Conversely, the Farm Workers Union sought foundation funds for their service centers, but union approaches to foundations have been rare.

The outstanding instance of the last motivation is seen in the work of the American Fund for Public Service, informally known as the Garland Fund, in the 1920s and 1930s. Its grants supported projects ranging from A. Philip Randolph's efforts to organize the Brotherhood of Sleeping Car Porters to workers' colleges that aimed to endow unions with a broader social vision—all in the name of "encouraging the emancipation of the working class and to promote a new social order."[41] The Garland Fund opened its doors in a period marked by a series of brutal strikes, in which troops intervened to escort strikebreakers. Antiradical sentiment crystallized in police raids, harassment, indictments, and deportations ordered by the Justice Department.

The Garland Fund grew out of the refusal of an idealistic young Bostonian, Charles Garland, to accept an inheritance of some $900,000 from his father, a Wall Street broker. Roger Baldwin of the American Civil Liberties Union persuaded Garland to accept the legacy and use it to support radical social and economic causes.[42]

The Garland Board was a hornets' nest of left-wing factionalism, but included such liberals as Henry Ward (Methodist minister and teacher at Union Theological Seminary) and Freda Kirchwey, a suffragist and later managing editor of *The Nation*. The Communists William Z. Foster and Elizabeth Gurley Flynn sat on the board, along with such labor leaders as Robert W. Dunn, general organizer for the Amalgamated Textile Workers Union, and Sidney Hillman, president of the Amalgamated Clothing Workers Union.

The Garland Fund supported the launching of the Vanguard Press, the legal defense of such celebrated defendants as Tom Mooney, a study of the use of the injunction against unions, and strike relief for shoe workers, miners, textile workers, fur workers, and farmworkers. Despite its ambivalence toward applications from Communists, the fund did support several Communist-affiliated publications—*New Masses, The Daily Worker, The Labor Herald*, and *Labor Age*—as well as such Communist-related activities as the International Labor Defense and the American Negro Labor Congress. The fund was attacked by the AFL as "Bolsheviks in patriots' clothing,"[43] kept under surveillance by the federal government, and cited extensively by the House Un-American Activities Committee in the late 1930s and 1940s and by congressional committees that investigated foundations in the 1950s.

A negative report on the Garland Fund by a liberal critic came from Eduard Lindeman, a scholar, teacher, and social work leader, who had been persuaded by Herbert Croly, founder of *The New Republic* and a close comrade in the Progressive movement, to write the first investigative study of foundations, *Wealth and Culture* (1936). Lindeman's study contrasted the philanthropic style of the Garland Fund with that of the William C. Whitney Foundation, in the conception of which Croly was influential. Few of Garland's new projects endured, said Lindeman, and its beneficiaries "could not . . . incorporate themselves within the cultural pattern of the nation." The Whitney Foundation, in contrast, concentrated on projects "designed to bring into existence or to test new conceptions of cultural value . . . to in-

Rand School bookstore, in New York City, ca. 1930, featured selections from the Vanguard Press, which was heavily subsidized by the Garland Fund, one of the country's most radical foundations. (Rand School Collection, Tamiment Institute Library, New York University)

crease the range of human freedom . . . especially in the realms of industry, education and politics."[44] This mission squared with Croly's belief in thoroughgoing industrial democracy, in which "militant unions, a cooperative government and enlightened employers could gradually attain the syndicalist goal of giving labor a powerful voice in management."[45]

Croly was chief philanthropic adviser to Dorothy Whitney Elmhurst Straight. With other family members, she established the William C. Whitney Foundation, named for her father, in 1936. After Croly died in 1930, Lindeman succeeded him as adviser. The Whitney Foundation was an important donor to such union-related organizations as the Brookwood Labor College, the American Labor Education Service, the Highlander Folk School, and the Southern Tenant Farmers Union.

Gloria Samson, the historian of the Garland Fund, concludes that Garland's directors "scattered their resources without giving each enterprise realistic funding or the time to become effective. . . . [They] scratched one another's ideological backs, funding anything left-of-center if a director promoted it. . . . Because most . . . came from the educated middle class, they awarded too much to research, not enough to actual activities, too much to publication, almost nothing to organizing."[46] Yet whatever its shortcomings, she says, the fund helped to keep the idea of industrial unions alive and to educate a group that would become part of the CIO cadre of organizers and labor educators.

Improving Labor-Management Relations

The standard instruments for dealing with labor unrest ranged from violent suppression by both private and public police forces to pacification through benevolent programs—bonuses and stock sharing, recreational facilities, clean washrooms—to the formation of worker organizations that fell short of unions. However, many reformers, business leaders, and conservative labor leaders, Karl and Katz point out, "understood perfectly well that . . . a new cooperative structure might provide an alternative to socialism and the welfare state, both of which seemed inevitable in contemporary Europe, in which the American private sector could retain its dominant position in the formulation of public policy. In this effort . . . the role of the philanthropic foundation might well prove central to the ambitions of the private sector."[47] In view of labor's perceived strength and political influence, corporate leaders were divided on whether confrontation was the appropriate response. The National Association of Manufacturers (NAM), representing small and mid-range businesses, advocated forceful measures to defeat the unions, but some of the most powerful industrialists believed that unions could serve as agencies for reconciliation. Such was the view of Mark Hanna, who in 1900 became president of the National Civic Federation. The NCF was modeled on the Chicago Civic Federation, a nonpartisan group formed in 1894 to reform municipal government and advance philanthropic and industrial interests. According to Herbert Croly, Hanna, a shrewd Cleveland industrialist and Republican Party kingmaker until his death in 1904, "was one of the first of our public men to understand that the organization of capital necessarily implied some corresponding kind of labor organization, and that the demands of organized labor were not incompatible with the desires of organized capital."[48] Incorporating social engineering alongside industrial efficiency, the NCF would become what one historian of the left has characterized as "the most important single organization of the socially conscious big businessmen and their academic and political theorists."[49]

In its drive to prevent American civic society from degenerating into unceasing industrial strife, the NCF recruited the distinguished corporate manager Gerard Swope (General Electric), the progressive intellectuals Herbert Croly and Walter Rauschenbach, and the reformer Jane Addams. It aimed to eliminate incipient class struggle by reconciling labor and capital on the basis of "reason and understanding." Because big-business moderates who signed on were willing to treat organized labor as a legitimate partner, Samuel Gompers approved.[50] He and John Mitchell, head of the United Mineworkers, were charter members of the NCF, and the leaders of a dozen other national unions joined, seeing the NCF as a counterforce against virulent antiunion employers. A third group was composed of corporate directors, a few clergymen, and academics—Nicholas Murray Butler, president of Columbia University, and Charles W. Eliot, president of Harvard University, both strong advocates of the open shop. A confidant of the Rockefellers, Eliot influenced the composition of the Rockefeller Foundation's board of trustees. John R. Commons, who worked for and admired Ralph Easley, the NCF's founder and director, observed that the federation "was two-thirds capitalistic and one-third laboristic." Still, he said, the organization was purely a conciliatory body, whose purpose was to bring about collective bargaining under the new name of "trade agreement." The NCF's strongest opponents, he noted, were the NAM, Communists, and anarchists.[51]

The NCF was initially financed by corporate and financial leaders and industrial magnates, including Carnegie and Rockefeller. Later the Carnegie and Rockefeller foundations contributed. Karl and Katz view this funding as evidence not of an antiradical, antilabor stance but of a sophisticated understanding of labor conditions and societal attitudes, which saw little urgency in the threat of radicalism. But during World War I, Easley turned into a patriotic zealot who sought to convert the federation into a leading antiradical agency. By 1920 Easley and the NCF had become such an embarrassment to Carnegie Corporation and the Rockefeller Foundation that they reduced their funding to their lowest prewar level.[52]

In its early years, especially under Hanna, the NCF helped settle strikes and, in a few industries where organized labor was relatively strong, promoted agreements whereby labor leaders, in return for union recognition, became mediators between workers and industry representatives, agreeing to enforce contractual agreements even against the wishes of their members. But, dominated by business interests as it was, the NCF did not formally affirm labor's right to organize until 1908, and then with reservations. This stance, along with the NCF's increasingly strident advocacy of the open shop over the years, caused union participants to resign. In his letter of resignation, James Duncan, head of the Granite Cutters Association and an AFL vice president, noted that although labor had reduced strikes wherever employers agreed to reasonable adjustment, few businessmen on the NCF Executive Committee represented industries that recognized unions, and still fewer signed agreements that provided a method of eliminating strikes.[53]

Only Gompers stayed with the NCF, despite its inability to promulgate anything more substantial than hope.[54]

Trade unionists had little use for another foundation-supported research and advocacy organization, the American Association for Labor Legislation (AALL), although its members included many liberal-minded reformers and even a few socialists. The association was supported by the Carnegie and Russell Sage foundations, the Milbank Fund, and individual donations. Ely's American Bureau of Industrial Research at the University of Wisconsin was a prime mover in setting up the AALL in 1906. He was its first president, and John R. Commons served as secretary from 1907 to 1909.[55]

Under the motto "Social justice is the best insurance against labor unrest," the AALL promoted model state legislation for protective labor regulation and social insurance so that employers in one state would not have advantages over others. It backed off, however, from legislation setting maximum hours and minimum wages.[56] The Russell Sage Foundation, along with the U.S. Bureau of Labor, published authoritative surveys of European workmen's insurance as early as 1910. The AALL was an important force in passage of legislation dealing with industrial disease and accidents and contributed research and ideas that found their way into the Social Security Act. The Rockefeller Foundation played a role, too, by bringing Sir William H. Beveridge and Sir Henry Steel-Maitland from England to explain the British social insurance program and to allay any fears of American business leaders and conservatives.

The AALL took no position on unions, but many of its members supported organized labor. One AALL founder said paternalistically that the organization would provide "guidance and advice" to unions whose previous attempts to secure legislation—eight-hour workdays, for example—had been "crude and ineffective."[57] Gompers was a vice president of the AALL, but as always he distrusted outside intellectuals, whom he suspected of having personal, class agendas. He finally resigned, in part over the AALL's frequent calls for impartial experts and commissions to resolve social problems. Viewing such measures as protective legislation as paternalistic and fearing they would weaken the labor movement, Gompers saw the AALL as an attempt "to rivet the masses of labor to the juggernaut of government." Not until the early 1930s did the AFL support social insurance legislation.[58]

Over its thirty-five years, the AALL advanced model legislation on industrial health and safety, unemployment insurance, and retirement benefits. Despite its progressive record, the AALL and other groups of professionals and policy intellectuals have long been accused by both the left and the right of hand-in-glove arrangements with big business, whose financial influence was palpable in universities, research institutes, and foundations.

During the Progressive era and the early 1920s, business struggled for the ideological loyalty of the American working class. As Elizabeth Fones-Wolf has noted, "business sought to construct a vision of Americanism that emphasized social harmony, free enterprise, individual rights, and abundance."[59] Alongside foundation-assisted approaches to improved labor-management relations, business developed "welfare capitalism." Carnegie viewed his support of community improvements in Pittsburgh—schools, churches, playgrounds, educational extension services in the mills—"as an antidote for radical proposals for redistributing property and a method of reconciling the poor and the rich."[60] Welfare capitalism also stressed improvements in facilities for workers (the railroads even gave money to the YMCA to provide decent overnight accommodations for railway workers and, by the way, to keep them from saloons) and benefits for victims of industrial accidents and sickness.[61]

A successor of sorts to welfare capitalism is corporate philanthropy—the donation of funds and services to a community beyond the bounds of the workplace. After World War II, when a small group of top corporate executives engineered a successful court challenge to legal restrictions on corporate giving (*Smith* v. *Barlow*, 1953, financed in part by the Ford Foundation), corporate philanthropy took on new life and broader scope. Corporate giving in many instances adopted the form of company foundations, which originally focused on grantmaking closely related to the parent firm. They also promoted industry-related research, such as the National Foundation for Unemployment Compensation and Workers' Compensation, which serves employers, labor, legislators, and government personnel with research on state and federal laws.

Relatively high tax rates in the 1940s and 1950s led to rapid growth in the formation of company foundations, and their philanthropic interests broadened. Not only do a few rank in size among the fifty largest foundations of all types (AT&T, GE, and General Motors), but several have earned reputations for professional grantmaking. By the early 1990s, corporate-sponsored foundations accounted for 3.6 percent ($6.9 billion) of the assets of foundations of all types.[62] Corporate foundations give to causes that are almost as varied as those of private foundations. Organized labor is hardly one of their priorities, but in encouraging educational improvement, some have made grants to tax-exempt spin-offs of teacher unions (the American Federation of Teachers and the National Education Association). Such support, along with funding of environmental and other advocacy organizations, has incurred the wrath of such conservative critics as Rady A. Johnson of the Capital Research Center, who wrote: "It is time to abandon the distorted definition of compassion that has characterized so much corporate and foundation giving . . . [to] failed programs of the past. . . . It is past time for the business community to apply rigorous business practices to the oversight of philanthropic contributions."[63]

Perhaps the most popular idea in the search for labor-management harmony was industrial democracy, a concept formulated by W. L. Mackenzie King, head of the Rockefeller Foundation's short-lived Industrial Relations Department. The system of paternalistic labor representation that the idea spawned played a major role in U.S. industrial relations for two decades. In his efforts to promote industrial democracy, John D. Rockefeller Jr. acquired the mantle of an industrial statesman, a role he modestly disclaimed: "I was merely King's mouthpiece. I needed education."[64]

By 1924, 814 firms reported employee representation plans covering 1,117,000 workers. Among those examined in detail by the Russell Sage Foundation was Filene's, the Boston department store, whose owner, Edward Filene, founded the Twentieth Century Fund. As early as 1901, Filene's had established an arbitration board of elected employee representatives to settle disputes over wages, discharges, and working conditions.[65] Although the AFL approved employee representation in factories during World War I, it reversed this view during the postwar open-shop campaign, and labeled plans such as Filene's "company unions." By 1928 company unions were increasing as membership in the AFL declined, and their members accounted for 44.5 percent of total union membership.[66]

The doubts cast by Van Kleeck's studies on the efficacy of worker representation plans were shared by a leading figure in the Rockefeller philanthropic galaxy, Raymond Fosdick, the foundation's president. In a letter to John D. Rockefeller Jr. of November 1, 1921, he wrote: "There is a psychological appeal in labor unionism which has not yet been analyzed. It seems to give the men a sense not only of power but also of dignity and self-respect. They feel that only through labor unions can they deal with employers on an equal plane. They seem to regard [worker representation plans] as a sort of counterfeit, largely, perhaps, because the machinery of such plans is too often managed by the employers. They want something which they themselves have created and not something which is handed down to them by those who pay their wages."[67] On another occasion, writing to his brother in America from strike-bound England in 1919, Fosdick said: "Labor should organize. I am coming more and more to believe that the open shop is fundamentally a wrong principle and while it may have fitted things as they existed five years ago (when King preserved it with his company labor representative grievance scheme . . .), it cannot possibly suit the temper of this age."[68]

A century after the National Civic Federation began a quest for solutions to labor disputes, foundations are still supporting work toward labor stability. Early on, the quest was motivated by fears of mass disorders, tempered by the Progressive spirit of reform and encouraged by a philanthropic ideology compounded of the Gospel of Wealth and faith in rational and scientific approaches to solving social problems. Near the end of the twentieth century, the stimuli were global competition, high technology, and dramatic change in work arrangements.

Management has held the upper hand since the passage of the Taft-Hartley Act in 1947, through the Landrum-Griffin Act in 1959 and the antilabor policies of the Reagan and Bush administrations. The old social contract was narrowly confined to bread-and-butter benefits. It left unions with virtually no control over the kinds of decisions that have been upending the workplace since the 1970s—production, relocation, and investment policies that result in the movement of plants to nonunion regions in the United States or overseas, the subcontracting of work to nonunion shops, and the sheer elimination of jobs under the rubric of "downsizing."[69]

The issue of whether and how workers want to be represented was addressed in a major survey of American workers' views of workplace representation conducted in 1994 and 1995 by Richard B. Freeman, of Harvard and the National Bureau of Economic Research, and Joel Rogers, of the University of Wisconsin, with support from the Joyce, Sloan, and Russell Sage foundations. The research was designed to underpin efforts by government (particularly the Dunlop Commission, formally the Commission on the Future of Worker-Management Relations), labor, and management to increase national competitiveness and to allow worker groups to express themselves on workplace conditions. In contrast to the Dunlop Commission, which interviewed labor officials but no individual workers, Freeman and Rogers interviewed 2,400 workers.[70]

Proponents of participatory programs—described in such terms as "quality circles," "total quality management," and "joint task forces"—view them as proving grounds for moving beyond "environmental" concerns of the workplace to more substantial issues of management prerogatives and policy, especially the design, introduction, and operation of new technologies. Others consider them analogous to the company unions of welfare capitalism in the 1920s. And although workers have a stake in productivity, it is not always the same as management's. Thomas Brooks pointed out years ago that "job enrichment programs have cut jobs just as effectively as automation or engineers' stopwatches."[71]

Freeman and Rogers found that managers and workers—whether unionized or not—favored various forms of employee representation and decision making. These researchers propose greater channels of representation and changes in labor law to promote more plant-level councils (common in Europe) and to modify the ban on company unions. Although most nonunion workers are not going to join AFL-CIO unions in the foreseeable future, they said, the government should toughen the protections of all workers who want to join unions.[72]

The Dunlop Commission recommended changes to make it easier for workers to join unions and win contracts but also proposed weakening workers' protection against company-dominated worker organizations. Douglas Fraser, retired UAW president and the commission's lone labor representative, wrote a dissent to that proposed change.[73] In any event, the Dunlop Commission's proposals were not enacted.

Foundations have played an active role in a major area of growth in the labor movement since World War II—unionism in government agencies. Because public-sector unionism raised the issue of encroachment on decision making by elected and appointed officials, early foundation programs sought to level the playing field by equipping ill-prepared government managers to deal with unions.[74] Over a five-year period beginning in 1970, for example, the Ford Foundation made grants totaling $1.2 million to the Labor-Management Relations Service (LMRS), which was established by associations of mayors and other officials. The LMRS managed programs to train government officials in collective bargaining and labor relations. However, that organization—and the foundation that supported it—ran afoul of Jerry Wurf, president of the American Federation of State, County, and Municipal Employees (AFSCME), who accused the LMRS of opposing federal collective bargaining legislation for local governments and of supporting the antilabor agendas of conservative members of city and county associations.[75]

Beginning in the mid-1990s, foundations have fostered union-government collaboration through a committee of public-employee unions and organizations representing state and local officials. Funded by the Ford and Annie E. Casey foundations, the project is an outgrowth of union disgruntlement at the absence of a representative of organized labor from a commission on "reinventing government" at the state and local levels. The unions' reaction came to the attention of a Ford Foundation program officer who was serving on a Labor Department task force, and to rectify the omission he invited a proposal from the AFL-CIO's Professional Employees Department (PED), which is composed of thirty-five international unions representing 4.5 million public workers. Statewide symposia funded by Ford resulted in concrete proposals to reform the workplace and encourage innovation as a matter of routine practice.

The Annie E. Casey Foundation also supported a major project that involved unions in restructuring human services. Its collaboration with the PED grew out of its "New Futures" project in six cities designed to make social service agencies more flexible and responsive to families' needs. "When I thought about who's involved in these reform efforts, it was clear that a key missing player was organized labor," recalls Janice Nattoli, a Casey Foundation program officer. The aim is to engage unions in efforts to meet the needs of families in their neighborhoods rather than through central agencies.[76]

Thus foundations have made important contributions to the understanding of economic instability, including the part played by labor-management relations. But it is stretching a point to conclude they have produced solutions, especially to major upheavals. In the early 1930s the Rockefeller Foundation appropriated $1.5 million (from which grants were made to the Brookings Institution, the Social Science Research Council, and other traditional agencies) "with the idea of expediting the search for some solution of the miseries and suffering caused by the financial depression." Raymond Fosdick later concluded, "It cannot be said that any startling results came from this emergency appropriation. It was based on hopes that were far too sanguine. There was no quick and easy remedy for the malady; there was not even the possibility of swift and accurate diagnosis. . . . The trustees discovered that economic maladjustment is a long-term problem, and that there is no short cut to a cure."[77] When a foundation took the rare step of directly intervening in public policy, however, as the Twentieth Century Fund did in the drafting and passage of the Wagner Act, the result was potent.

2

Dimensions of Connection and Mistrust

As disparate as they are in origin and structure, foundations and labor unions share certain characteristics. On a narrow legal basis, both are nonprofit organizations, exempt from taxation under the Internal Revenue Code. Unions, however, are defined as self-help organizations, in a class that analysts call "clubs." That is, their benefits accrue essentially to their members, as distinguished from collective-type nonprofit organizations (for example, the Sierra Club), which benefit nonmembers as well as members. Contributions to the latter are tax deductible; contributions to unions and other club-type nonprofit organizations in the same category—social clubs and professional business groups—are not.[1] Under law, for a benefit to be public "it must not be fully captured by the *quid pro quo* but must spill over into society at large."[2] Some scholars, however, would argue that unions also produce certain public benefits, such as establishing a floor of improved wages and working conditions. Moreover, as David Hammack has noted, labor unions and other movements intended to empower the poor have often depended on support from large numbers of poor people.[3] Such arguments have not persuaded the Internal Revenue Service.

Unions and foundations differ, of course, in their financing and governance. Unions derive their income from members' dues and are governed by elected officials, though instances of undemocratic practices have been common. Private foundations, the major type of foundation (89 percent of all foundations) and the one mainly dealt with in this book, function with the income from assets contributed by a wealthy individual or family. They are governed by self-perpetuating boards of trustees. They conduct or help others conduct charitable, educational, religious, or other activities serving the public good, primarily by making grants to nonprofit organizations.

The usual relationship between foundations and other tax-exempt organizations—grantmaker and grant recipient—rarely applies to relations with unions. Foundations are permitted to make grants to unions, but they involve restrictions (grouped under IRS provisions known as "expenditure responsibility"). Moreover, unions rarely turn to foundations for financial assistance, though, as will be seen, indirect assistance has been given in many instances. And a few unions have set up fund-raising arms to which foundations and other donors may more readily make tax-deductible donations— such as the National Education Association's National Foundation for the Improvement of Education. These usually are "public foundations," which do not have endowments, but use funds from donors or the founding organization to make grants or otherwise advance charitable purposes.

The first modern American foundation, the Peabody Education Fund, was created in 1867 with $3 million from George Peabody, a New England banker who was also responsible for establishing the Boston Public Library. His foundation sought to repair some of the ravages of the Civil War by improving education in the South, especially among blacks. Peabody believed that foundations did not improve with age, so he specified that his was to be liquidated fifty years after its founding—not so with the majority of foundations, some of which are approaching the century mark.

Labor organization began well before the Civil War, overcoming a court judgment in 1806 that unions were criminal conspiracies. The U.S. labor movement was born when Philadelphia unions banded together in 1827 to promote the ten-hour day, and the following year the Workingman's Party was organized. The Panic of 1837 virtually destroyed the burgeoning labor movement, but by the 1850s several national unions had been founded and had won the ten-hour day in large cities.

The first great period of foundation growth—1900–1920—saw the establishment of the Russell Sage, Carnegie, Milbank, and Rockefeller philanthropies. By 1915 at least $500 million had been invested in foundations; in 1931 the twenty largest had assets totaling $859 million.[4] Over the next six decades, the number of foundations has grown enormously, from fewer than 1,000 in the 1930s to 40,000 in 1996 (the last year for which data are available), with assets of $268 billion and annual grants of $13.8 billion. For such a vast enterprise, they employ relatively few people, some twelve thousand.[5]

Before the great foundations were created, the Knights of Labor had flourished (730,000 members at its peak in 1873) and declined, the American Federation of Labor (AFL) had been organized (1886), and individual unions had grown in strength following the depression of the 1890s. In contrast to the radicalism of the Industrial Workers of the World (IWW), the skilled craftsmen of the AFL developed a brand of unionism marked by a strong set of business values—accepting the inviolability of contracts, the inevitability of industrial concentration, the practical sovereignty of management in the making of general industrial policy, and the obligation of union executives to become technical experts in their particular industry. Industrial America had been bruised by riots as railroad workers struck to protest wage cuts, the Haymarket bombing during a demonstration for the eight-hour day, and the bitter Homestead, Pullman, and anthracite strikes. By World War I, the number of international unions affiliated with the AFL had risen to 120, and union membership stood at a remarkable 2.1 million.

From a focus on education and public health early in the twentieth century, foundations expanded their interests to virtually every avenue of social, cultural, and scientific enterprise. In cash terms, foundation funding relating to organized labor has been minuscule compared to the billions of dollars spent annually in major fields of foundation support: education, religion, the arts, health care, poverty, and delinquency. A survey of labor-related grants by foundations since the mid-1980s discloses some 630 grants by 169 foundations. During a one-year period in 1994 and 1995, there were 187 such grants, totaling $11.7 million. These represented only 0.3 percent of the 73,000 grants that foundations made during that period in all fields, and 0.2 percent of the $6.1 billion granted. Tiny proportions hold for the earlier years for which data are available.[6]

These small sums are consistent with the limited engagement of foundations with social movement philanthropy. Surveys by Craig Jenkins, a leading scholar of that field, disclose that the number of foundations involved with social movements has never exceeded 150; total grants to advance such movements have typically ranged between 0.6 and 0.7 percent of all foundation giving, although the figure increased in the 1980s to 1.1 percent. Even in the heyday of foundation support for social movements—the 1960s and 1970s—foundations, Jenkins noted, "were not particularly interested in such controversial and unconventional topics as peace, union organizing and workplace reform, or recruiting in the cities through tenant organizing and community movements."[7] Put another way, grants related to labor are paltry compared with the hundreds of million dollars foundations have devoted to the education of business leaders at the graduate level.

The principal media of exchange between foundations and unions, then, have not been cash grants but foundation-supported research on labor, joint support of projects, or grants to third parties for programs in which unions play a role but are not necessarily identified in the public record. For example, the collaboration between foundations and unions to establish community development corporations in inner-city neighborhoods is not counted in foundation records or data bases as union-related activity. The bitter dispute in New York City between the teachers' union and the Ford Foundation in the 1960s is classified under something like the rubric of school reform.

Controversy and Commitment

Central to the question of foundations' engagement with organized labor is the dilemma of controversy. From the outset, foundations have been beset by ideological strains—accused on one hand of fomenting radical social change and on the other of defending conservatism and the status quo. When the great foundations were launched, there was no more controversial issue than organized labor. Yet by the first decade of the twentieth century social scientists, intellectuals, and prominent clergymen—groups to which the foundations had a natural affinity—were calling for justice for labor rather than benevolence. Were it not for the chill of the Rockefeller Foundation's association with the Ludlow massacre, foundations would have been more attentive to the labor movement sooner.

Among the critics accusing organized philanthropy of detachment from social problems was Jane Addams. She said donors who supported churches, libraries, and recreation facilities were unwilling to work toward "social righteousness in its most advanced form, that is, toward changes in legislation and working conditions so as to maintain a higher standard of living for all." Addams illustrated the point with a story about a group of manufacturers who offered Hull House $50,000 if she would drop her advocacy of anti-sweatshop legislation. She refused.[8]

The theme of detachment recurs. A former president of the Russell Sage Foundation, Donald Young, chided foundations in 1962 for having yielded leadership in such controversial areas as race relations, medical care, mental health, and the prevention of poverty. In the past, he said, foundations had used their advantage of independence "to pioneer with projects far too controversial or uncertain of results for support by tax money under political control."[9] Young was referring to the Russell Sage Foundation's pathbreaking studies of working conditions and unionism. In a more recent appraisal of foundations, Waldemar Nielsen, a respected analyst of the field, observed a continued reluctance on the part of the majority to delve deeply into controversial social issues. These issues, he wrote, were becoming the province of neoconservatives represented by Irving Kristol's journal *The Public Interest* and the Moral Majority. No longer were foundations the progenitors of policies concerning government responsibilities.[10]

Foundations continue to insist that they are independent organizations free of ideological slant, working in the public interest, which is not to say that they steer clear of public policy, including issues related to organized labor. Chapters 4 and 12 describe foundations' roles in the Wagner Act in the 1930s and the NAFTA legislative dispute in the 1990s. Effective philanthropy must have viewpoints, and even traditional charity, and especially scientific philanthropy, require information and ideas. That these may be disputable does not negate the charitable nature of the enterprise. Given the diversity of American society, someone is sure to regard foundations as biased.

Generalizations about foundations, including attitudes and behavior toward organized labor, have become less valid as the field has become more diverse. For one thing, the vast majority of foundations—82 percent—were established after World War II, and more than half since the late 1970s. For another, the foundations created in the first two decades of the century (Carnegie and Rockefeller in particular) were initially governed directly by the founders along with close advisers, business associates, and class allies. As foundations evolved, most of the larger ones came to be administered by professional stewards. They and the trustees elected to guide foundations after World War I were for the most part prominent businessmen and academics from the Northeast. The Depression hastened the trend. Founders may remain as trustees, and their values and ideologies may still be reflected in foundation activity, but in time many foundation boards become independent. Far from being monolithic, the philanthropic world has always been subject to internal dissension, bureaucratic maneuvering, ideological debate, and organizational self-interest. And in the last two decades of the twentieth century foundation staffs (and, to a lesser extent, boards) have become more diversified as to race and gender.

Attitudes

How have foundations and organized labor viewed one another? Early on, the institutions appraised each other with suspicion, if not hostility. The men who established the early foundations generally feared the "radical" consequences of unionization, viewing militant labor as the vanguard of socialism. The men they chose to direct their philanthropies generally shared those views, although some sought conciliation and industrial peace. For their part, unions were predictably suspicious of centers of philanthropic power spawned from fortunes created from the blood and sweat of exploited labor.

The roots of union distrust of organized philanthropy may also be traced to mid-nineteenth-century charitable practices. As David Montgomery noted, "control of relief for unemployed but able-bodied men and women was commandeered by bourgeois reformers who reshaped charity to reinforce industrial discipline."[11] Workers preferred government control. Said a labor editor in 1828, "I think that no such thing as charities should exist; for though it is very proper that schools should be instituted for the instruction of youth, and asylums provided for the aged, the sick and the infirm, yet these things ought not be left to the uncertainty of private charities, but to be institutions founded and supported by the government itself."[12]

When foundations appeared, unions viewed them as surrogates for capitalist power. Resentment of trusts, voracious railroad builders, and monopoly capital was also shared by the public and the owners of innumerable small companies that failed in a series of financial panics and depressions of the late nineteenth century. Populism and the Populist Party were principal outgrowths of this resentment.

Not surprisingly, union suspicion of foundations was fed by the views of two of those Theodore Roosevelt called "malefactors of great wealth"—Carnegie and Rockefeller, who, in the words of two foundation historians, "fought against organized labor with the kind of brutality many in their position considered appropriate."[13] Rockefeller was "so bitter against the way the unions had acted he would not have a union man on his estate," his own son reported.[14] Carnegie seemed to take a different stance. He declared at one point, "The right of workingmen to combine and to form trades unions is no less sacred than the right of the manufacturer to enter into association and conferences with his . . . fellows. . . . My experience has been that trades unions upon the whole are beneficial both to labor and capital."[15] But when his own enterprises were at stake, as in the bloody strike at Homestead Steel in Pennsylvania in 1892, he fought the unions. On the eve of the Homestead strike Carnegie was in Scotland, but he cabled his support to Henry Clay Frick (his antiunion manager) "not stopping short of a contest. We are with you to the end."[16] In the battle between striking workers and armed Pinkerton detectives hired by the company, three Pinkertons and several workers were killed, and Frick persuaded the governor to send state militia to take over the town.

The *Locomotive Fireman's Magazine* scorned Carnegie's "Gospel of Wealth" as "flapdoodle" and "slush." It required patience, said the magazine, to read about " 'the right modes of using immense fortunes known to be the product of cool, Christless robbery." And the conservative *National Labor Tribune* sneered, "Oh, most adorable Carnegie, we love thee, because thou are the almighty iron and steel king of the world; thou who so much resembles the pharisee. . . . We thank thee . . . for the hungry men, women and children of the land . . . for all the free gifts you have given the public at the expense of your slaves."[17]

Most industrial giants, Karl and Katz note, "never ceased to think of themselves as friends of labor. . . . Their paternalism—wishing to help employees in need and reward virtue—made opposition from organized labor seem almost conspiratorial, an affront to their generosity. . . . They justified the employment of armed guards to protect their property as a regrettable but necessary response to the threat of violence they thought inherent in the strike weapon."[18]

Foundations often supported Progressive views on various issues—in medicine, social welfare, and governmental economic policy. And some foundation leaders did become sensitive to criticism that they used their power against workers' interests. In his history of the first four decades of the Rockefeller Foundation, Raymond Fosdick, its president for twenty years, addressed charges that the foundation would use its power for "unsociable purposes": "Fears were frequently expressed that the . . . Foundation would be used to crush labor unionism, or warp education for capitalistic ends, or foster religious strife, or undermine the aims of progressive legislation in promoting forward-looking social practices. . . . Time and the persuasive argument of performance have answered most of these charges . . . their absurdity is [also] evidenced by the character and high integrity of the trustees."[19]

For their part, such liberal intellectuals as Ira Steward, Henry George, Edward Bellamy, and later Henry Demarest Lloyd and Clarence Darrow articulated pro-labor ideas that reflected an indigenous American radicalism. Despite the ambivalence of the Progressive Movement toward unions, certain leading Progressives (Jane Addams, Florence Kelley, John Dewey, Louis Brandeis, and Frank Walsh) were closely associated with organized labor.

Nonetheless, unions' wariness of foundations is of a piece with their attitudes to intellectuals and universities, with which foundations have been strongly identified. One need not look far for reasons, beginning with Harvard's Charles W. Eliot, a confidant of Rockefeller, who glorified the strikebreaker as an "American hero" and pleaded that employers should allow "no sacrifice of the independent American worker to the labor union."[20] In 1902 an AFL study complained that private universities were appointing trustees who were not likely to antagonize wealthy donors and that public universities were dependent on state legislatures, "which . . . are controlled by corporate interests that have some axe to grind."[21] Similarly, Gompers was suspicious of the appointment of college and university presidents to foundation boards. He urged communities to reject grants from Carnegie Corporation to build public libraries, because the money was "tainted."[22]

In contrast, Rockefeller lamented the drift of some professors "toward socialism and some forms of Bolshevism." Many of these professors, he said, "would not have had their opportunities for education but for the funds contributed gratuitously by the people whom they seem so readily to assail."[23]

Testifying before the Walsh Commission, Gompers was most critical of the Rockefeller Foundation and its new department titled Investigation of Industrial Relations. And the trade union conservative John Frey quoted Gompers, "God save us from our intellectual friends. All I ask is that they get off our backs."[24] The bitterness continued in a 1918 AFL Executive Committee resolution on intellectuals, which declared, "Although we welcome the advice and suggestions of any and all that are willing to give them to our men and women, we decline to yield the leadership of our movement to those who do not work. We object to those who undertake to be the censor and mentor of the American labor movement."[25] (In an unkind cut, the AFL also opposed the granting of pensions by private foundations to retired faculty of public universities.)[26]

Some labor scholars actually endorsed distance between intellectuals and union leaders. Commons's colleague Selig Perlman believed that "American workers, left to their own devices and free of the noxious influence of intellectuals, were practical people interested in better wages, hours, and working conditions—not in such radical notions as combining to improve their position as a class. Of paramount interest, then, as the truest vehicle of workers' self-expression, was the 'pure and simple' labor union."[27]

Unions also resented foundation support of ardent proponents of scientifically molding worker behavior. The most prominent system was devised by Frederick Winslow Taylor in the decades surrounding the turn of the twentieth century. Originally viewed by Progressives as an enlightened approach to labor relations, Taylorism came to be regarded as a management response to inefficiency; by fragmenting, simplifying, and routinizing work, management could more firmly control work processes. Taylor's "scientific management" linked wages to productivity through "time and motion" studies, keyed to the speed and output of the individual worker. Unions, fearing Taylorism's time studies, premium and wage bonus plans, and production standards as a "speedup," sometimes responded with strikes. Labor obtained federal legislation preventing government arsenals and navy yards from employing time and motion studies.[28] Workers who struck against the system at Westinghouse Electric near Pittsburgh in 1914, for example, called the Taylor system "the last word in man killing."[29] "To organized labor [Taylor] was a soulless slave driver, out to destroy the workingman's health and rob him of his manhood," his biographers observe. Taylor himself hated unions, but later proponents of Taylorism counseled managers to come to terms with organized labor, and AFL leaders softened their opposition in the 1920s.[30]

The leading psychologist in the human relations field during the interwar years, Edward L. Thorndike, received approximately $325,000 in grants from Carnegie Corporation between 1922 and 1938. His research concluded that employers could promote conditions that best advanced the contentment of the worker without sacrificing productivity: "This did not require increasing wages or reducing the work day but rather mastering the art of human relations. If the employer satisfied the psychological needs for recognition and social distinction, workers' grievances would largely disappear."[31] (Thorndike also favored eugenics theory, a field in which the Rockefeller and Carnegie foundations were active.)

Intellectual support for labor peaked during the New Deal years, but gradually declined after World War II, turning sometimes to sharp criticism, as in studies in the late 1950s and early 1960s supported by the Center for the Study of Democratic Institutions, an offshoot of the Ford Foundation.[32] A prominent official of the UAW, Brendan Sexton, described such critics as a "vocal, widely published, and . . . somewhat more influential than one might expect based upon known scholarly achievement or demonstrated creativity. . . . No group has been more savagely critical of trade unions . . . [or] focused only on the omissions of trade unions. . . . The disenchanted intellectual discounts or ignores . . . the . . . fact that a large number of union officers and staff members stoutly resist the corrupting influences endemic to our society."[33]

Because many union leaders supported the Vietnam War and opposed affirmative action, revisionist labor historians of the 1970s discounted unions, shifting to history from the bottom up, examining the working class through cultural and political as well as economic prisms.[34] Michael Frisch and Daniel Wolkowitz suggest that the history of the labor movement in the nineteenth century may have seemed to New Left scholars more relevant to radicalism than the era of the AFL-CIO.[35] Organized labor also saw itself under attack by advocates for the poor and minorities whose causes it had long championed. Since these groups enjoyed the support of activist foundations, union and other members of the urban, lower-middle working class felt that foundations ignored them in favor of their perceived adversaries.[36]

As this is written, the pendulum seems to be swinging again. Signs of a rapprochement between intellectuals and organized labor began appearing after the changing of the guard at the AFL-CIO in 1995.

Surveys

As part of the research for this book, I surveyed contemporary union and foundation officials to gauge their opinions of each other's institutions. Their attitudes are generally marked more by indifference than by distrust, and little contact was reported. Union leaders were largely unaware of connections with foundations, and traces of Gompers-era animus toward them remain. Similarly, foundation officials' knowledge of past interaction with organized labor is thin, and even some who have had programmatic contact with unions share some of the negative stereotypes held by the general public.

Following is a sampling of union officers' views:

"Most unions don't consider foundations to be a relevant part of their lives," said Robert Emerson, a Michigan state legislator who was formerly president of a union local and later on the regional staff of AFSCME. "Attitudes are probably negative, though not deeply so. It's simply a feeling that the money with which foundations were built came from people who had no close relations to labor and in many cases exploited labor. And down to the present, there is a feeling that most foundations are controlled by corporate executives."[37]

Robert S. Keener, president of the National Federation of Federal Employees, considers foundations to be "very worthwhile and generally public-minded." The difficulty, he says, "seems to be in learning of the existence of the various foundations and their funding availability. Since [our union] has never been contacted by any foundation, it appears that the lack of awareness is reciprocal."[38]

Ron Myslowka, president of the United Textile Workers of America, believes that foundations are "helpful for promotion of business interests and are used essentially for private purposes."[39]

Charles E. Bradford, director of occupational safety and health and community services for the International Association of Machinists and Aerospace Workers, wrote: "I view foundations as helpful, generally public-minded with some private purposes, [but] foundation staff are probably totally unfamiliar with the labor movement."[40]

Gordon H. Bream, executive assistant to the president, United Paperworkers International Union, wrote: "I consider foundations helpful and public-minded, although I believe most to be controlled by conservative directors not sympathetic to the labor movement."[41]

Anne C. Green, director of research and education for the International Chemical Workers Union, noted: "Discussion has taken place about setting up an appropriate arm under the IRS code to permit foundation grants. However, [we believe] this would be inappropriate. Our mission is to organize workers, to bargain collectively, and to educate workers about a variety of issues. Our feeling is that grants would narrow what we could do or say to our members or potential members."[42]

Moe Biller, president of the American Postal Workers Union, remarked: "It would make sense for unions and foundations to work together when they are serving common purposes. Labor unions have always shown concern for others in their community and have been more than willing to work to help those in need (i.e., raising funds for charitable causes)."[43]

An unusual perspective—that of a former union official now responsible for raising funds from foundations for a nonprofit advocacy organization—is provided by the president of the National Committee on Pay Equity, Susan Bianchi-Sand. Formerly president of the Association of Flight Attendants and a vice president of the AFL-CIO, she finds it more difficult to deal with foundations than with airline management. "In collective bargaining," she notes, "we represented a workforce. With foundations we're dependent. Foundations realize that much of our support comes from unions. It doesn't seem to bother them, but they share the general public's perception of unions as dwindling dinosaurs. Some foundations are aware of what unions have done on the social justice issues, but there's little discussion between the two." She also finds that even in some foundations that focus on women's issues, unions are unpopular. "By the same token I don't think unions have a clue about what resources are available to them and what sort of collaborative work could be done with foundations."[44]

Men and women in mainstream foundations that have had some interest in labor unions since the mid-1980s:

Terry Saario, former president of the Northwest Area Foundation, commented: "Particularly as one focuses upon such populations as those who are hard to employ, those who are marginally employed, the working poor, or migrant workers, for example, one must take into consideration the role of unions both in the protection of the rights of these workers as well as sometimes creating barriers that make it difficult for such workers to obtain a reasonable job at a living wage. Therefore, I think it is in a foundation's best interest to recognize that labor unions and organizations are certainly a factor that has to be dealt with positively and negatively as they think through grant strategies."[45]

One of the few labor officials who went on to serve at a foundation—Larry Kirkman, who worked for the AFL-CIO before becoming executive director of the Benton Foundation—expressed surprise at how little understanding those in the labor movement have of foundations. Conversely, he says, foundations have little understanding of unions. For example, the film *Roger and Me* (about General Motors and its workers) was shown at a Council on Foundations annual meeting and, Kirkman reports, "I was stunned at the ignorance among foundations of what unions and the labor movement are up to. Foundation officials don't view unions as innovators. They stereotype [them], and yet many unions play a similar role to foundations—conducting research and advocating change." Some of the mid-level staff of the AFL-CIO are very bright, says Kirkman; "they are the match of many grant makers and as advanced as any of them."[46]

Kirke Wilson, executive director of the Rosenberg Foundation, observed,

"In contrast to the post-war period, when labor organizations were seen as agents of change and potential allies in community development, in the post–civil rights environment trade unions and their leaders are too often either opponents of social change or outside the debate. For example, trade unions have been slow to join the efforts to improve the wages, benefits, and working conditions for part-time, contract and other contingent workers."[47]

Noting that the Charles Stewart Mott Foundation has never had a grant program focused on labor organizations, Willard J. Hertz, a retired Mott vice president, remarked, "This is hardly surprising considering the bitter anti-UAW prejudices of the founder, who was General Motors' largest single stockholder. Nor is it surprising that the Foundation has never had any labor person on its board. C. S. [Mott] would turn over in his grave."[48]

Thomas Lambeth, executive director of the Z. Smith Reynolds Foundation in Winston-Salem, noting that unionized workers are a very small part of the work force in North Carolina, says nevertheless that his foundation would have no reluctance to support a project because of union involvement. The foundation has supported several worker centers in the fields of health and women's rights and made a grant to the A. Philip Randolph Institute in Raleigh to bring together black trade union members with community people to work on issues of common concern.[49]

"The irony of having the vestiges of robber baron wealth supporting proletarian causes is not lost on us, although our endowment came from success in generally nonunionized industries," said Joel D. Getzendanner, vice president of programs at the Joyce Foundation.[50]

Peter Bell, when he was president of the Edna McConnell Clark Foundation, wrote, "In our Program for Disadvantaged Youth we are aware that teachers' unions can advance or block . . . reform, and [we] try to enlist them into playing a positive role. Similarly in our Children's Program, we know that public employees' unions can advance or block the incorporation of family preservation services, and [so we] try to include them on the side of reform or work around them if necessary."[51]

Less typical is the statement of Larry Kressley of the Public Welfare Foundation: "I think the extent to which a foundation is open to funding labor organizing activities of any kind has been an indication of a foundation's true progressive bent. Few mainstream foundations seem to have any interest in, or even understand, the rationale behind supporting workplace organizing as a means of improving the social and economic status of poor and working people."[52]

Paradoxically, even some outspoken advocates of social change, such as members of the National Network of Grantmakers (NNG), share the conservative critique of the labor movement. They regard it as a special interest group, serving only its members and antagonistic to nonmembers, including victims of race and gender bias, and bureaucratic (if not corrupt), focusing on organizational preservation and perks for its officials. Worse, unions are often associated with corruption. On the other hand, small foundations currently demonstrating greater interest in organized labor come mainly from the self-styled "progressive foundations" (such as the Haymarket People's Fund, the Unitarian Universalist Veatch Program, and the North Star Fund), many of which are members of the NNG.

Their attitude toward foundations aside, several unions have adopted the foundation form to honor prominent figures in the labor movement. The Communications Workers of America, for example, established the Joseph Anthony Beirne Foundation (named after the CWA's late president) in 1975. It has awarded scholarships to children of union members and made grants to such organizations as the Center for Public Integrity, the Institute for Southern Studies, and the National Organizers Alliance.

The Sidney Hillman Foundation, created in 1946 to honor the founder of the Amalgamated Clothing Workers Union, gives awards to outstanding officials, public figures, and journalists such as Herbert H. Lehman, William O. Douglas, Harry S Truman, Martin Luther King Jr., and Michael Harrington.

The Cesar E. Chavez Foundation was set up by family friends and colleagues after Chavez's death in 1993 at age sixty-six. Connected to the UFW and the Farmworker Service Centers, it also receives support from corporations and foundations. The focus is on producing educational materials and promoting events commemorating Chavez's union organizing and historical and religious legacy.

The American Federation of State, County, and Municipal Employees (AFSCME) established a $1 million Jerry Wurf Fund in 1982 to honor its late president. The fund supports labor-management activities at Harvard.

The Bayard Rustin Fund was established in 1988 to commemorate the civil rights leader who was chairman of the A. Philip Randolph Institute and who championed alliances between organized labor, churches, and liberals as a means of advancing black progress. The fund financed services by Rustin Fellows in labor unions and human-rights organizations, and sponsored lectures and student conferences, but has cut back sharply owing to lack of funding.

3

Congressional Intervention

Ahalf century after the first great foundations were established, a congressional committee provided a sober perspective on the relationship between foundations and organized labor: "The rise of a powerful labor movement refuted the prophecy that the foundation could be a strategic weapon in industrial warfare and foundations had become increasingly evaluated in terms of their programs and dissociated from judgments about their donors."[1] Congressional investigations have scrutinized unions and foundations separately and in some cases explored the links between them. Labor unrest was the focus of the first U.S. Commission on Industrial Relations, which Congress authorized in 1898. A second commission was urged on President William Howard Taft by Progressive reformers associated with *Survey* magazine (supported by the Russell Sage Foundation), following the 1910 dynamiting of the building of the antiunion *Los Angeles Times*, one of a series of violent episodes that accompanied the remarkable expansion of unionism around the turn of the century.

Industrial Relations Commission (Walsh Commission)

The second Industrial Relations Commission, which Congress authorized during the Taft Administration, actually came into being in 1913. Its nine members, nominated by Woodrow Wilson and confirmed by Congress, included Frank Walsh as chairman. Congress charged it to investigate underlying causes of industrial conflict and make recommendations to temper a tense environment. In addition to members giving equal representation to labor, business, and the public it had a substantial staff of investigators. Its investigation of foundations, unlike later ones, was not conducted by members of Congress.[2]

The Progressive era's crusades against gross inequalities and industrial monopolies was reflected in growing congressional hostility toward philanthropists and the foundations they created. Thus Congress rejected requests for federal incorporation of large foundations on the ground that their activities "were but thin disguises for institutions established to protect and defend 'the robber barons,' their industrial empires, and their fortunes."[3] Congress had approved federal charters for Rockefeller's General Education Board (1902), the Carnegie Institution of Washington (1904), and the Carnegie Foundation for the Advancement of Teaching (1906). But by 1910, when the Rockefeller Foundation applied for a federal charter, the climate had changed. With Rockefeller's Standard Oil Company a prime target of antitrust agitation, the foundation was viewed as a creature of big business. Anti-Rockefeller attitudes would lead several senators in 1914 to move to prohibit the Department of Agriculture from accepting grants from the General Education Board for farm demonstration work in the South.[4] For three years, the Rockefeller Foundation fought for a federal charter against opposition within and outside Congress. Rockefeller was willing to have the president and other high-ranking public officials sit on the board of a federally chartered foundation and to give Congress a veto over its actions. Fortuitously, Congress's rebuff to such a direct federal role bolstered the independence of foundations. Finally, in 1913 Rockefeller withdrew the application in favor of a New York State charter, which that legislature granted in less than two weeks.

The first confrontation between organized labor and a philanthropic foundation became a focus of the Walsh Commission's work. On April 24, 1914, state militia killed ten striking employees of the Colorado Fuel and Iron Company (CF&I) in Ludlow, Colorado; eleven children and two women suffocated to death when one of the tents to which miners' families had moved when they were evicted from their company-owned homes was torched. This event, which became known as the Ludlow Massacre, was part of a larger conflict—two hundred deaths during an unsuccessful strike by nine thousand coal miners against twenty coal companies. The strike lasted fifteen months, during which arrests and armed clashes became routine.[5] The strikers, according to one member of the militia, were "being rapidly debauched and degraded by conditions over which they have no control" and "living under a despotism so absolute that the radical labor press is not far wrong in calling them slaves."[6] Eventually, President Wilson declared a state of insurrection and sent in two thousand federal troops.

A striking miners' tent colony in Ludlow, Colorado, was torched by militia in 1914, resulting in the deaths of two women and eleven children. The disaster occurred at a Rockefeller-owned coal mine, and in the aftermath the Rockefeller Foundation hired a Canadian labor authority, W. L. Mackenzie King, to investigate, triggering bitter criticism of the foundation. As part of a public relations effort, King (center) and John D. Rockefeller Jr. pose with an employee of the Colorado Fuel and Iron Company. (Rockefeller Archive Center)

CF&I was part of the Rockefeller industrial empire. John D. Rockefeller Jr., while frequently denouncing the United Mine Workers, unsuccessfully sought backing among his business associates for a private organization that would conduct research and education to find peaceful and cooperative solutions to labor-management problems.[7] Nationwide revulsion to the violence at Ludlow prompted him to hire W. L. Mackenzie King, a former Canadian minister of labor, to investigate the affair and devise plans for improved industrial relations. He was placed on the payroll of the Rockefeller Foundation, which had been chartered only a year earlier, where he created an Investigation of Industrial Relations. King favored a government investigation of the facts, during which time employer lockouts and worker strikes would be prohibited.

The Rockefeller trustees explained the King project as follows:

It seemed to [us], especially in view of the industrial conflict in Colorado, that the Foundation could do no greater service than by instituting a careful and thorough inquiry into the cause of industrial unrest and maladjustment, with the object, not of passing judgment upon the merits of any particular controversy, but rather on assembling in a purely objective way, and with scientific accuracy, the experience of this and other countries, as illustrating both the evils inherent in modern industrial conditions, and the successful or promising experiments that had been made.[8]

Rockefeller, guided by King and the publicist Ivy Lee, held meetings in mining communities, and the foundation made a $100,000 grant to alleviate poverty among the miners and their families.[9] A combination of CF&I intransigence, the use of strikebreakers, and the exhaustion of strike funds finally broke the strike in December 1914. The workers agreed to give up representation by the militant UMW and voted overwhelmingly to join a newly organized company union (under what came to be known as the Colorado Industrial Plan), with which management promised to negotiate fairly. Over time, however, the mine workers lost faith in the company union, and in the 1930s the UMW defeated it by a vote of 877 to 272.[10]

Responding to the public outcry over the Ludlow Massacre, the Industrial Relations Commission, which had been examining conditions at several work sites for the past two years, began in 1915 to explore the role of foundations generally, and the Rockefeller Foundation's program directed by King specifically. The commission's chairman, Frank Walsh, soon announced to the press that "the Rockefeller Foundation is entirely without the realm of Government control."[11] Furthermore, he stated that the commission had been informed that "the creation of . . . foundations was the beginning of an effort to perpetuate the present position of predatory wealth through the corruption of sources of public information . . . [and] that if not checked by legislation, these foundations will be used as instruments to change the form of the government of the U.S. at a future date, and there is even a hint that there is a fear of a monarchy."[12] A questionnaire that the commission distributed to foundations asked if "industrial warfare was related to possible defects and maladjustment in industry and whether existing private and public agencies deal effectively with these problems." It went on, "Do the large resources of endowed foundations constitute a possible menace? If so, what regulation or supervision is desirable?" Asked by the commission about the foundation's hiring of King on a business-related matter (to study labor relations following the Ludlow Massacre), Rockefeller replied, with more candor than discretion, "Our office staff is a sort of family affair. We talk over all kinds of matters of a common interest. We have not drawn sharp lines between business and philanthropic interests."[13] Walsh's inquiries extended to Carnegie philanthropies and other major foundations—Russell Sage, the Baron de Hirsch Fund, and the Cleveland Foundation.

Walsh called upon leading Progressives (Louis Brandeis, the future Supreme Court justice, and John Haynes Holmes, a noted Unitarian minister) to bolster his case against the Rockefeller Foundation. Brandeis, then a corporate attorney active in labor matters, feared the development of corporate "absolutism" that, though initially benevolent, would expand beyond the reach and control of both business and government. Samuel Gompers testified before the commission, "I believe that such Foundations as the Rockefeller cannot impartially investigate problems in the field of industry. . . . The results of the industrial investigations [by] foundations would not carry conviction to the workers or influence their action, would not decrease or alleviate industrial unrest." John R. Lawson, a UMW representative who had been active in the Colorado strike, commented at the hearing, "It is not their money that these lords of commercialized virtue are spending, but the withheld wages of the American working class. . . . The Rockefeller foundations were spending millions for health, education and conservation throughout the world, but not a dollar for those suffering the effects of the Ludlow Massacre."[14] The commission heard views favorable to foundations, however, from such sources as the *New York Times* and the former president of Harvard, Charles Eliot. The commission's final report termed foundations "reflections of creeping capitalism."[15]

Foundation policies "must inevitably be colored, if not controlled, to conform to the policies of . . . corporations from whose wealth they were founded," the report continued.

> [Their] funds represent largely the result . . . of the exploitation of the American public through the exaction of high prices. . . . The power of these foundations is practically unlimited. . . . [They] are subject to no public control, and their power can be curbed only by the difficult process of amending or revoking their charters. . . . The extent of the possible influence of these Foundations [in shaping education and opinion] . . . is shown by a large amount of evidence in the possession of the Commission (such as a degree of control over the teachings of professors) . . . which constitutes a most serious menace.[16]

In the final analysis, the commission majority termed the Rockefeller Foundation connection "tangible proof of the apprehension then felt concerning foundation penetration into the field of industrial and social problems." Walsh and two labor union members of the commission, James

Lennon and James O'Connell, recommended, in effect, that Congress dissolve the Rockefeller Foundation, confiscate its wealth, and distribute it among the unemployed. "This [proposal] . . . proceeded from the assumption that the money of the foundation came from workers' wages which were 'withheld by means of economic pressure, violation of the law, cunning and violence' by the Rockefellers."[17]

The commission majority disagreed, but recommended that federal funds be appropriated to take over much of the work done by foundations. The commission's eleven-volume report called for congressional regulation of the activities of American foundations, including a limit on their size and a requirement that those with assets over $1 million obtain a federal charter. Congress took no action.

In 1917, when the fires of the Colorado mine strife and the Walsh Commission had been banked and World War I was consuming the public interest, the Rockefeller Foundation quietly closed down its Investigation of Industrial Relations. So stung were its trustees by the Ludlow-Walsh trauma, according to Raymond Fosdick, that they decided to alter the basic strategy for spending the Founder's money. "Except for a narrow range of noncontroversial subjects, notably public health, medicine, and agriculture, the Foundation [would] become primarily not an operating agency but a fund-dispensing agency." Only in this way could both giver and recipient be freed from any "suspicion of ulterior interest."[18]

The Royal Little Investigation

Foundations were free of congressional attention for more than thirty years, but returned to the spotlight in 1947 in an investigation of foundations that owned profit-making businesses. The impetus was complaints from the CIO Textile Workers Union (TWU) against the misuse of a Rhode Island foundation whose funds came from the profits of the Textron Corporation. In Senate hearings, the TWU and Senator Charles Tobey (R.–New Hampshire) accused the foundation of providing funds to enable Royal Little, Textron's president, to purchase textile plants that he would then liquidate and revive in a low-wage state, resulting in the loss of several thousand jobs (unless the union was willing to "cut its own throat" on wages, hours, workloads, seniority, and arbitration).[19] Little defended the practice of "speculating" with funds set up as charitable trusts as a method of obtaining venture capital. But Emil Rieve, president of the TWU, accused Little of using "so-called charitable foundations which he set up" for self-serving business advantage, and, he went on, "Quite a few industries have also found [foundations] convenient . . .

as a means of avoiding taxes."[20] The Subcommittee concluded that through the manipulation of Little's trusts, Textron had gained an unfair competitive advantage over other textile manufacturers, and that the tax burden had been thrown more heavily upon the shoulders of all other taxpayers.[21]

Reflecting uneasiness over the mixture of charity and business, the Revenue Act of 1950 required arm's length dealing between a tax-exempt organization and substantial contributors, and penalties for financial misuse of tax-exempt organizations. Although many charitable organizations were exempted from the application of these provisions, private foundations were the main target.[22]

The Cox and Reece Committees of the 1950s

As the Cold War created a climate of militant anti-Communist suspicion and fear, private and government agencies examined alleged subversion. A House of Representatives Select Committee launched an investigation in 1952 into foundations and other nonprofit organizations, looking for "un-American activities." The committee was headed by Eugene E. Cox, a leader of the conservative southern wing of the Democratic Party. He made a distinction between foundations confined to medical research and culture and those that operated in the fields of social reform and international relations.

Howard W. Keele, the Cox Committee's general counsel, noted that Frederick Gates, the Baptist minister who had been the chief architect of the Rockefeller philanthropies, "was unalterably opposed to the Rockefeller endowments entering the controversial field of social sciences, which has proved to be the friction point. He argued . . . unsuccessfully that they should confine themselves to medical and scientific research."[23] Oddly, Keele introduced into the record an article in which Edwin R. Embree of the Rosenwald Fund accused foundations of shying away from controversial social issues. Noting "the recent diatribes of the *Chicago Tribune* that foundations are 'fostering the red menace,' " Embree had written, "the real criticism is not that foundations are vicious, but that they are inert."[24]

Keele cited a report of the House Un-American Activities Committee that Communist leadership was "strongly entrenched" in several unions, and equated such unions with foundations that supported union-related activities and "communist-front organizations." The William C. Whitney Foundation, the Field Foundation, and the Twentieth Century Fund were those he named. He pointed out, for example, that the Whitney Foundation had made grants to twenty organizations, including Commonwealth College in Arkansas, which had been "cited, criticized, or appeared" on the attorney-

general's 1947 *Guide to Subversive Organizations and Publications*. Charles Dol-
lard, president of Carnegie Corporation, was also questioned about small
grants ($5,000) twenty years earlier to Commonwealth College.[25]

Michael Straight, president of the Whitney Foundation, responded,
"There is no question that in [the fields of labor organization and education]
the Communist Party was a very active underground force. . . . I think it
would have been very remarkable, probably more a matter of luck than in-
tuition, had we had a perfect record . . . from your point of view." Straight
quoted Philip Murray, president of the CIO from 1940 to 1952, as saying that
Whitney Foundation support was useful in the CIO's struggle against the
Communist Party and expressed pride in a series of grants to the American
Labor Education Service, "working in a field which we feel is very important
and somewhat neglected by the trade unions themselves."[26]

In a letter to Cox of December 10, 1952, Solomon Barkin, director of research at the TWU, proposed a drastic measure to curb foundations—to limit
their lifetime to twenty-five years. Recalling his union's role in the 1950 Revenue Act, he urged that all states set up special offices to supervise charitable
trusts, as Rhode Island had done under pressure from his union. "The attorneys general of most States have shown little, or at best rare, interest in the
foundations and trusts to insure protection of the public interest," he wrote.[27]

Two professional anti-Communist witnesses testified about "subversive"
foundation-union connections. Maurice Malkin, a self-described "consultant" to the U.S. Immigration and Naturalization Service, said the Communist Party had succeeded in placing two Communists (William Z. Foster and
Benjamin Gitlow) and sympathizers on the Garland Fund board, and that
Anson Phelps Stokes's wife was a charter member of the Communist Party,
but its influence on the Phelps-Stokes Fund ended when Stokes divorced
her. These foundations, according to Malkin, supported the Worker's School
in New York, "which was actually the training school for Communist leadership in the U.S." He also claimed that Communists had penetrated the
Robert Marshall Fund, the Heckscher Foundation, the Guggenheim Foundation (citing their grants to various "Communist front" labor groups), and
Carnegie Corporation, where, he said, the Party organized office workers in
competition with the AFL: "We actually penetrated to the filing cabinets of
the foundations and charitable institutions [s]o we knew actually what was
going on and were able to act on it accordingly."[28]

Mary Van Kleeck of the Russell Sage Foundation, who had studied working conditions and organized labor for thirty years, was singled out by Malkin
and another Justice Department informer, Manning Johnson, as a member of
the Communist Party. "The imposing array of positions which she holds,"
said Johnson, "carries a lot of weight before congressional committees and

front organizations." He claimed that a report she and others submitted to a congressional committee had been prepared by Robert W. Dunn, head of the Party's labor research. Donald R. Young, who became president of Russell Sage two months before Van Kleeck's retirement, acknowledged the common assumption that she was "to the left of center," but he paid tribute to her work, calling her early books outstanding and influential.[29]

The informers' testimony, riddled with errors, carried little weight with the Cox Committee, which conducted its hearings in a friendly manner with no attempts to browbeat witnesses. The committee concluded that the Communist Party was not very successful in infiltrating foundations and making use of foundation grants, and it made only two recommendations: (1) full public accounting by foundations, and (2) reexamination of tax laws to encourage more support for education and philanthropic work from private sources.[30]

The Cox hearings were followed a year and a half later by a distinctly antagonistic investigation of foundations headed by Representative B. Carroll Reece (R.–Tennessee). Foundation representatives were not permitted to testify, and their written submissions were long afterward published as an appendix to the main hearings and soon permitted to go out of print. Hostile testimony was directed against the Fund for Adult Education (FAE) for a grant to the American Labor Education Service (ALES), whose conferences on farm-labor cooperation were attacked as antibusiness. Also challenged was FAE support of the Inter-University Labor Education Committee for publications that were prepared by the Union Leadership Project at the University of Chicago.[31] The committee staff examined the ALES intensively. The backgrounds of its personnel, together with its conferences, "suggest an interlocking directorate of individuals and groups who have been associated with militant socialism and even, in some cases, with Communist fronts."[32] The report named men and women who had also been cited by the House Un-American Activities Committee—Eduard C. Lindeman, Mrs. Sherwood Anderson, and J. Raymond Walsh, along with recipients of ALES awards, such as Albert Maltz and Clifford Odets, and such institutions as Brookwood Labor College in Katonah, New York, Commonwealth College, the Southern Summer School (which met at various locations), the Institute of Management and Labor Relations at Rutgers University, and the Highlander Folk School in Tennessee.

The final report of the Reece Committee called for study of some labor organizations to determine whether they had crossed the border from privilege to license in political matters. It echoed earlier charges that Communists had infiltrated foundations, citing foundation funding for the National Education Association and the Progressive Education Association, organizations described as "propagandizing for socialism."[33]

Occasionally, testimony reached the level of absurdity. For example, Representative Hays (D.–Ohio), a strenuous critic of the committee's slant, asked a committee staff member to characterize certain paragraphs in an unidentified document describing the plight of workers. The staff member replied, "All of these—I do not know your source—are closely comparable to Communist literature that I have read." Whereupon Representative Hays reported that they were quotations from the encyclicals of Pope Leo XIII and Pope Pius XI, illustrating "the danger of lifting a sentence or paragraph out of context."[34]

Representative Patman and the Tax Reform Act of 1969

Although no legislation resulted from either the Cox or Reece hearings of the 1950s, they frightened the foundation community, and for several years most foundations avoided controversial programs and organizations. After a seven-year respite, foundations again came under intense congressional scrutiny in 1961, when Representative Wright Patman (D.–Texas) a populist and chairman of the House Select Committee on Small Business, arraigned them as concentrations of economic power designed to escape taxes, control businesses, and serve their trustees' personal interests.

Patman's incessant shrillness finally persuaded Congress in 1965 to request a report from the Treasury Department. The report called for legislative changes regarding foundations that provided the framework for the Tax Reform Act of 1969.[35] During congressional deliberations on the act, Senator Albert Gore (D.–Tenn.), a liberal Senate leader, revived Barkin's proposal for a twenty-five-year limit on the lifetime of foundations. "One of the strangest anomalies in our history," said Gore, "is that my liberal friends think this is a liberal cause for which they are fighting. They are fighting for the vested wealth of this country to be tied up in perpetuity for the descendants of a few people who have waxed rich." Several other liberal congressmen withheld support from the foundations because of the vigorous opposition of the AFL-CIO to foundations as "tax shelters for the wealthy."[36]

George Meany, then president of the AFL-CIO, testified at the hearings:

> As a nation, we recognize that philanthropy is desirable and it should be encouraged. . . . The philosophy underlying the private foundations . . . is "the systematic use of private funds for public purposes." Unfortunately . . . studies . . . have shown that in many cases the opposite situation prevails. . . . Family foundations frequently are used as a means whereby the wealthy can avoid income, gift, and inheritance taxes, yet maintain control

over wealth. . . . Generous tax treatment is appropriate for charitable organizations since private philanthropy is an important adjunct to public
programs serving the goals of the nation. However, this special treatment
is justifiable only if those organizations are in fact using the foundation,
and their tax-exempt privileges, for the public good and not merely for the
private advantage of a select well-heeled few.[37]

Through strenuous foundation lobbying and the help of Senator Walter
Mondale, the limited lifetime proposal was defeated.

Beneath the visible surface of concerns over financial manipulation lay social and political issues. Southern congressmen resented foundation support
of civil rights generally and voter registration of blacks in particular. Others
were troubled by the Ford Foundation's recent (1967–68) conflict with the
New York City teachers' union over school decentralization (described in
Chapter 8). Two New York union officials appeared before the House Ways
and Means Committee to raise questions of conflict of interest and foundation intervention in the political process. Walter J. Degnan, president of the
Council of Supervisory Associations, recommended that the definition of political activity be expanded to ban grants to groups engaged in social action
programs that tax-exempt organizations could not undertake. Dan Sanders,
assistant to the president of the United Federation of Teachers (UFT), charged
that following publication of the school decentralization plan designed by
McGeorge Bundy (president of the Ford Foundation and chairman of the
Mayor's Committee on School Decentralization), the foundation had made
grants to every influential organization connected with education except the
UFT, whose own plan was based on a different framework.[38]

The Tax Reform Act imposed limits on foundations' self-dealing (such as
lending money to a manager of the foundation), excess business holdings
(more than a 20 percent interest in the voting stock of a corporation) and
lobbying, and established an excise tax and requirements for distributing income to charitable organizations. Although the limitations were at first perceived as a blow, refinements over several years softened their impact. On
the positive side, the act increased the foundations' public accountability and
improved the public perception of philanthropy. But by reinforcing the tendency of most foundations toward caution, the act sounded a discouraging
note for relations between unions and foundations that regard the labor
movement as a controversial arena. Labor's unsympathetic comments about
foundations when they came under fire in Congress also chilled the climate
for many years, though relations improved with the passage of time.

4 | Research

Research is the largest single area in which foundations have demonstrated an interest in organized labor. In their various fields of interest foundations have granted hundreds of millions of dollars for studies by individual scholars, for centers ("think tanks") whose staffs make their own studies and commission others from outside researchers, and for other sponsoring groups such as the Social Science Research Council.

The funding of labor research coincides with the earliest chapters in the history of modern foundations—the Carnegie Institution's support of John Commons's history and the Russell Sage Foundation's exploration of social conditions. Although Rockefeller-related instrumentalities were most prominent in labor research in the 1920s, the Twentieth Century Fund and the Ford Foundation played major roles later. The Twentieth Century Fund in particular took on an audacious policy-influencing role of a sort from which most foundations later would flinch.

To the extent that social science research enthusiastically supported by the foundations in the first three decades of the twentieth century produced recommendations for systemic change, they echoed a rich American history of social change movements, ranging from abolition to populism to women's suffrage. The Carnegie Institution of Washington, one of the nation's oldest foundations, financed the monumental *Documentary History of American Industrial Society* (edited by John R. Commons and published in eleven volumes in 1910–11), and two volumes of a four-volume *History of Labour in the United States* (1918).[1] The institution's Department of Economics and Sociology was organized in twelve sections, each representing an aspect of the American economy (commerce, manufactures, and so on), each responsible for producing an authoritative history of its subject. Commons's labor history was one of these projected works, which were farmed out mainly to researchers in universities, who collaterally produced more than one hundred monographs and scores of articles. Commons headed the division devoted to labor, but because of his duties on the U.S. Industrial Relations Commission and the Wisconsin Industrial Commission, he turned it over to Selig Perlman and other University of Wisconsin graduate students, pooling his Carnegie money with other funds.[2] For Henry Farnam, a Yale economist and adviser to the project, the research was utilitarian: "our studies in economic history . . . have an important bearing upon practical questions. In these days of rapidly increasing governmental regulation of business and labor, the one safe guide is the experience of the past."[3] Eighty years later, Peter Hall, a leading scholar of philanthropy, saw this early funding for research on labor as "an effort to legitimate labor as a force to be reckoned with, a force to be taken seriously, a force whose actions and opinions could no longer be dismissed as products of illegal conspiracies in restraint of trade [then the generally accepted legal doctrine] or [of] anarchist/communist covens."[4]

Originating in industrial conflict more than in planned scholarship, W. L. Mackenzie King's *Industry and Humanity* appeared the same year as the first two volumes of Commons's history—1918. Although public agitation after the Ludlow massacre had persuaded the Rockefeller Foundation to dismantle its Investigation of Industrial Relations, the foundation did enable King to complete his treatise, which called for reconciling the interests of labor, capital, management, and the community at large, suggesting that the role of government was simply to investigate disputes and inform the public. An informed appraisal of King concludes that he was a far better adviser than scholar.[5]

To address social and economic issues, the Rockefeller Foundation had first considered an economic institute along the lines of the Rockefeller Institute for Medical Research. But Frederick T. Gates, Rockefeller's chief adviser on philanthropy, was opposed. "What is urgent in economics is not research," he wrote, "but a clearer apprehension by the masses . . . and the voters . . . of the . . . more fundamental economic laws." He envisioned the teaching of elementary principles of economics to "reading and thinking people" and to "a low stratum, viz., the sort of men who have the capacity to get elected to Congress, and demagogues, laborites, socialists, editors, ministers and other people who know little of practical life and live in a dreamland."[6]

Muckrakers assumed that research done through foundation grants must necessarily be weighted toward the status quo. The Walsh Commission's final report questioned whether "foundations set up by corporate capitalists should fund research on socially controversial issues . . . that in a democracy should be decided by a public unswayed by interpretations manufactured by social scientists on foundation payrolls."[7] The Walsh Commission's position and the Ludlow incident had a profound impact on the direction of the Rockefeller Foundation. Imposing a prohibition against social research, the foundation confined itself to medicine, public health, and war relief in the following years. Most other foundations also avoided so controversial a field as labor unions. The Carnegie Institution shut down its Department of Economics and Sociology in 1917. The Commonwealth Fund (formed in 1918) was initially interested in economic and legal research but dropped those subjects in favor of medical care, concluding that an attempt to explore industrial questions "is so controversial that it seems impossible to enter the field without being suspected of taking sides."[8]

Early Think Tanks

From the vantage point of more than a half century, a leading foundation official and social scientist termed the 1920s "especially important as the period in which the aspirations of the social sciences merged with the ambitions of private philanthropy, each finding in the other the opportunity to advance its own agenda."[9] Creating independent research centers enabled foundations to pursue social issues "cleanly" through a growing community of experts. Collaboration among political economists, foundations, and government agencies permitted a broader agenda and approach to social science investigation and data evaluation than did reliance on university departments, which might be susceptible to business or political interference or to the intransigence of tradition-bound department chairmen.[10]

The forerunner of the new social science centers that flourished in the 1920s was the Brookings Institution. Initially named the Institute for Government Research, it was founded in 1916 by a St. Louis businessman, Robert Brookings. In 1927 it merged with two other organizations, one of which, the Institute of Economics, was financed primarily by Carnegie Corporation, which gave it $1.65 million over the first ten years.[11] Brookings would became a major center of research on labor, but its early focus was the promotion of efficient government; for example, it developed a framework for the Bureau of the Budget, which came into existence in 1921.

After the government declined to continue a modest World War I planning and statistical unit, another early think tank, the National Bureau of

Economic Research (NBER) obtained a charter in 1920 to carry on the work. It was funded by Carnegie Corporation, the Commonwealth Fund, the Laura Spelman Rockefeller Memorial (LSRM), and the National Research Council. LSRM funding was its mainstay for many years, which troubled such liberal NBER board members as George Soule: "In spite of Mr. Rockefeller's good intentions, the fact is patent to all that many of his most important properties pursue an anti-union policy and this serves to keep the traditional hostility alive." Yet Soule admitted that the risk of such support must be borne to prevent the bureau's extinction.[12]

The NBER went to great pains to proclaim its objectivity by including on its board men from several sectors, including labor. John P. Frey, a conservative labor leader, was chairman, and Hugh Frayne of the AFL a director. Leo Wolman, who had been with the Amalgamated Clothing Workers of America, served for many years on the NBER research staff.[13] A review of the NBER's first three years by the Laura Spelman Rockefeller Memorial expressed doubts as to whether such a broad-based, fact-finding organization would work in the long run: "To get business men and engineers, accountants and economists, trade union officials and socialists all to agree upon facts which underlie some of the most controversial issues before the American people was a formidable undertaking." The NBER's first analysis—of the distribution of income in the United States—"put the organization to a severe test," the account said. It was "a matter concerning which there have been heated discussions for a long time . . . which has obvious bearings upon most contests between labor and capital."[14] The bureau's 1924 annual report expressed satisfaction that the National Industrial Conference Board was cooperating in a study by making a survey of company unions: "That . . . organizations representing opposing interests in the business world can work with us in trying to establish economic facts is not merely a pleasant recognition of our own standing but also a promising sign of social progress toward the aims which the National Bureau was created to promote."[15] The NBER in the 1920s also produced important studies of business cycles and the impact of restricted immigration on the use of labor-saving machinery and on the labor supply.

A union presence at the NBER continued through the Depression and after World War II. Boris Shishkin, a leading AFL economist, was its president in 1948–49 and later chairman of the board. In recent years bureau research has covered such labor matters as unjust-dismissal legislation, the effect of unions on wage distribution, and the effects of deunionization on earnings. Currently one fourth to one third of NBER financial support comes from foundations.[16]

Labor and the Social Sciences

After the first generation of economic historians had pioneered research on la-bor, the discrete field of industrial relations developed in the 1920s, with roots in Commons's work at the University of Wisconsin, where the first academic program in industrial relations was established as a concentration in the eco-nomics major. Commons, Richard T. Ely, Selig Perlman, David Saposs, and their associates not only conducted research and wrote landmark works on the union movement and other aspects of industrial relations. They were also scholar-activists, consulting with union, business, and government officials, heading government agencies created at their own urging, and serving as me-diators and arbitrators in industry. They structured workers' compensation systems, unemployment agencies, mediation bureaus, and other state agencies to regulate labor relations.[17] After a lifetime of labor research and policy en-gagement, Commons reminisced: "I concede to my radical friends that my trade-union philosophy always made me conservative. It is not revolutions and strikes that we want, but collective bargaining on something like an organized equilibrium of equality. It seems to me the only way to save us from Commu-nism, Fascism, or Nazism. Yet many of my employer friends are opposed to it, or seeking to control it. I think they are leading us to Fascism."[18]

The Rockefeller family, if not the foundation, again ventured into the dan-gerous area of social inquiry with the establishment of the Laura Spelman Rockefeller Memorial, a tribute to John D. Rockefeller Sr.'s wife. Under the leadership of Beardsley Ruml, a respected academic economist and Progres-sive who viewed social science as a means to a more rational, democratic gov-ernment, the Memorial, like independent research centers, was fashioned as a device to circumvent the narrow "classic" focus of the universities. Instead of attempting to strengthen and sustain a broad spectrum of elite American colleges and universities, major foundations in the 1920s committed them-selves above all to furthering the advancement of knowledge, chiefly by fa-cilitating graduate-level research. In a confidential memo, Ruml noted, "All who work toward the general end of social welfare are embarrassed by the lack of knowledge which the social sciences must provide."[19] Still, he estab-lished principles to insulate the LSRM from certain controversial behavior: no support would be given for efforts to secure reform legislation; no in-house social research would be conducted; and no attempt would be made to influence the conclusions of researchers.[20]

After a decade of directing the Memorial, Ruml recalled the early motiva-tion: "It was felt that through the social sciences might come more intelli-gent measures of social control that would reduce such irrationalities as are represented by poverty, class conflict, and war between nations."[21] Ruml and

A seminar in labor economics at the University of Wisconsin, headed by Professor John R. Commons (second from right), ca. 1925. The Carnegie Institution's support of Commons's monumental history of American industrial society (1910–11) was one of the first instances of foundation backing for labor-related research. At the far right is another distinguished labor historian, Selig Perlman. (Courtesy Mark Perlman)

leading activist scholars such as Wesley Mitchell (economics) and Charles Merriam (political science) strived to raise the social sciences to the precision of engineering. But some critics faulted the preoccupation of social scientists with empirical problems such as labor and other current social and political issues at the expense of what Harold Laski of the London School of Economics termed "the vision and the insight of the individual thinker." Deprecating the interconnection between social investigators, universities, and philanthropy, he accused foundation executives of having no idea of the very meaning of research in any effectively creative sense.[22]

A major exception to Ruml's skeptical view of university-based social research was his funding of the Social Science Group (later renamed the University Social Science Research Committee) at the great research university that Rockefeller had founded in Chicago three decades earlier, in 1891. The group facilitated large-scale empirical research that frequently dealt with labor, including eight labor-focused projects during 1926–27, which resulted in such publications as *Industrial Relations in the Chicago Building Trades, The Railroad Labor Board*, and *The Chicago Federation of Labor*.[23] Another study, *Chicago Strikes with Special Reference to the Problem of Policing*, gave an account of each major strike in the first quarter of the twentieth century.[24] At the second annual Institute for Social Research, papers titled "Group Behavior and the Strike" and "Industrial Morale" were presented. The university agreed to keep a low profile about the Memorial's funding, a condition of which was that it be matched by other sources (in this case, grants came from the Commonwealth Fund, the Wieboldt Foundation, and the philanthropist Julius Rosenwald, who was head of Sears, Roebuck).

Ruml also sought to surmount the shortcomings of university-based social science by creating a vehicle to stimulate and coordinate research—the Social Science Research Council, founded in 1923. Although several foundations contributed to the SSRC, 92 percent of the $4 million it received in its first decade came from the LSRM and later from the social science division of the Rockefeller Foundation into which the LSRM was folded when the foundation reorganized in 1928. The SSRC maintained a committee on industrial relations from 1926 to 1930, with an advisory group composed of business representatives, Leo Wolman, and several academics, including Commons. In addition to providing advice to governmental and nongovernmental agencies seeking to plan and monitor the effectiveness of emerging social welfare systems, the committee sponsored basic research—studies of the national labor market, for example. In the early 1930s, the SSRC helped the Rockefeller Foundation "search for some solution of the miseries and suffering caused by the financial depression." Despite extensive research, the results were meager, according to Fosdick, the foundation's president. The effort was "based on hopes that were far too sanguine." Not even a major foundation could make inroads into such a massive societal problem. "There was no quick and easy remedy for the malady," he observed. There was not even the possibility of swift and accurate diagnosis.[25] After World War II the SSRC set up committees dealing with economic growth (1949–68) and economic stability (1959–70).

Some critics charge the SSRC with having made a Faustian bargain with foundations on behalf of the conservative social control agenda of its patrons, diverting the social sciences from attention to the exploitative side of

American capitalism. The SSRC's view is that while it was deeply involved in developing the nascent social sciences, it also grappled even-handedly with vital social issues, not least Social Security and other New Deal initiatives. It was certainly to labor's benefit that the SSRC was on the same wavelength with New Deal policy.[26]

Despite representation in think tanks, most unions preferred to remain apart from organized social research, declining to participate in joint labor-management research committees. Van Kleeck traced this reluctance to "labor's fear that privately supported research institutions exist primarily to defend capitalism as it is, and hence cannot be trusted to speak the truth about controversial economic questions."[27]

Middletown

The classic sociocultural study of a small American industrial community—Robert and Helen Lynd's *Middletown* (1929) and its sequel, *Middletown in Transition* (1937)—highlighted the cleavage among social scientists over whether such research should provide knowledge that questions the prevailing order. This issue was a sharp one for social research on labor in modern industrial society. The Lynds clearly called for the transformation of social science from what they deemed an instrument of class rule into one of human liberation and fulfillment. In dissecting Muncie, Indiana, the scene of the research, both volumes devote major attention to factory workers and unions and to the city's power structure, particularly its ruling family, whose fortune created an important regional foundation.[28]

The Rockefeller Foundation played a key role in the genesis of the Middletown project, which was carried out under the auspices of John D. Rockefeller Jr.'s Institute of Social and Religious Research, an organization dedicated to "class harmony under corporate capitalism." The institute, an outgrowth of Rockefeller's extensive interest in interchurch movements and the YMCA, was established as a stimulus to liberal church unity through empirical social studies. Robert Lynd's appointment in 1923 to conduct the project was in itself remarkable, for earlier he had feuded publicly with Rockefeller about conditions among workers in the Rockefeller-controlled oil fields at Elk Basin, Wyoming. Drawing on observations made there while he was a seminary intern, in letters to Rockefeller and in published articles Lynd challenged Rockefeller's stance as an industrial liberal (Lynd's findings concerning Elk Basin were later confirmed in a study by the Russell Sage Foundation). Nevertheless, Lynd impressed Rockefeller. His background as a theology student, his research on Elk Basin, and his stated intent to inquire into the spiritual life of the Muncie community accorded with the institute's be-lief that a small-city study would determine "precisely what is the spiritual life of the community, with especial reference to dynamic aspects, i.e., how do new spiritual impulses arise?"[29]

As the Lynds' research departed from the church-oriented agenda, they quarreled with the institute staff. Raymond Fosdick, a chief adviser to Rocke-feller, was also critical of the Lynds' emphasis on class divisions as the key to understanding social processes because it strayed from the rational, "scien-tific" structure of social science research then being shaped by Rockefeller funds.[30] The institute balked at publishing the work, but two years after its completion *Middletown* was published commercially and became an instant sensation. It did indeed apply a scientific lens to the small-city social and po-litical dynamics popularized in fiction by Theodore Dreiser and Sinclair Lewis in that, methodologically, it was marked by the participant observer technique and the application of social anthropology to a contemporary community. Thirty years later, Fosdick himself termed it a pioneering study.

The Lynds presented a blistering analysis of a business ethos and perva-sive business control that contrasted starkly with the community's putative ideology of equality and moral unity. It included an account of the decline in positive community attitudes toward organized labor from the late nine-teenth century to the mid-1920s. In Muncie and other small manufacturing centers during the industrial heyday of that period, unions often were major community institutions. By the early 1890s, Muncie was one of the best-organized cities in the country. As the Lynds described it, "Organized labor formed one of the most active coordinating centers in the lives of some thou-sands of Middletown working class families, touching their getting-a-living, educational, leisure-time . . . activities. . . . [T]he unions brought tangible pressure for a weekly pay law, standardized wage scales, factory inspection, safety devices . . . and other improvements, and helped in sickness or death, while crowded mass meetings held in the opera house collected large sums for the striking workers in Homestead and elsewhere." When Samuel Gom-pers came to town he dined at the mayor's home before addressing a great crowd. The press wrote approvingly of union activity, urging public support of union solicitations for union purposes.[31]

The most prominent industry in Muncie was the Ball Brothers plant, whose major product for many years was the famous "Ball Jar," used for pre-serving fruit, vegetables, and a variety of other foods. The union that repre-sented its workers, the Glass Bottle Blowers' Association, had good relations with the company. When, for example, several technological innovations in the glass industry forced the union to accommodate reduced employment of certain skilled workers, negotiations enabled union members to operate new automatic machinery.[32]

The Ball family amounted to a reigning oligarchy, the Lynds observed, controlling banks, newspapers, school administration, and other areas of the city's life. In 1926 they established the Ball Brothers Foundation, which became a major benefactor of Ball State University (successor to a failed private academy that the family bought at auction in 1918 and persuaded the legislature to fold into the state university system). Other major beneficiaries were the Ball Memorial Hospital and the Minnetrista Cultural Center, which has collections in history, the arts, and Native American culture.[33]

By the mid-1920s, the Lynds' second volume reported, public attitudes toward unions in Muncie had turned from warmth to coolness, if not hostility. The local press had little good to say of organized labor, and churches avoided the subject. Labor Day, a great day in the 1890s, was barely noticed. Furthermore, Muncie's business class reflected the bitter post–World War I national view of unions, the prevalent attitude appearing in a statement by one of the city's leaders: "Working men don't need unions nowadays. There are no great evils or problems as there were fifty years ago. We are much more in danger of coddling the working men than abusing them. Working people are just as well off now as they can possibly be except for things which are in the nature of industry and cannot be helped." The Lynds concluded that many workers had abandoned the group solidarity of trade unionism for the individualistic rewards of consumption. Americanization campaigns during the early twenties and advertising through the decade encouraged this reorientation.[34]

The labor-friendly New Deal atmosphere notwithstanding, efforts to revive organizing bogged down in a jurisdictional dispute between two unions, while at the same time the company pushed its Benefit Association. Ultimately the Glass Bottle Blowers' Association held sway in the Ball plant, but relations between the union and the company deteriorated in the 1960s. By the end of the decade the Ball Corporation expanded into aerospace manufacturing, moved most of its operations out of Muncie except for the company headquarters, and became a partner in international operations of glass manufacturing companies. Muncie is no longer a company town, and union membership is dwindling.[35] The union and the Ball Brothers Foundation have had little to do with each other. According to the foundation's executive director, however, it has used its influence to ensure that labor representatives serve on committees and "have a place at the table" in discussions of community issues affecting union members.[36]

Because scholars worldwide have continued an intense interest in Muncie/Middletown as a laboratory of sociocultural analysis, a Center for Middletown Studies was established in 1980 and became part of Ball State University four years later. The center maintains the archives of the Lynds' books, sponsors lectures and exhibits, and assists the research of both local and visiting scholars.[37]

Scientific Management and Behavioral Research

The institutional flowering of social research, heavily nurtured by foundations, embraced a technocratic approach to progressive reform through which social scientists established themselves as "disinterested professionals [who] serve a public cause." Such research aimed, among other things, to ensure the stabilization of the U.S. economy through creation of an essentially non-statist system of economic planning.[38]

Frederick Taylor's system of scientific management played a major role in labor-management relations from World War I through the 1930s. As one scholar noted, "Serious people believed . . . that scientific management's ability to raise productivity within the firm could become the basis for a new utopia."[39] After Taylor's death in 1915, the Taylor Society was transformed into "a larger conception . . . one that would now include unemployment and worker dissatisfaction among the ills to be remedied through better management."[40] This change in outlook drew into the Taylor orbit social scientists, policy intellectuals, and reformers (including Mary Van Kleeck of the Russell Sage Foundation) who were initially intrigued with applying the concept of scientific management to government, business administration, and social policy. But foundations (with the exception of the Russell Sage and Van Kleeck herself, who reflected a fashionable Marxist interest in the subject) cooled toward Taylorism. The Rockefeller Foundation's Fosdick and the LSRM's Ruml refused to include funding for the Taylor Society among programs aiming to apply scientific inquiry to social issues. In a strenuous effort to return to the center of scientific social reform, the society staged a major dinner conference in 1927 to which leading social investigators, journalists, and officials of eight leading foundations were invited. Only Russell Sage officials attended.[41]

Elton Mayo was another towering figure in industrial relations research during the 1920s and 1930s, and more acceptable to foundations than the Taylorites. He was brought to the United States from Australia under grants from the Rockefeller and Carnegie foundations to continue his research on adapting the methods of clinical psychologists and anthropologists to shape management's approach to dealing with industrial labor. Mayo broke new ground in exploring the psychological and social habits of industrial workers, studying in particular Western Electric's Hawthorne Works near Chicago. He proposed to reduce widespread conflict in industry through the use of more adaptive methods under which a trained administrative elite would resolve human as well as technical problems in the total industrial environment as well as in individual factories.[42] Despite his Rube Goldberg–style use of such variables as worker daydreaming and pulse rate, Mayo's approach appealed to Ruml and Fosdick, who thought that his projects—linking physiology to the control of industrial labor—would likely appeal to John D. Rockefeller Jr.'s deep concern about improving industrial relations. The Memorial appropriated $155,000 in 1927 to the Harvard Business School for a four-year grant to study "individual industrial efficiency."[43]

Critics argued that there was no place in Mayo's philosophy for conflict and that he did not understand the role of unions in a free society. "While Mayo has been charged with being anti-union, it might be more accurate to say that he was simply indifferent to unions," William F. Whyte observed.[44] Mayo's greatest impact was through graduate schools of business and the relatively new university-based centers for industrial relations. A major player in this development was Clarence J. Hicks, chairman of the board of Rockefeller's Industrial Relations Counselors, Inc., who promoted several Rockefeller-funded centers of industrial relations at universities in the 1920s (Princeton, California Institute of Technology, Stanford, University of Michigan, and Massachusetts Institute of Technology). Hicks had been assistant to the president of the Colorado Fuel and Iron Company and executive assistant to the president of Rockefeller's Standard Oil of New Jersey (1917–33).[45]

Important technocratic believers included Van Kleeck, Wesley C. Mitchell and Herbert Hoover. Van Kleeck searched for modern secular tools to carry out the Christian Gospel. Russell Sage's Industrial Studies Department, Guy Alchon writes, "reflected Van Kleeck's stubborn faith in the potential of social research to provide the path to social transformation." As a founding member of the Taylor Society, Van Kleeck was "deeply committed to the social potential of scientific management. Her pursuit of what she later termed 'social-economic planning' took shape . . . in her swelling disillusionment with capitalism's potential for self-correction, and in her growing involvement with labor and radical politics."[46] Along with Mitchell, a leading economist, and Owen D. Young, the chairman of General Electric, Van Kleeck was an enthusiastic member of Hoover's Business Cycles Committee, an effort to improve and stabilize society by applying technical expertise to complex economic problems. "The idea was that . . . new knowledge . . . about the business cycle and the benefits of scientific management would be broadcast to the national's businessmen by a Commerce Department eager to see them stabilize their operations and tailor their investment decisions to the cycle's swings. . . . [T]he sum of individual actions would add up to a national economy of greater stability and less unemployment."[47] She grew skeptical of the Hooverian approach by the onset of the Depression, however, and concluded that without a strong and independent labor movement to drive it, scientific management would never fulfill its promise of a rational and abundant economy.

Even before he became secretary of commerce, Hoover was "troubled by the alienation and disenfranchisement already prevalent among American workers, [recognizing] the need to reduce employer domination over employees. . . and [looking] toward extending of technocratic authority as the most promising means of restructuring industrial relationships." As secretary of commerce (1921–29), Hoover was one of the earliest government officials to understand and appreciate the value of foundations, spurring the business community to include them in business and university alliances. Hoover frequently turned to foundations for help in advancing his approach to industrial and social harmony (which he termed the "associative state" or the "administrative state"): developing trade associations, professional societies, and similar organizations among farmers and laborers to form a structure parallel to and working with government.[48]

Despite attacks on foundations as "invisible governments," government at all levels looked to private donors, among them foundations, to fund the research on which officials sought to base new social and economic policies.[49] Hoover carried such reliance into his presidency, when he requested Rockefeller Foundation support (with a grant of $560,000 to the Social Science Research Council) for a major review of American society, coincidentally at the onset of the Depression. The Russell Sage Foundation provided facilities and some staff for the research. In the resulting two-volume study, *Recent Social Trends*, union leaders and foundation officials were sparsely represented among the 624 persons the research group consulted. Business and industry figures were heavily represented, ranging from Edward Bernays, the public relations mogul, to the head of the New York State Hotel Association.[50] (The staff, concentrating on its research agenda, became wary of Hoover as he pestered it—not surprisingly—for current findings to help him understand and control the effects of the Depression.)[51]

Two pages of the final report dealt perfunctorily with private foundations. A fifty-five-page chapter titled "Labor Groups in the Social Structure" took a rather Darwinian view of the American economic system: "The basic feature of our present economic organization is that we get our livings by making and spending money. This practice offers prizes to those who have skill at money making; it imposes penalties upon those who lack the ability or the character to render service for which others are willing to pay." On industrial relations: "insofar as increasing production may be due to . . . harmony in relationships between employer and employees, the past decade may have been an exception and friction and strife may arise more frequently in the future." While organized labor had achieved success in improving earnings and shortening hours of work, "there has been no such success against the terror of unemployment . . . a major cause of suffering."[52]

The Committee on Social Trends was organized on the eve of the Depression by Herbert Hoover with funds provided by the Rockefeller Foundation. Its two-volume report, *Recent Social Trends*, a major review of American society, said that despite union weakness, industrial growth depended on cooperation with labor. Left to right: Wesley Mitchell, Columbia University; William F. Ogburn, University of Chicago; Charles K. Merriam, University of Chicago; Alice Hamilton, Harvard School of Public Health; Shelby Harrison, Russell Sage Foundation; Edward Eyre Hunt, executive secretary; and French Strother, administrative secretary to President Hoover. (Herbert Hoover Presidential Library)

Describing the nature of industrial relations, the report stated, "On the part of owners and managers of industry, there are signs, however feeble, that the cooperative and democratic nature of industrial relations are being increasingly recognized. At the same time that trade unions in American society have remained surprisingly weak and inarticulate, there is accumulating evidence that the safe and successful conduct of large-scale industry involves the creation of machinery for enlisting the cooperation and winning the consent of labor." Significantly, the report noted the first decline of the manufacturing sector of the labor force, along with substantial gains in "trade, professional service and variety of mechanical and personal services."[53]

Two years later a highly significant foundation contribution to organized labor was made by the Twentieth Century Fund, which was then exceptional among foundations for its concentrated interest in the policy-making process and legislation affecting unions and collective bargaining. Edward A. Filene, the Boston department store magnate who established the fund in 1919, was an ardent supporter of the New Deal. Filene's employee relations were based on his espousal of consumerism as the key to economic well-being in a capitalist society. If workers won their reasonable demands, he believed, they would have the wherewithal to participate in the economy.[54]

The fund has focused on economics and the application of scientific methods to economic affairs, reinforcing Filene's theory "that men were chiefly imprisoned by their poverty, due to the incapacity or perhaps the unwillingness of the economic and social systems in which they lived to provide adequate conditions for human life."[55] Filene argued in books, speeches, and articles that organizations such as credit unions and labor unions would lubricate America's new mass consumption economy by placing more money in buyers' hands through higher wages, thereby expanding purchasing power. Thus the fund's view of its research was pragmatic: research was not an end in itself but was justified to the degree that it contributed to sound public policy; and policies are useful to the degree that they result in action, which depends on widespread public knowledge. Like many businessmen of the time, Filene believed that if one had to choose, foundations were better institutions for national planning than government.

Citing resistance to higher wages as an example of cupidity and short-sightedness, he resolved to fight business conservatism with its own methods—publicity and the use of experts (though he had been one of the founders of the U.S. Chamber of Commerce, he resigned at the beginning of the Depression).[56] He was an inveterate publicist in his own right, reaching to the highest levels to share his views; (after a cross-country investigative tour, for example, Filene reported to FDR on criticism of the National Industrial Recovery Act [NIRA]). A survey by the fund in the early 1930s showed that the study of economics and the evolution of economic policy was a "poor relation" in American philanthropy. Such matters were controversial and "foundations normally do not like controversy." But as the first executive director of the fund, Evans Clark, observed: "Controversy is almost an index of the importance of a public problem. People do not think, talk or act violently about things that are of little importance to them."[57]

Fund board members have held influential positions in every administration from Herbert Hoover's to Richard Nixon's. But they were opposed in principle to having the fund's work become "part of any power mechanism, commercial or political."[58] Notwithstanding, the fund has been viewed as parts of a network of "mass consumption experts" who advocated a strategy of "government-sanctioned" wage increases as the way to improve the economy and society.[59] Among them were Sidney Hillman, who had become ac-

Edward A. Filene, department store magnate, established the Twentieth Century Fund in 1919. During the New Deal the fund's staff helped draft landmark labor legislation, for which Filene himself lobbied. (Reprinted with permission from the Twentieth Century Fund/Century Foundation, New York)

quainted with Filene when he sought to enlist support for the Amalgamated Clothing Workers Union among Boston manufacturers, and who testified before the Senate Finance Committee in 1933, and Mary Van Kleeck, who mobilized an array of statistics to buttress her underconsumptionist argument.[60] Late that year, the fund formed a special committee on labor, directed by William Hammatt Davis, assistant to Senator Robert F. Wagner in drafting the NIRA, whose Section A gave workers the right to organize. After the Supreme Court invalidated the NIRA, Davis provided critical statistics and economic analyses to Wagner's staff, submitted important congressional testimony explaining the logic behind the successor National Labor Relations Act (1935), and worked with Wagner's chief adviser, Leon Keyserling, to draft the NLRA.[61] By enabling workers to bargain collectively for higher wages, the bill was intended to address the diagnosis that the country's biggest problem was underconsumption. In giving the force of law to the process of collective bargaining, the Wagner Act became the first, and remains the only, serious legislative defeat of business on the labor issue. Filene labored long and hard to persuade old friends from the Progressive movement—from businessmen to economists—to support it.

The first published study by the fund's Labor Committee, *Labor and the Government*, which appeared in 1935, recommended creation of a national labor mediation service and a permanent federal labor relations board [which became the Wagner Act's National Labor Relations Board] to enforce legal guarantees of workers' right to organize; advocated the "effective development of collective bargaining"; and urged federal and state legislation to protect wage agreements. The study stated, "American trade unions must still overcome any weaknesses before they can adequately carry on collective bargaining. . . . [The] majority . . . are still unorganized and still almost completely uneducated in the need for union organization."[62]

Judging from the minutes of the fund's Labor Committee (called Labor and Government until 1940) over the decade 1937–47, the members were compassionately concerned with labor—labor law, acceptance of the Wagner Act, the success of unions and collective bargaining, and the democratic functioning and responsibilities of unions. The committee included William H. Davis (chair), William L. Chenery, Edwin E. Witte (professor of economics at the University of Wisconsin and former executive director of the President's Committee on Economic Security), William M. Leiserson, and Summer H. Slichter. (The last three were students of Commons). The committee eagerly recruited businessmen and labor leaders—from business, Gerard Swope of General Electric and Frazier MacIver of the Phoenix Hosiery Company of Milwaukee; from labor, Philip Murray of the CIO (invited but declined), Clinton Golden (Steelworkers), and Robert Watt of the AFL.[63]

By the late 1930s the fund's Labor Committee was concerned with union responsibility—internal democracy, financial management, compliance with labor agreements, and responsibility in the conduct of strikes. Sterling Spero of Columbia University (co-author of *The Black Worker* [1931]) urged the Labor Committee to study these factors.[64] Another proponent of in-depth research on unions by the fund was Louis Stark, labor reporter for the *New York Times*. "Wherever I go I hear a lot of tommyrot about labor," he wrote Clark. "Some well known businessmen talk about communism and trade unionism as if they were synonymous. . . . the Twentieth Century Fund can do a good service . . . by bringing out the facts. Particularly it would be timely in view of the continued recession campaign for wage reductions, for union busting, for 'reduced costs' at the expense of labor."[65]

The Second Half Century

As the country mobilized for World War II, the Twentieth Century Fund's Labor Committee issued a report—*Labor and the National Defense*—discussing machinery for handling industrial relations in defense industries. But the fund's principal project at the time was a survey and analysis of fourteen industries to guide employers in working within the framework of the Wagner Act. Harry Millis, the fund's research director and editor, was appointed by President Roosevelt to head the NLRB.[66]

During and after World War II, the fund was, in Andrew Workman's words, "closely involved with public members of the War Labor Board, shaping their ideas on labor policy."[67] The Labor Committee's activism increased as widespread postwar strikes broke out and demands for curbing union power grew. Committee members testified as individuals before Congress, but Witte urged the Labor Committee to analyze a panoply of regressive labor legislation that was flooding Congress, including bills for the repeal of the Wagner Act, and (as proposed by Senator-elect Joseph McCarthy, R., of Wisconsin) the drafting of strikers. As the committee sought ways to neutralize the most draconian bills, concerned that collective bargaining might be killed, for example, Davis suggested a joint board (Congress, labor, and management) to determine which labor disputes constituted a national emergency. Lloyd K. Garrison, dean of the University of Wisconsin Law School, warned, "We should be prepared to point out why [legislation to curb unions] won't work," but he also questioned the virtual total union immunity with respect to strikes. Some strikes were so frivolous as to be without any public interest, he declared.[68]

By the late 1940s clearly the days of the Twentieth Century Fund's influence on the character of federal labor legislation were over. Postwar research on labor was also shaped by liberal and conservative think tanks and the appearance of the Ford Foundation as a major source of large-scale support. Industrial peace was a prominent part of the public agenda, and research focused on the balance of power between labor and management and the impact of collective bargaining and productivity demands. Labor studies commissioned by the Twentieth Century Fund included an examination by Charles C. Heckscher of the Harvard Business School of the potential of a new movement in labor-management relations—association unionism (1988). Five years later, Richard C. Edwards (University of Massachusetts), recognizing that an erosion of workers' rights was likely, explored an alternative system of labor-management relations to protect both employers' competitiveness and the legitimate interest of workers.[69]

Rockefeller Foundation grants reflected an interest in labor-management relations as a case of organizational behavior, influenced by the arrival in the United States of refugee social scientists. In 1947, the Bureau of Applied Social Research at Columbia University, then home to a group of distinguished social scientists (Robert Lynd, Paul Lazarsfeld, Robert K. Merton, C. Wright Mills), was sponsor of a Rockefeller grant to J. B. S. Hardman, labor journalist and former head of education for the Amalgamated Clothing Workers, for a study of labor union leaders, with particular attention to socioeconomic and psychological aspects.[70] A grant proposal to the foundation from the University of Michigan Survey Research Center stated, "We have much to learn about unions as organizations . . . because as large-scale organizations they are a relatively recent addition to our society." The resulting study, in which the economist Kenneth Boulding and Brendan Sexton, the UAW director of education and research, participated, focused on four UAW locals and the rubber workers' union. It explored the theory that greater diversification of responsibility and authority, democratic supervision, and wider worker participation would lead to greater motivation, job satisfaction, and productivity.[71]

The Brookings Institution's most important contributions in the labor field were two books by Summer H. Slichter, *Union Policies and Industrial Management* (1941) and *The Impact of Collective Bargaining on Management*, with J. J. Healy and E. R. Livernach (1960). Slichter, a student of Commons, was a leading labor economist.[72] His 1960 work, supported by the Maurice and Laura Falk and Ford foundations, engaged a team of scholars who revised his 1941 study in light of enormous changes in labor-management relations during World War II. Contrasting sharply with the earlier work, the new study "shifted toward a management perspective in which 'industrial relations' represented an adversarial rather than a liberating mechanism for solving social and economic conflict."[73] Slichter argued that "the American environment has produced strongly individualistic and highly competitive employers who have been aggressively hostile to unions." He contended further that unions in mass production industries should be undemocratic in administration. "Because union leaders are sensitive to technological and market changes including employers' competitiveness," he said, "they should be enabled to negotiate and make policies without ratification by the rank and file."[74]

On the strength of the outstanding reputation Brookings had established for its research on labor/management affairs and their interface with government, it received a $400,000 grant from the Ford Foundation in 1967 for a series of studies of unionism in public employment. Membership in government employees' unions rose from 915,000 in 1956 to 1.5 million in 1964, a 50 percent increase. Put another way, by 1964 one of every twelve union members was a government employee, many of them white-collar workers who heretofore had shunned unions but grew militant because their pay scales lagged behind those of blue-collar public employees, who had been unionized for years. The project resulted in several books, including *Unions and the Cities* by Harry H. Wellington (1972), *The Impact of Collective Bargaining on Compensation in the Public Sector,* by Daniel J. B. Mitchell (1980), and *Local Government Bargaining and Management Structure* by John F. Burton (1972), and journal articles.

By the 1990s, however, organized labor had little place on Brookings's agenda. Its staff included a labor economist, Gary Burtless, but his focus was social insurance. He attributes the decline in research to the decline of unions as a percentage of the labor force (excepting public employee unions) and to a lack of interest in union issues among graduate students in labor economics. Burtless tried unsuccessfully for ten years to have Albert Shanker appointed a Brookings trustee. "I had great respect for his intellect but he may have been too contentious for the Brookings board."[75]

Academic research and teaching about labor matured with the growth of postwar multidisciplinary industrial relations programs at many universities. Distinct from labor history, the separate field of industrial relations was also reflected in a new academic body, the Industrial Relations Research Association (IRRA), established in 1948, and a new journal, *Industrial and Labor Relations Review.* (Two heads of the IRRA, George P. Shultz and John Dunlop, went on to become secretaries of labor).[76] Most of that part of corporate America that was still unionized had reconciled itself to living with organized labor. IRRA seminars, books, and pamphlets were aimed at showing business how to cope without jeopardizing its management prerogatives.

"It is customary," James Cochrane says, "to consider industrial relations as having been developed through the integration of four contributing disciplines: labor economics, behavioral sciences, and labor history and labor law. Specialists in this area focused on three 'mainstream' areas: collective bargaining, unions, and manpower." They had not only academic backgrounds but ample experience at very high levels of industry, labor, and government decision-making. "They . . . noticed a substantial lag, partly the result of a lack of research done during the war, between everyday practice and textbook generalizations on labor."[77]

Two motives animated the field. One was scientific—a desire to advance the state of knowledge of the employment relationship, especially the causes of friction between employers and workers. The other was problem-solving—a desire to discover the means to resolve labor problems through improved methods of organization and practice in industry. For its first two decades, industrial relations research had focused on problem-solving—fact-gathering, descriptive analyses of institutions and practices, multidisciplinary study of labor relations, and a strong policy-oriented perspective—and had reached a high level of respectability by the end of World War II. In 1947 Witte noted that more members of the American Economic Association listed labor as their major field of interest than any other. Literature on the subject had reached a critical mass with the appearance of the trilogy by Harry Millis and Royal Montgomery (under the auspices of the Twentieth Century Fund).[78] Some scholars deplored what they termed a bifurcation in the field—between economic and behavioral science views. Thus, some viewed the trade union and the firm as economic entities, others as major components of the community power structure, as sources of new opinions, and so forth. The problem of internal union democracy, which an economist might dismiss as irrelevant to the determination of wages or working conditions, may be regarded as crucial by the political scientist, who sees the trade union as one of the key institutions sustaining democratic processes in the larger community.[79]

By the late 1960s the two major strands of industrial relations—personnel management and institutional labor economics—began to unravel. One casualty was the waning of academic industrial relations as a course of study because of the decline of its intellectual and job-market appeal. Many programs were subsumed into business school curricula and took such titles as "human relations" or "human resources." According to Bruce E. Kaufman, the IRRA's focus on and support of the traditional system of labor-management relations after World War II, even when labor union membership was declining, tended to isolate it in the academic community.[80] Thus at the first annual IRRA conference, Dunlop declared, "In a world of powerful economic groups—unions, management, farmers,—there must be an attempt at coordination of [their] interests. Political compromise . . . is a requisite to economic stability."[81]

As mentioned earlier, a series of analyses of disturbing trends in labor unions was commissioned through the 1950s and early 1960s by the Center for the Study of Democratic Institutions, the main activity of the Fund for the Republic, itself an autonomous foundation established by the Ford Foundation in 1952. The center's general outlook, while acknowledging the achievements and strengths of unions, reflected a certain pessimism about the future and a drift of intellectuals away from bonds with the labor movement. In addition to discussions of labor issues, the project also included studies of the governance of seven major unions. The director of the studies was Paul Jacobs, a journalist attached to the Institute of Industrial Relations at the University of California, Berkeley. Noted contributors were Solomon Barkin, director of research for the Textile Workers Union of America, and Clark Kerr, chancellor of the University of California system. Generally, the reports criticized labor's "stagnation and complacency," but, more important, they raised issues: why unorganized workers were unwilling to join unions, why once sympathetic liberals were estranged from the union movement, the movement's declining public image, and unions' lack of social consciousness and reluctance to help the poor and victims of discrimination. "Have unions lost their appeal because of anachronistic goals, aspirations, and policies, because of inadequate and unsophisticated performance?" asked Barkin. "Do the difficulties lie within the movement, or among the employees, or in the environment, or in all three?"[82]

On a scale even grander than the effort behind the Carnegie Institution's eleven-volume documentary history of labor (1910–11) was the post–World War II Inter-University Study of Labor Problems in Economic Development (later called the Inter-University Study of Human Resources in National Development), a twenty-year effort that produced thirty books and forty-three articles. The project received substantial Ford Foundation grants, supplemented by Carnegie Corporation funding. Clark Kerr, John T. Dunlop, Frederick H. Harbison, and Charles A. Myers, the lead authors, would not have characterized themselves as just economists: They were social scientists who, among other things, had been instrumental in developing the independent field of industrial relations.

Among the conclusions of the Inter-University Study were:

- Labor problems are not unique to capitalism;
- The adaptability of labor and the evolutionary character of most workers' movements ease the industrialization process;
- Organized workers are more a glacial force for change than a revolutionary movement;
- Industrial relations systems tend to become tripartite in nature, with the state an increasingly influential participant.

While the Inter-University Study had little policy influence and certainly no impact on the continuing slide of the labor movement, foundations in the late 1980s and 1990s did respond to a distinctly policy-directed research center, the Economic Policy Institute (EPI), established in Washington in 1986. One view has it that the EPI grew out of frustration with the failure of the AFL-CIO's Industrial Union Department to attract media interest in its studies. "Union officials decided they would be better off following the corporations' example," noted one analyst, "funding a group that was committed to their principles and ideas but not tainted directly by their label."[83] The EPI now draws its major support from foundations, which view it as a credible counterpart to business-oriented think tanks such as the Committee for Economic Development and the American Enterprise Institute. "Initial concerns that organized labor would exert undue influence or control over the Institute's agenda have proven to be baseless," a Ford Foundation evaluation concluded.[84]

Roger Hickey, a former EPI vice president, noted:

> EPI had its start with money from the Stern Fund and a few small foundations, but several international unions soon came on board with major assistance. The basic idea was to revive the tradition of connection between the labor movement and academia, which had been so productive during the New Deal and the New Frontier. The economic issues we deal with are important to unions' survival. We convinced them of the need for an independent think tank, not connected with the AFL-CIO. Unions' own research departments are limited mainly to bread-and-butter matters.

With a staff of thirty, plus outside researchers, the EPI's studies range over such topics as urban investment strategy, trade deficits and labor unions, the changing financial conditions of U.S. households, the consequences of part-time work, export controls, and telecommunications policy. The EPI's flagship publication is its annual *State of Working America*, whose first issue (1988) galvanized a debate about the decline of real wages and income. "Scholars at other places—Brookings for example—said at first that the decline was a temporary phenomenon. Others tried to debunk us. Now it is accepted, though of course people have different policy proposals to reverse it," says Hickey.[85]

After five years of grants, the Ford Foundation in 1992 commissioned an independent evaluation of the EPI, which earned very high marks across most of the political spectrum. As a result the foundation refunded the EPI, for research on such topics as labor markets and living standards, trade and competitiveness, reforms in the workplace, health care financing, and the relationship between welfare spending and economic performance.[86]

Despite continuing support from mainstream foundations (MacArthur,

Ford, and Sloan), along with several corporations (Metropolitan Life, LTV Steel, and Milliken), the EPI has its detractors. The organ of the conservative Capital Research Center says, "EPI is concerned not so much with scholarship and research as with achieving political ends [such as] big government and the ideology of wealth redistribution." A *Wall Street Journal* commentator wrote, "In EPI's view there are few problems . . . that cannot be solved by spending a few score more billion dollars collected from whatever wallets are within reach."[87]

Not surprisingly, avowedly conservative think tanks have opposed policies favorable to unions, and they have been assisted by company and private foundations. The Heritage Foundation, for example, which receives 40 percent of its funds from foundations, has argued against legislation requiring businesses to notify workers, unions, and state governments of their intention to close plants. Other targets were antistriker replacement legislation ("by shifting the balance decisively in favor of unions, the legislation would slow job creation.") and measures to increase the minimum wage and to provide comparable pay for women.[88] Heritage also reprinted and distributed a talk by Reed Larson, president of the National Right to Work Legal Defense Foundation, opposing the use of union dues to influence public policy and contribute to political campaigns. "The pro-socialist policies advanced by union officials using their multi-billion dollar forced-dues resources," he said, "do not reflect the views of America's working people, including most of those who are compelled to pay in order to keep their jobs."[89]

Fifteen years before the EPI was established, the distinguished labor economists Derek Bok and John Dunlop, in a prominent Rockefeller Brothers Fund study, called attention to an imbalance between foundation support of business schools and their inattention to union-based research. Proposing a research institute cosponsored by foundations and the AFL-CIO, they wrote: "By making grants to business schools, foundations have spent millions of dollars to educate executives to become more proficient at their trade and more responsive to the broader needs of society. If foundations are serious in pursuing these aims, they would do well to consider giving assistance to similar endeavors within the labor movement."[90]

In light of the growth of conservative foundations, has a greater imbalance developed in foundation support for union-related research? An AFL-CIO official who has enjoyed foundation funding for a major research and demonstration project says, notwithstanding, "A lot of mainstream foundations are very skittish about giving money to what they perceive as left-of-center groups that would do research in policy areas, whereas right-wing foundations just proliferate with research on privatization and issues they find appealing. We lack that in the progressive community."[91]

On the other hand, the Alfred P. Sloan Foundation in 1992 began a significant program to address the vexing issue of competitiveness. Titled "Standard of Living, Competitiveness, and Economics," it examines such factors as the role of organized labor, job generation, and required workforce skills and training. Consisting mainly of eleven university-based research units, the program deals with service sector industries as well as manufacturing. The program director, Hirsh Cohen, a mathematician with extensive industry experience, says: "In addition to building new knowledge we hope the results would be of direct benefit to the companies involved in the studies." In some of the industries it has proved useful, he reports. The automobile industry contributes 70 percent of the cost of the MIT study of that sector.[92]

The role of unions is examined in a set of grants called the Sloan Human Resources Network, supervised by Thomas Kochan of MIT. A key element is whether performance is related to unionization of a given industry or plant. A former UAW official, Don Ephlin, is a full-time participant, and union officials Jack Shenkman and Jay Mazur have played important roles in the Harvard study of the apparel industry, which focuses on relations between manufacturers and large mass retailers. Other industry studies are pharmaceutical, trucking, restaurants and retail food, semiconductors, powdered metal, finance, and managed health care.[93]

The Russell Sage Foundation and the Rockefeller Foundation in 1994 launched a large-scale research initiative concerning low-skilled labor, including the role of unionization. The $2 million effort marks a return of sorts by the RSF to a focus on workers after a fifty-year hiatus. The foundation is concentrating on labor market opportunities available to the poor, according to Eric Wanner, its president, "both because these play such a dominant role in determining the possibility of escaping poverty and because the evident deterioration in the labor market position of low-skilled workers over past two decades has lengthened the odds of escape for many Americans."[94] In a Russell Sage book, Richard Freeman concludes that the decline in unionization contributed roughly 20 percent to the increase in earnings inequality in the 1980s. The decline, about one percentage point a year, was unprecedented in American economic history.[95] The RSF also commissioned research on outcomes of policies, such as greater investment in education and training, which have long been a staple of foundation programs.

5

Black Workers

"**O**rganized labor holds the main gate of our industrial and economic corral; on the day that it throws open that gate . . . there will be a crack in the wall of racial discrimination that will be heard around the world," wrote James Weldon Johnson in the early 1930s.[1] But through most of American history, the public policies that shaped the fortunes of black workers were slavery, legal segregation, and discrimination. As unions arose, they reflected the mores of the larger society, excluding blacks or segregating them in separate units. As for foundations, no subjects were more controversial than unions and race. Nevertheless, after the Civil War and into the twentieth century several foundations actively supported the improvement of black education in the South.[2] Because they accommodated to a segregated framework, such efforts have been severely criticized by black scholars who charged that northern philanthropy "became a powerful instrument for fortifying 'white supremacy' and 'keeping the Negro in his place.'"[3] Race relations per se did not appear on foundation agendas until after World War I, and organized philanthropy paid virtually no attention to blacks as industrial workers, much less in the labor movement, until the 1960s.

Moreover, the predominant view of labor unions among black leaders for at least a half-century after the Civil War was as suspicious as the attitude of white workers toward blacks was antagonistic. The black educated class that sought entry into the professions focused not so much on economic opportunity as on political equality and equal citizenship, largely ignoring the black working class. The focus on political rights by black leaders like Frederick Douglass, P. B. S. Pinchbeck, and John Langston prevailed against the judgment of those of a mind with Wesley Howard, who told the 1869 State Convention of Colored Labor in Baltimore that the franchise without the organization of labor would be of little benefit.[4]

Before the Civil War, racial tensions between white and black workers heightened as employers sought to apprentice slaves into skilled trades. Conversely, beginning with Reconstruction, blacks in the South were steadily eliminated from skilled and semi-skilled occupations. When blacks began to move into heavy industry, they had to accept lower wages than whites (both native-born and immigrant) and were frequently enlisted as strikebreakers. Booker T. Washington's antiunion views epitomized the attitudes of black leaders and of influential black publications, some of which actually endorsed the use of blacks as strikebreakers.

Blacks were finally welcomed into the mainstream union movement by the Knights of Labor (organized in 1869 and, within a decade, the nation's largest labor union) whose leader, William H. Sylvis, declared, "We are all one family of slaves together. The labor movement is a second Emancipation Proclamation."[5] The Knights grew rapidly in the South, especially among blacks and farmers, with as many as 50,000 southern workers. Local assemblies were racially segregated, but both black and white locals sent representatives to district and state assemblies. But by the late 1880s the Knights of Labor was disintegrating.

Barred from crafts, trade unions, and apprenticeships by the hostility of southern white workers, steered away from industrial employment, reliant on cotton plantation culture and its farm tenancy and peonage, blacks in large numbers began to move north. Although an 1890 AFL resolution opposed exclusion of persons from unions because of race or color, exclusion was a fact. Ten years later the AFL endorsed organizing blacks in separate unions, which the organization would then admit. In 1918, Thomas J. Jones, a well-known sociologist and the educational director of the Phelps-Stokes Fund, together with officers of the Anna T. Jeanes Fund, signed a letter to the AFL suggesting more concrete steps to advance the position of Negro workers. The federation's annual convention approved a meaningless resolution in favor of black advancement. In 1924 the National Association for the Advancement of Colored People (NAACP) was moved to issue an open letter to the AFL calling for action. "Is it not time that black and white labor got together?" the letter asked. "Is it not time for white unions to stop bluffing and for black laborers to stop cutting off their noses to spite their faces?"[6]

Interracial Efforts

The National Urban League (NUL) was formed in 1906 at the instigation of William Baldwin, a railroad executive who was president of Rockefeller's General Education Board and a trustee of the Tuskegee Institute. The league dedicated itself to "[Making] the Negro's position [in northern cities] following the great migration of the last two years from the South one of helpfulness to the community rather than a menace."[7] From 1918 to 1928, the Laura Spelman Rockefeller Memorial was the league's largest source of foundation funds, joined by the Altman Foundation and Carnegie Corporation.[8] In an appeal to the LSRM in 1920 for funds to hire an industrial secretary, the league's L. Hollingsworth Wood wrote: "You will realize the delicacy of the industrial situation for the Negro. He has been brought in great numbers into the steel industry and was the main agency which broke the recent steel strike. . . . The AFL recognizes this [and is] going out to organize [blacks], but the prejudice of the various local unions has to be overcome." Resentment against blacks serving as strikebreakers might fan the race issue into a race riot, he noted. "Consequently we feel that an Industrial Secretary who will keep in touch with all the developments in the labor situation and be able to advise Negro workers sanely and wisely is a necessity."[9]

The league's Industrial Department worked with employers to encourage hiring and promotion of blacks and with unions to enable black workers to affiliate with them. Its research resulted in a study of blacks in unions edited by Ira DeReid, the league's industrial secretary.[10] In a report to the LSRM summarizing its activities for 1920, the league noted that, following a conference with the Executive Council of the AFL, the federation "decided definitely to admit Negroes to full membership in all its internationals." Yet eight years later, the league reported, "discrimination [is] pursued by the labor unions . . . and even when discrimination is not decreed by formal constitution there are various practices at work that keep Negroes out of unions and consequently out of employment." But despite reputable scholarship, the NUL never earned the respect of black intellectuals and activists because a good part of its funds came from foundations and individual white philanthropists. The Depression increased the league's dependence; between 1932 and 1939 more than half its income came from Rockefeller philanthropies, Carnegie Corporation, and the New York and Friedsam foundations.[11]

The NAACP was relatively late in addressing union matters, but by the end of World War I it joined with the NUL in pressuring organized labor to admit blacks. The NAACP favored protest and agitation, however, rather than the NUL's investigation, negotiation, and persuasion.[12] During World War II the NAACP also fought against discriminatory labor practices within the federal government and in plants holding government war contracts. Over the following decades, the organization focused almost totally on civil rights, but maintained an interest in organized labor by appointing Herbert Hill, a former Steelworkers' organizer, in 1948 to develop and conduct a labor program. At times the organization's activities on behalf of black workers led to quarrels with organized labor and liberal, Jewish, and civil rights groups—allies of the NAACP on other issues. The NAACP had long prided itself on being self-sustaining through membership dues (unlike the Urban League), but its support from foundations began in 1965 and continued to rise to a peak of $1.8 million in 1995.

The historians Sterling Spero and Abram Harris labeled leaders of the Urban League and various committees of interracial cooperation "Negro administrators of white philanthropy . . . [who] are interested in greater economic activity for the colored worker. . . . The lifting of trade-union barriers is but one of the methods. . . . Their principal appeal is to employers and members of the professions. Their efforts [also seek] the cooperation of prominent trade-union officials, [but] make no attempt to reach the white or black rank and file."[13]

A decade later, Gunnar Myrdal disagreed. He found that in many cities, especially in the South, local opinion hindered local Urban Leagues from taking any action to integrate Negro workers into labor unions. However, he wrote, "As the trade union movement and collective bargaining are gradually becoming normal and appreciated factors in American society, the Urban League is increasingly holding the lead as a pro-union force working among the Negro people."[14]

The LSRM sponsored an important meeting titled the National Interracial Conference in New Haven, Connecticut, in 1927. Addressing the conference in a brilliant and prescient speech, A. Philip Randolph declared:

> One of the basic methods for improving race relations in this country is going to lie with the change in the general psychology of the worker, black and white, towards each other. As long as you have great masses of people competing in the industrial field for jobs, in the relationship of organized and unorganized, there will naturally grow up bitterness; it would be inevitable even if both groups were white, but when you have one group black and the other group white, there is the additional element of color and race which makes it all the more intense and antagonistic and hostile. So that by way of remedying this whole question of race relations, if we are able to bring the Negro workers into the general field of organized labor and break down the superstition and belief in the mind of the white worker

that the Negro is a natural scab, a strikebreaker, and that he is trying to pull down the standards of life built up by organized labor, then you are going to remove that feeling of antagonism in the mind of the white worker toward the Negro worker, and he is going to feel that here we have a common interest, common struggle, a common cause.[15]

One of the few foundations ever to deal directly with unions and the labor movement was the Garland Fund, which did most of its work in the 1920s. Its board—singular among foundations then and since—included several labor leaders and a black member, James Weldon Johnson, writer, diplomat, intellectual, and the first black to head the NAACP. Garland funded A. Philip Randolph's efforts to organize the Brotherhood of Sleeping Car Porters as a challenge to the Pullman Company's Employee Representation Plan. And Randolph obtained a grant and a loan for his magazine, *The Messenger,* which opposed "the capitalist exploitation of the workers, especially the Negro." Garland also subsidized publication by the Vanguard Press of *Negro Labor in the United States,* by Charles H. Wesley, chairman of the history department at Howard University. Garland grants were made to the NAACP's Committee on Negro Work and to the Trade Union Committee for Organizing Negro Workers. However, Garland rejected an application from the National Urban League for union organizing of blacks because the league was "supported largely by corporate interests."[16]

The Depression stimulated foundation-funded research on the status of blacks in the economy, including their role in labor unions. In 1929, the LSRM resolved to "delve more deeply" into studies of Negro life. At the Russell Sage Foundation, Mary Van Kleeck launched a major study of labor. The effect of National Recovery Administration codes on blacks, said to continue wage discrimination, was examined in a Twentieth Century Fund study, *Labor and the Government.*[17] The Rosenwald Fund sponsored a conference on the economic status of the Negro in 1933. Then, using a secret $50,000 grant from the Rockefeller Foundation, Rosenwald established a Committee on Negroes in the Economic Reconstruction, which commissioned three seminal scholarly studies on labor economics in the South: *The Collapse of Cotton Tenancy, A Preface to Peasantry,* and *Black Workers and the New Unions.*[18]

A Phelps-Stokes Fund conference, "Economic Conditions among Negroes" was held in Washington, D.C., in May 1935 (cosponsored by the Joint Committee on Economic Recovery and Howard University's Department of Political Economy). From this conference grew a large meeting in Chicago in February 1936, formally establishing the National Negro Congress (NNC). According to Lester Granger of the National Urban League, the

NNC's "amazing attendance" comprised eight hundred delegates (including trade unionists) from 551 organizations, with five thousand men and women present at the opening session. Granger noted, "The Congress [demonstrated] the growing importance of labor leadership and the power of the labor movement. Delegates were present from 80 trade unions, as contrasted with only 18 professional and educational groups."[19]

During the CIO's massive organizing drives in the steel, auto, mining, packinghouse, and rubber industries in the 1930s, 500,000 blacks signed up. Blacks in many southern communities became the strongest supporters of the union movement. At the same time, many whites resisted biracial unionization drives by the CIO.[20] By 1946, 1.6 million black members constituted over 10 percent of total union membership. Although some gains were wiped out after the war, they had established a beachhead in the labor movement that would have been impossible before the rise of the CIO. The CIO's formal egalitarianism, embodied in constitutions, led to a political alliance with the NAACP and other black leadership elements, strengthening the position of organized labor as a whole. Still, black advancement in industrial unionism just before and during World War II was blocked by strikes against integrated work in war plants.[21] Bombarded with complaints from the NUL and the NAACP, CIO president Philip Murray appointed a Committee to Abolish Racial Discrimination, and the threat by Randolph of a march on Washington led to FDR's establishing a federal Fair Employment Practices Commission.

Anson Phelps Stokes, head of the Phelps-Stokes Fund, spearheaded the Committee on Negro Americans in Defense Industries (1941), which included religious, business, labor, and educational leaders. In a report two years later Stokes praised the committee's work, but he also reported "friction in various centers," due in part "to the failure of some leaders of industry and labor to adjust themselves to the conditions needed for our American democracy to wage a successful fight at home and abroad against Nazi ideas of totalitarianism and extreme racism."[22]

The experience of blacks in industry in World War II, including their relations to unions, was vividly chronicled by the black novelist Chester Himes, assisted by a grant from the Rosenwald Fund in 1944. Himes's *If He Hollers Let Him Go* depicts working conditions in a California shipyard. In an earlier novel, *The Lonely Crusade*, he describes the efforts of a labor union to organize black aircraft workers. Himes's works, wrote one literary critic, were "searing proletarian novels that point up the social stresses under which the protagonists suffer and the turbulent atmosphere brought about by the constant tension between industry, laborers, and unions."[23]

Protests against wartime discrimination, along with growing unionization, aroused fears, even among liberal philanthropists and moderate, middle-class blacks and white businessmen, of radicalization of blacks through unions and other militant organizations. In *An American Dilemma*, Gunnar Myrdal declared that the white upper classes (from which foundation officials were largely drawn until the 1960s) "have probably to a large extent been dominated by a fear that lower-class whites and blacks might come to terms and unite against them."[24]

The Rosenwald Fund and the LSRM had funded a Commission on Interracial Cooperation as early as 1919 (eventually it became the Southern Regional Council). The rationale for interracial committees, as Ralph Bunche wrote, was that "solutions can be obtained through the cultivation of interracial goodwill," but by and large, "this conception steers clear of the more ominous aspects of the problem, such as strife between black and white labor."[25]

In a shift in policy from racial accommodation to integration, the Rosenwald Fund established the American Council on Race Relations in the 1940s. The change arose from the fears of Rosenwald's president, Edwin Embree, "that unless influential liberals acted quickly, a black proletarian movement would emerge and destroy the 'good will' that had been developing between the races."[26] This concern was echoed later by Dana Creel (senior philanthropic adviser to the Rockefeller family in the 1950s and 1960s and president of the Rockefeller Brothers Fund from 1968 to 1975) in a survey of African American welfare as a prelude to possible expansion of Rockefeller philanthropy in this area. Once an "intelligent and ambitious Negro" is identified as a racial leader, Creel wrote, "he is condemned within the Negro community if he proposes a middle-of-the-road approach, but if he takes an 'all or nothing' stand he is held suspect by the white community." To avoid such frustrations, talented Negroes "were turning toward organized labor, militant newspaper activity, etc."[27]

Myrdal and *An American Dilemma*

The towering racial analysis of the era was *An American Dilemma*, by Gunnar Myrdal, which was funded by Carnegie Corporation.[28] Myrdal perceived the invitation to direct the study as an opportunity to write a major interpretation of "the Negro problem" (certain that it was really a "white man's problem" of national dimensions) that would serve as a guide for both policy makers and an informed public. He believed that any discussion of the social quagmire of discrimination should necessarily include equality of opportunity as well as civil rights efforts.

Given his socialist orientation, it was natural that Myrdal included labor unions within the scope of the study; it would not have been so for most scholars. Nor did he flinch from hiring radicals such as Ralph Bunche on a staff that represented all the important schools of thought on race relations. Several commissioned studies of black labor were incorporated into *An American Dilemma*. Paul Norgren, an economist who went on to a twenty-year career in minority manpower studies, submitted a 767-page manuscript that examined every facet of black labor, from bartending to railroads. He stated flatly that "in almost every sphere of employment examined [Negroes] are concentrated at or near the bottom of the occupational ladder." However, in coal mining, iron and steel production, and automobile manufacturing—where large numbers of blacks were employed—a more favorable situation prevailed. The increasing power of unions, Norgren believed, was significant for blacks, despite the past history of exclusion.[29] Of unions, Myrdal himself wrote, "The trade union movement . . . in America has always been comparatively inconsequential. . . . The observer is struck by the importance played by salaried 'organizers' and the relative unimportance of, or often the lack of, a spontaneous drive from the workers themselves." But Myrdal concluded that the growth of unionism would, in the long run, favor black workers, and suggested that unions be a tool to reach the white middle and lower classes to affect their political views toward moderation and racial integration. His European experience led him to conclude that strong American unions must have a base of all-inclusive labor solidarity.[30]

Assigned by Myrdal to study the political status of blacks and their organizations and leaders, Bunche traveled throughout the South, interviewing a wide spectrum of people, from gas station attendants to Justice Hugo Black and Eleanor Roosevelt. In his memorandum "Conceptions and Ideologies of the Negro Problem," Bunche forcefully made the case that the best strategy for American blacks lay in forging an alliance with the white working class. In terms that would not be heard again for another two decades, he wrote, "The strength of the working class is in its . . . ability to present a unified front to the bosses. Therefore, white and Negro workers must cast aside their traditional prejudices, in their own welfare; they must lock arms and march shoulder to shoulder in the struggle for the liberation of the oppressed working masses." He also observed, "The Negro has long exploited his humility, his ability to talk low, to bow and scrape, in his relations with the white employer and the white philanthropist. If he must, he can employ these artifices to much better advantage for himself in nudging into the good grace of organized labor."[31] Bunche had little use for the civil rights tactics of the NAACP (he argued that the vote had not done much for the poor whites of the South), concluding that the most critical aspect of black life was economic. Myrdal himself differed, believing the problem was social, cultural, and behavioral—"the economic factor was no more 'basic' than any other."[32]

The ultimate choice facing the United States, Myrdal predicted, was to provide jobs for blacks or to accept them as chronic relief clients; there was no viable alternative to integrating blacks into the white economic system. But he could not envisage the degree of social and economic deterioration that would lead to development of an "underclass" (a term he used).[33]

The Civil Rights Movement

Addressing the AFL-CIO convention in 1961, Martin Luther King observed, "Negroes are almost entirely a working people. There are pitifully few Negro millionaires and few Negro employers. Our needs are identical with labor's needs—decent wages, fair working conditions, livable housing, old-age security, health and welfare measures, conditions in which families can grow, have education for their children and respect in the community."[34] In a Labor Day address in 1966, A. Philip Randolph said, "The only institution in this society whose economic programs coincide with the needs of the civil rights movement is the labor movement."[35]

Black workers along with white have been affected by foundations' direct intervention in union affairs through support of "union democracy" movements—efforts by dissident union members to oust corrupt or ineffective officials. Black mine workers charging union neglect formed a rival National Miners' Union in 1928, which dissolved after strikes failed in Pennsylvania and Kentucky. By the 1950s, when corruption had seeped into the UMW, black members were active in insurgencies that foreshadowed the formation of Miners for Democracy. The MFD received support from the Field Foundation and the Stern Family Fund, but appeals to a dozen other foundations, including several self-styled "progressive" ones, failed.[36]

After the NAACP established a tax-deductible arm, the Special Contributions Fund, initial grants came from small foundations. The organization had splintered in 1957, under pressure from Congress and the Internal Revenue Service, and the NAACP Legal Defense and Education Fund split off separately, producing confusion among donors. The Rockefeller Foundation, whose trustees included Ralph Bunche, made sizable grants for NAACP litigation on employment discrimination by unions, corporations, and municipalities. "The major breakthrough came with grants from the Ford Foundation," recalls Gilbert Jonas, who directed the organization's fund-raising from 1965 to 1995, and Ford became the single largest foundation donor, but earlier grants from smaller foundations like Field, New World, and New York were critical.[37] At the peak, Jonas says, support came from some fifteen foundations. Unions themselves were small contributors—$120,000 annually against more than $4 million from corporations. In contrast to foundations and most corporations, unions tried to exact a price, he adds.[38]

Title VII of the Civil Rights Act of 1964, against discrimination in employment, facilitated foundation programs in minority employment and union representation. Labor historians differ on the degree to which organized labor's treatment of blacks improved, even after Title VII and notwithstanding the CIO's reputation for racial even-handedness. According to the NAACP's Hill, the bill that organized labor supported was limited to future discriminatory practices and would have insulated established seniority systems, "thus preserving the racial *status quo* in employment for at least a generation." He also charges that organized labor failed to implement the statute and "repeatedly resisted the law once the federal courts began enforcement."[39] And Robert Zieger, in his history of the CIO, writes that by the 1950s "the CIO relegated African-American workers to the margins."[40]

Although Henry Ford's relations with Negro workers were regarded as progressive by the black community in Detroit, the foundation that bore his name had virtually no connections with minorities in the labor movement for some twenty years after his death in 1947. Then, over a ten-year period, the Ford Foundation carried out one of the most sustained foundation efforts in this area. Mitchell Sviridoff, the former labor official who become a vice president of the Ford Foundation, was eager to strengthen connections between the labor movement and minority leaders. By 1965 the National Urban League had expanded and deepened its contacts with union groups. In a major three-year grant to the league that year, the Ford Foundation addressed obstacles to black participation as a result of union practices in many blue-collar occupations. An internal foundation paper characterized national efforts toward equality as having "failed to alter discrimination in local union hiring practices. Some unions, notably in the building trades, remained virtually closed to blacks."[41]

Under a Ford Foundation grant, the league set up a Labor Education and Apprenticeship Program (LEAP), to conduct seminars with black community leaders and organized labor in several cities. The AFL-CIO granted $30,000 and the federal government awarded $1,250,000 in contracts for LEAP. LEAP ran apprenticeship outreach projects in which nearly a thousand black apprentices were introduced to the building and construction trades, and negotiated agreements with electrical industry unions and employers to recruit black journeymen and other workers. The league also developed materials informing the black community about job prospects in the blue-collar labor

market and the rights and responsibilities of union membership, and chan-
neled black youth toward job preparation in the skilled trades.

Even more extensive than LEAP was the Ford Foundation–supported Joint
Apprenticeship Program (JAP), sponsored by the Workers Defense League
and the A. Philip Randolph Educational Fund. By providing minority appli-
cants with rigorous tutoring for apprenticeship admissions tests and devising
journeyman upgrading programs, the JAP opened doors to many minority
workers. Ford grants for the JAP, totaling more than $400,000, were com-
plemented by a legal effort, also with foundation support, through the NAACP
Legal Defense Fund. "Nothing has done more to increase the number of minorities in employment generally—and this includes unionized employment—than that broad effort," Sviridoff said.[42] A contrary assessment was
offered by Herbert Hill: "Apprenticeship and other training programs in the
skilled craft occupations of the building trades failed to eliminate the traditional pattern of exclusion based on race. . . . While there has been an increase in non-white participation in apprenticeship training, there has been
little change in the percentage of black journeymen admitted into unions
controlling employment in the skilled job classifications."[43] Hill's findings
appear to be supported by a study funded by the Ford Foundation on the impact of unionism on the industrial and occupational distribution of blacks, in
which Leonard A. Rapping found that unions heightened entry barriers not
only into craft unions but into industrial unions as well. Rapping used data
over the period 1910–60.[44]

Black workers dissatisfied with union efforts to combat bias took matters
into their own hands from time to time. In a typical case, the organization
Fight Back was established in 1964 to overcome racial discrimination in the
construction industry through militant site confrontations. It received support mainly from the North Star Fund, which also funded *Hard Hat News*, a
newsletter on job security, organization of low-wage workers, and discriminatory union practices.

More than a decade after Title VII, grounds for continued pessimism existed. In a Ford Foundation–assisted study, a leading authority on employment discrimination declared:

Trade unions are the focal point of racial discord in our society, [repre-
senting] both the new immigrants and older groups who are pulling themselves up the ladder and who perceive their competitive status to be unsta-
ble and threatened. Paradoxically, the unions represent some of the most
reactionary and insecure elements in American society as well as the "underclass," which is disproportionately black as well as Chicano and Puerto
Rican. A principal obstacle to a more progressive labor movement is its un-

warranted self-satisfaction and smugness about organizing new categories
of workers. The effect is to disregard the interests of those who need protection most—the significant number of the poor who are members of
racial minorities.[45]

Another initiative in opening jobs to blacks has been the A. Philip Randolph
Institute (APRI), a national organization of black trade unionists, founded in
1965 by Randolph and Bayard Rustin, a leading civil rights and labor activist
and strategist, and an organizer of the 1963 March on Washington for Jobs
and Freedom. APRI has received funding from several foundations, beginning with the Taconic Foundation, for activities ranging from voter registration to opening of wider job opportunities for blacks, especially in the
building trades and construction industries. An annual AFL-CIO grant supports the APRI's administration. The institute has some 150 chapters in
thirty-six states.
    One of its announced principles is to work within the labor movement:

> The vast majority of blacks are workers. While we realize that the labor
> movement is not a perfect institution, black trade unionists must work
> within the broad movement of organized workers of all races. The Institute
> is firmly committed to racial integration; it rejects the idea that black work-
> ers can or should solve their own problems in isolation from the overall la-
> bor movement. Thus, the tactics and strategies of the Institute must paral-
> lel the tactics and strategies of the mainstream trade union movement.[46]

Addressing the paucity of minority union leaders, in 1973 the Ford Foundation granted $100,000 to APRI for a national leadership-training program.
(At the time only two small unions out of 114 affiliated with the AFL-CIO
had black presidents, although 15 percent of total union members were black.)
Many of the several hundred black union members who participated went on
to win union elections. The number of black union officials has increased,
especially in the expanding public service sector.
    The U.S. Department of Labor became the main funding source for an
APRI outreach program in twenty-one cities, building on a Ford Foundation
pilot program to recruit and train black apprentices. In New York in the
mid- and late 1960s, a foundation-funded APRI program provided intensive
preparation of black candidates for the apprenticeship examination for the
sheet metal workers union. So high did they place that the union brought
suit, alleging that the tests had been stolen; the court ruled against the union.
In Los Angeles in the 1990s, black bricklayers formed their own contracting
cooperative because so relatively few had been employed under a union

To widen access for minorities to skilled trades, foundations supported apprenticeship training programs starting in the 1960s. (George Meany Memorial Archives, AFL-CIO)

agreement with 140 contractors. The effort was launched with grants of nearly $500,000 from six foundations. It originated when the head of the national bricklayers' union called the APRI's attention to the situation. Other foundation funding has supported strategic analysis; thus the APRI obtained a Sloan Foundation grant to conduct a black-oriented study parallel to the AFL-CIO's 1986 study on the changing situation of workers and their unions related to the changing nature of work.

If foundations and unions draw closer together, will minority workers receive special attention? Given foundations' early concerns for black education and later engagement with minority civil rights and equity, that seems likely. The late John N. Sturdivant, once the nation's highest ranking black union official (he was president of the American Federation of Government Employees), believed that although foundations "generally buttress the ideological interests of their sponsor," they are helpful to society. His union jointly funded or collaborated on projects with foundations in occupational health research and safety and voter registration and education. Foundation staff people know little about the labor movement, he said, but collaboration could help both unions and foundation be more responsive to social needs.[47]

6

Working Women

Florence Kelley, a pioneer of women's rights, compared bourgeois philanthropy unfavorably with working-class philanthropy. Under the latter, efforts by trade unions and benefit societies to promote human welfare, she argued, "strengthened [workers] in their daily encounters with the capitalist system and helped mitigate inequities that someday the revolution would sweep away." She viewed bourgeois philanthropy as "a means by which capitalists returned to the workers a small fraction of the wealth stolen from them in order to control 'the dependent and dangerous classes' and avert the revolution."[1]

In fact, foundations, which institutionalized "bourgeois philanthropy," championed working women's interests when unions were inhospitable toward them. A few foundations (notably Russell Sage and the Garland Fund) were openly sympathetic to female membership in trade unions. After the flowering of feminism in the late 1960s, foundations supported a variety of programs to improve the status of working women, in unions and elsewhere—programs to open nontraditional occupations to women, to advance women in union office, and to support women's rights in the workplace. Foundations are now supporting worker centers that seek to improve conditions for working women on the lowest rungs of the economic ladder, mainly minorities and new immigrants.

Research on Women's Work

Foundation interest in women's working conditions began with the Russell Sage Foundation, whose concern was influenced by the fact that it had been established by a woman and women were, uncharacteristically, a substantial proportion of its first board of trustees. Moreover, its agenda was sympathetic to Progressive reformers, individual philanthropists, and charitable organizations whose socioeconomic goals went beyond ameliorating social ills.[2]

In 1910 a Committee on Women's Work became an integral part of the foundation, a development all the more remarkable because the public had not yet absorbed the fact that the number of women in industry had been growing rapidly, with resulting alterations in their status and roles.[3] By 1900 women made up nearly one-fifth of the labor force, and from 1890 to 1910, the number of women employed outside the home doubled, from 4,005,532 to 8,075,772. Despite these numbers, women remained an inconspicuous part of the labor movement.[4]

In surveying the conditions of women's employment, the Russell Sage project director, Mary Van Kleeck, pledged to base her research on accurate, disinterested reporting as opposed to propaganda or support of a particular economic theory First off, the trailblazing Russell Sage–supported study *The Pittsburgh Survey* devoted one of its six volumes to women. Noting that the 22,000 women employed for wages in Pittsburgh constituted "a new labor force," the study proposed practical measures, including legislation, to promote the welfare of such workers and "advance their material and spiritual standards."[5] But as later research has concluded, women workers were not seen by legislators or the courts as entitled to the living wage that men should receive.[6]

Paralleling the Russell Sage studies were the nineteen-volume *Report on Condition of Woman and Child Wage Earners in the United States*, conducted by the U.S. Bureau of Labor and published in 1910–13, and investigations by the National Consumers League of wages and living standards among working women. An elite organization of well-educated women, the NCL grew out of protests in 1890 by retail shop girls in New York against low pay and deplorable working conditions. It differed from other women's organizations, however, in its support of trade unionism. State leagues throughout the country conducted "White Label" campaigns, certifying manufacturers and stores with better working conditions.[7] The league's legal actions, assisted by a grant from the Russell Sage Foundation, defended maximum hour and minimum wage laws in several states. Its chief counsel, Louis Brandeis, at the behest of his sister-in-law Josephine Goldmark and Florence Kelley, successfully defended the Oregon Ten-Hour Law in 1908 (*Muller v. Oregon*), opening the way to other protective laws. When Brandeis was named to the U.S. Supreme Court, Felix Frankfurter replaced him as NCL counsel.[8]

Underpaid, overworked women workers, usually young, sometimes immature, and unused to working in groups and facing intense opposition from employers, generally resisted unionization. The AFL made little effort to organize women, and some locals prohibited their membership or sharply restricted apprenticeships. When the AFL did organize women, its major incentive was to protect the earning power of men. Even unions formed by women were denied affiliation, despite proclamations by some national unions. Among the arguments marshaled against women as union members was that their employment was temporary until they married, and that their wages were unnecessary to their families' well-being.[9] The exception to women's general apathy toward unions was an upsurge of women's organizing in the New York garment industry, spurred by the strikes of 1909–13, which were supported by many wealthy women. By 1914 the International Ladies Garment Workers Union (ILGWU) was the third largest union in the AFL.

Van Kleeck's studies of women's work led the Russell Sage Foundation to take the position that the problems of women in industry largely reflected conditions affecting men, too. Accordingly, the name of its Committee on Women's Work was changed in 1916 to the Division of Industrial Studies, which encompassed labor union studies, the first of which (1916) dealt with the cigar-making industry.[10]

The largest and longest-lasting labor-related women's organization was the Women's Trade Union League (WTUL), founded in 1903 by liberals and social workers as well as trade unionists.[11] More than the NCL, it carried the message of unionism to women in trades where they were widely employed—clothing, textile, laundry, glove, and millinery industries. By 1929, the WTUL had twenty-seven branches and had published the magazine *Life and Labor* for eighteen years; it was sustained by individual contributions and occasional foundation grants.[12]

In New York City, the WTUL had difficulty surmounting language and cultural barriers to organizing Italian women, so it made common cause with the Russell Sage Foundation. A resulting study declared, "Bargaining power in settling the terms of the work agreement should be as evenly balanced as possible between employer and employee [and] recognize the right of employers and employees alike to organize or form unions." The WTUL organized the Italian Girls Industrial League, an evening club to educate young women about trade unions. In response to pervasive negative views of immigrant working women, Carnegie Corporation undertook, at the same time, a study of Americanization, *Fusion of the Native and Foreign-Born,* but ignored the role of unionization.[13]

On the eve of the Depression, the role of women workers was specifically explored in one of the monographs in a study supported by the Rockefeller Foundation. While many national union leaders are still "stale, pale, and male," the author observed, "women's union leadership is increasing at all levels."[14]

Education for Women Workers

Education for women workers on economic and social issues attracted foundation support as early as the 1920s, with the emphasis on knowledge rather than union activism. Attracting union and nonunion women, the sessions provided middle-class women with exposure to the labor movement while giving working-class women, in the words of two scholars, "opportunities to interact with women of a different race, ethnic group, or region on common personal, workplace, union and community issues."[15]

Foundation and government grants and contracts provided critical support for pilot programs that demonstrated the potential of labor education when unions and universities were not prepared to undertake them.[16] But the labor-focused Garland Fund, in one of its contrarian acts of false purity, denied a grant for the WTUL's Training School for Women Organizers, which included courses for credit at the University of Chicago, on the grounds that it emphasized bureaucratic and administrative skills rather than organizing. Garland also appeared to view negatively the Training School's reformist sponsors and its desire to link up with the AFL. Student dissatisfaction with the school's fieldwork, combined with financial problems, led to its closing in 1926.[17]

The Bryn Mawr School for Women Workers (1921–38) was a suffragist-inspired social feminist institution, dedicated to bridging economic and social classes. Support came from Bryn Mawr alumnae, a few unions (Amalgamated Clothing Workers of America, the ILGWU, the Brotherhood of Sleeping Car Porters, and the Electrical Workers Industrial Union), and such philanthropic sources as John D. Rockefeller Jr. and the Carnegie Corporation.

The idea of such a school at a staid, elite college was "neither an anomaly nor an exercise in *noblesse oblige*," according to the feminist scholar Rita Heller. The family of the college president, M. Carey Thomas, had connections to the British Fabians. Bryn Mawr established the first American graduate school of social work, and its students had "a passionate interest . . . in justice and [an] intense sympathy with girls less fortunate than themselves."

Thomas knew little about unions, but invited union women—Mary Anderson, chief of the Women's Bureau, and Rose Schneiderman, president of the Women's Trade Union League—to participate.[18]

In the charged political atmosphere of the 1930s, some alumnae of the college accused the school of Communist sympathies and participation in strikes. It was evicted from Bryn Mawr in 1935, then returned for three more years, but by then "much of the momentum was gone and its idealistic energies spent." Notwithstanding, it had "enabled a generation of women to discover new inner and outer worlds, [grooming them] for leadership."[19]

In 1927 southern women working with the YWCA Industrial Department created the Southern Summer School for Women Workers, which ran six-week residential sessions, first at Sweet Briar College and afterward at various schools in Western North Carolina. The Garland Fund granted the school $12,000 to initiate a year-round program. In doing so, it compromised its own dedication to black causes, since in order to ensure cooperation from the AFL, the school enrolled only white women. Of the twenty-five women who attended the first summer session, seven were union members (from the textile, tobacco, and telephone industries). The percentage of students belonging to unions rose and fell with union membership in the South: 45 percent as labor revolts broke out in 1929 and 1930, 9 percent in the early Depression, and 38 percent following pro-labor New Deal legislation. In 1937 a group of women sharecroppers from Arkansas recruited by the Southern Tenant Farmers Union enrolled. Men were admitted in 1938, and by 1940 union locals were sending more males than females. The school lasted until World War II.[20] Foundations also contributed to Brookwood Labor College in Katonah, N.Y., a major training ground for future CIO organizers. Brookwood allotted its admissions equally between men and women although a greater number of applications were received from women.[21]

The Affiliated Schools for Women Workers, organized in 1928, served as a national clearinghouse for instructional materials and information on fund raising, teacher recruitment, and curriculum. Affiliated Schools received a major grant ($70,000) from the Rockefeller Foundation's General Education Board in 1933, permitting it to develop New Deal worker education projects through the WPA. When funds ran out, the agency reorganized as the American Labor Education Service (ALES), leaning more toward general workers' education and becoming more dependent on organized labor for financial support. The ALES closed in 1962, foundering on "the tension between the commitment to freedom of discussion and the increasing political conservatism of organized labor."[22]

The ambivalent motivation behind foundation support of these projects has been noted by a leading teacher and authority in the field, Joyce Kornbluh of the Labor Studies Center at the University of Michigan:

> When courses expanded beyond traditional academic subjects to include subjects such as union organizing, economic and political power, and class divisions, mainstream foundations, such as Carnegie Corporation, became apprehensive. Foundations were more ready to give grants for worker education when they viewed women as downtrodden and oppressed individuals. The focus was on *worker* education rather than on *labor* education. Labor unions were viewed as institutional threats; confrontational. CIO organizing campaigns were particularly threatening.[23]

In 1957, the National Manpower Council, established at Columbia University under a grant from the Ford Foundation, published *Womanpower* (the sixth in a series of reports on conferences in sixteen cities), which illuminated the extent to which women were indispensable to the national economy. In analyzing factors that influenced their participation in paid employment, the report called union discrimination against women comparable to the problem of integrating whites and blacks. Although World War II produced tremendous psychological changes in women's attitudes to paid employment outside the home, unions were no less hostile toward women in the workplace, particularly on the issue of seniority protection. No orientation was offered to male workers or foremen with regard to women employees.[24]

After the women's movement came to stay, model university programs for women workers were established at Cornell University and the University of Michigan in the 1970s. New organizations such as the Coalition of Labor Union Women (CLUW), and 9 to 5 (the National Association of Working Women) also provided labor education.[25] Cornell's Institute for Women and Work received a grant from the Muskiwinni Foundation to train minority women as labor educators, in cooperation with the CLUW and the AFL-CIO Department of Education.

Nontraditional Employment

Three-fourths of working women still have low-paying jobs with little security, few benefits, and scant room for advancement. In 1992, Congress passed the Women in Apprenticeship Occupations Act, designed to prevent sexual harassment and break down barriers to advancement by helping employers and unions create a workplace more receptive to women.[26] Despite that stimulus and the Non-Traditional Employment for Women Act of 1991—in whose passage the foundation-supported Wider Opportunities for Women played an important part—the percentage of women employed in well-paying trades such as construction, transportation, and fire fighting has barely budged since the late 1970s. So foundations have devised programs aimed to open doors to traditionally male jobs with better pay and benefits.

These ventures were facilitated by Title VII of the Civil Rights Act of 1964, which guaranteed nondiscrimination in employment. In Appalachia, for example, the Coal Employment Project has been the advocacy organization for women miners since the early 1970s, while the Southeast Women's Employment Coalition targeted highway jobs.[27] More than half the Coal Project's budget came from a wide range of foundations—from mainstream Ford and John Hay Whitney to such alternative sources as the Muskiwinni Foundation and the Ms. Foundation for Women. Using lawsuits and a media campaign, the Coal Project raised the number of women in coal mines from less than 1 percent of new hires in 1974 to 4.2 per cent (1,100) of all new hires by 1979.[28] In addition it can take credit for a family leave clause in a new UMW contract with the Bituminous Coal Operators Association. The Southern Appalachian Leadership Training program is another example of strategic foundation support, leading to a court settlement requiring building trades unions to issue permits to women and minorities to enable them to work on union jobs in Charleston, West Virginia. After an evaluation of these efforts in the early 1980s, the Ford Foundation granted funds that enabled these groups to expand into new programs. The Coal Employment Project, for example, moved west to include women in the deep mines and strip mines of Utah and Colorado.[29]

Philadelphia-based Public/Private Ventures used Ford Foundation funds for a six-site project that apprenticed low-income women as painters, plasterers, plumbers, and carpenters. The participants, many of them young mothers on welfare, earned from $8 to $10 an hour while training with experienced union journeymen. The women succeeded not only in entering these trades but also in surmounting barriers to participation in union activities. A similar project, with greater breadth, is Chicago Women in Trades (CWIT), established in 1980, whose members work in construction and manufacturing as electricians, machinists, pipe fitters, painters, and other predominantly male jobs. The Woods Charitable Trust, the MacArthur Foundation, the Chicago Foundation for Women, the Robert R. McCormick Tribune Foundation, and several other private and corporate foundations fund CWIT.

Working with both sides—contractors and unions—CWIT publicizes apprenticeship openings (termed "underground information" in that it is usu-

The Coal Employment Project, to help open jobs for women in the coal industry, received grants from foundations beginning in the 1970s, as one of several efforts to help women gain entry into nontraditional employment. (© 1976 Earl Dotter, Impact Visuals)

ally confined to males within the trades) and conducts its own pre-apprentice tutorials. CWIT's director is Lauren Sugarman, a former elevator repair woman. "We upset the apple-cart," she says, by having the U.S. Department of Education investigate a major trade school that unions were operating in conjunction with the Chicago Board of Education, charging discrimination against women in recruitment and admissions.[30]

Programs similar to CWIT in Milwaukee, Wisconsin, Hartford, Connecticut, and Montana are conducted by Wider Opportunities for Women (WOW) with help from the Ford Foundation, and in the San Francisco Bay Area by WOW and Tradeswomen, Inc. supported by foundations and companies. The national figure for the proportion of women in the skilled trades was at least 6.6 percent in 1994.[31]

Union Women's Organizations

Foundations provided critical support for new labor-related women's organizations such as the Coalition of Labor Union Women (CLUW), founded in 1974 as an outgrowth of both the women's liberation movement and the activism of union women. Thirty-two hundred union women attended the founding conference, more than four times the number expected. Like its forbear, the WTUL, the CLUW demonstrated that middle-class feminists could productively join forces with working women.[32]

The CLUW itself does not organize working women in unions and will not side with one union over another, but it believes in working with the labor movement. For several years a deep ideological struggle went on between its leadership and radical members who were highly critical of established unions. Conflict also arose over seniority rights versus affirmative action, and resolutions on union democracy, which many members viewed as antiunion. The leadership prevailed. George Meany, addressing a CLUW conference in 1977, said, "If supporting a living wage for all workers makes me a feminist, move over sisters. . . . [women trade unionists] have provided special expertise to the labor movement on such issues as day care, minimum wage, pregnancy benefits and national health insurance."[33]

9 to 5 originated in 1973 as an association of clerical and middle-management women. Operating in more than two hundred cities, it has highlighted health and safety in offices, workplace discrimination, and sexual harassment, and publicized the best and worst employer practices.[34]

The founder of 9 to 5, Karen Nussbaum, was appointed director of the AFL-CIO's new Working Women's Department in 1996. It aims to "inject women's concerns into every nook and cranny" of the organization.[35]

Shortly after joining the AFL-CIO, Nussbaum chided a gathering of liberal foundation officials for not taking more of an interest in the labor movement.

Research and Leadership

Since the 1960s foundations have carried forward the tradition of research on women's work and the relation of women to unions pioneered by the Russell Sage Foundation. With the aid of a Ford Foundation grant in 1979, for example, the CLUW collaborated with the UAW and the Communications Workers of America in a unique series of interviews at work sites; heretofore most research on women workers was general and concerned statistical matters ranging from job upgrading to comparisons of male/female work content and pay.[36] Child care, a key issue on the CLUW's agenda, was the subject of a $96,500 grant from the German Marshall Fund of the United States that enabled the CLUW to join in a study of programs in three foreign countries. In the 1970s two agencies were established to explore the problems and needs of women in low-paying jobs—the National Commission on Working Women and the Center for Women and Work. They were funded by the National Institute of Education and the Ford and Rockefeller foundations.

Foundations have also addressed the issue of women in union leadership roles. In the mid-1970s no women sat on the thirty-nine-member Executive Council of the AFL-CIO, and within the 185 trade unions listed by the Bureau of Labor Statistics, only six top elective posts were held by women. The CLUW's Joyce Miller (who later became the first female member of the Executive Council) declared, "Women need representatives at the highest policy levels within unions, as well as at all middle levels, if their voice is to be heard throughout the movement." By the mid-1990s although many more women held executive positions, improvement overall had been modest.[37] Beginning in the late 1960s, the Ford Foundation funded programs on the leadership issue, including a study by the New York State School of Industrial and Labor Relations (SILR) at Cornell University that led directly to a Trade Union Women's curriculum, ranging from three-day sessions to one- and two-year training courses. The program produced organizers, editors of union newspapers, national and state executive board members, shop stewards, and negotiators.[38]

Pursuing a traditional civil rights strategy, foundations have backed working women's litigation against companies or unions, with grants to the ACLU Women's Rights Project, the NAACP Legal Defense and Educational

Fund's Minority Women's Employment Program, the Mexican-American Legal Defense and Educational Fund's Chicana Rights Project, the League of Women Voters Education Fund, and public-interest law firms engaged in sex discrimination work. Thus the NOW Fund won a district court victory in a landmark case (*Robinson v. Jacksonville Shipyards*) in which extensive pornography and repeated verbal abuse were held to violate the "hostile environment" standards of sexual harassment laws. Together with the Association for Union Democracy Women's Project, NOW prepared a *Manual for Survival for Women*, which describes strategies for combating gender bias.[39]

Until recently policy makers, unions, and women's groups have all been slow to address the work-related problems besetting large numbers of immigrants from Latin America and Asia. In the vacuum, ethnic-based labor organizations have sprouted within immigrant and minority communities. Foundations have given important support to such efforts—Asian Immigrant Women Advocates, for improved conditions in the garment, restaurant, electronics, hotel, and nursing home industries in Los Angeles, Mujereres Undidas y Activas/The Immigrant Women's Advocacy and Education Project for similar work in San Francisco, La Mujer Obrera in El Paso, Fuerza Unida in San Antonio, Korean Immigrant Workers Advocates in Los Angeles, and in New York, the Chinese Staff and Workers Association.[40]

Increased sensitivity to the role of women in the labor movement was illustrated dramatically in the 1995 contest for the presidency of the AFL-CIO. Thomas Donahue's slate had a woman nominee for vice president. John Sweeney, who defeated Donahue, persuaded the convention to create the post of executive vice president, which was filled by Linda Chavez-Thompson, a vice president of AFSCME. As noted earlier, a Working Women's Department was created in the AFL-CIO after the election.

In the foundation world, the rise of women to top ranks since the late 1980s has been so dramatic that it has been termed "the feminization of philanthropy." With four of the country's eleven largest foundations headed by women, it is not unreasonable to assume that these institutions will be disposed to pay special attention to women in unions and to unions that make a special effort to organize and empower women.

7

Farm and Southern Labor

Union organizing to address the plight of farm workers
has ranged from such visible efforts as the Southern Tenant Farmers Union
before World War II to Cesar Chavez's United Farm Worker movement in
California beginning in the 1960s. Funds and hands-on assistance to improve farm workers' economic and social status have come from foundations, church groups, and unions.

The Southern Tenant Farmers Union
and Agricultural Policy

As early as 1914, the U.S. Commission on Industrial Relations (the Walsh
Commission) was investigating conditions for tenant farmers (at that time in
Texas).[1] By the Depression, rural poverty in the South, pervasive for years,
had reached an acute stage. More than eight million people were living in
desperate conditions, bordering on peonage, in the cotton fields. Most
sharecroppers were black, and tenant farmers were generally white. (Tenant
farmers, with their own tools and livestock, farm someone else's land, pledg-
ing one quarter to one third of the crop to the landlord. Sharecroppers, who
provide only their labor, pledge the landlord close to half of what they raise.)
Despite flagrant injustices of decades' duration, concerted action by agricultural workers was late in coming, given such elements of rural culture as individualism, poverty, illiteracy, disease and malnutrition, the plantation sys-

101

tem of paternalism, and dependence on a single crop (cotton), to say nothing of the enduring antagonism between blacks and whites.

The Southern Tenant Farmers Union (STFU) was not only a union movement, but also a protest movement—a unique biracial organization of sharecroppers, other tenant farmers, and some small businessmen, founded in Tryronza, Arkansas, in 1934, triggered by farm workers' exclusion from the New Deal's National Industrial Recovery Act and the stringencies of the Agricultural Adjustment Act. Despite efforts by liberals in the Agricultural Adjustment Administration (AAA) to protect landless farmers in the allocation of New Deal benefits, the policies and programs of the agency were discriminatory in their application: government payments were sent to landlords who refused to honor contract-sharing, and there was no enforcement. The AAA also provided incentives for mechanization, which, coupled with a sharp drop in cotton prices, drove thousands of agricultural workers—about 20 percent—off the land. Those who stayed were offered work as day laborers, a situation that allowed even more benefits to accrue to the landowner.[2]

The founders of the STFU were two active Socialists, Harry L. Mitchell and Henry Clay East. Personally inspired by Norman Thomas, Mitchell and East decided to redirect their energies from organizing Socialist Party locals to organizing sharecroppers, although their attitudes to New Deal agricultural policy always retained an element of Socialist criticism.[3] The Reverend Howard Kester, a Presbyterian and Congregational minister who was southern secretary of the New York–based Fellowship of Reconciliation, was sent to Arkansas as Thomas's personal representative.

In its active years, the STFU generated nationwide sympathy and support, a result in part of the terrorism (shootings, burnings, beatings, and jail) unleashed on both southerners and northerners by vigilantes and sheriffs' deputies who did the bidding of large-farm and plantation owners. Southerners hated the STFU especially because it was integrated.[4] Kester and the activist Gardner Jackson, a wealthy railroad heir ousted from the AAA, led a nationwide consciousness-raising movement for funds; National Sharecropper Week, first held in 1937, stirred interest and support. Most funding, however, came from the Garland Fund and the Strikers Emergency Relief Committee, the latter originally set up in New York City by the League for Industrial Democracy in 1929 to raise money for then striking cotton mill workers. Other donors included the ILGWU, the ACLU, the AFL, the Federal Council of Churches of Christ, and some wealthy individuals.[5] The Garland Fund decided to end its $200 monthly contribution in 1939, when the STFU was in desperate financial straits. Norman Thomas persuaded the foundation to reverse its decision, but Mitchell "disliked having his union serve primarily as a pet for philanthropists."[6] Charles Garland himself had become greatly interested in farmers' organizations in the 1930s. Although it had been agreed that he would leave distribution of grants entirely to the fund's board and not try to influence their decisions, he proposed in 1936 that the balance of assets be turned over to him to use in furthering a united front among farm organizations. The board refused, but agreed that it would allocate a substantial amount to this work. Through the fund's lifetime it appropriated $79,000 to farm organizations, some 4 percent of the total assets.[7]

The STFU's most memorable moment occurred in 1939, when, to call attention to the plights of evicted tenant farmers and sharecroppers, Owen Whitfield, a charismatic black minister and STFU organizer, led a massive sit-down strike along the main highway between Memphis and St. Louis. The Farm Security Administration was forced to provide shelter and field kitchens for the destitute protesters.[8]

More efficacious than direct but limited philanthropic support of the STFU were grants from the Rockefeller Foundation and Rosenwald Fund for path-breaking research on the entire framework of the South's land tenure system and its overdependence on cotton. Under the supervision of Rosenwald's president, Edwin R. Embree, the study (by the Committee on Minority Groups in the Economic Recovery) was conducted jointly by Will W. Alexander, director of the Commission on Interracial Cooperation, and Charles S. Johnson of Fisk University. The resulting book, *The Collapse of Cotton Tenancy*, closely examined the 1.1 million white and 699,000 black tenant farmers (whom the study referred to as "peasants"). Between 1920 and 1930, it noted, more than 200,000 whites became tenant farmers, mainly because they lost their land through foreclosure or sale, and at the same time black tenants decreased by some 2,000 (many blacks simply left to go to large cities of the South and North). Only governmental relief prevented wholesale starvation and rioting among black and white farmers in the South.[9]

The violence that confronted the STFU prompted an extensive investigation by the Senate Civil Liberties Committee, chaired by Robert La Follette (D.–Wisconsin), in 1936, but Roosevelt's disinclination to act against southern politicians during a reelection campaign (one of his closest allies in the Senate was Joe Robinson of Arkansas) forestalled a federal administrative investigation. After the election, however, Roosevelt laid the groundwork for passage of the Bankhead-Jones Farm Tenant Act and the establishment of the Farm Security Administration (FSA)—both in 1937—when he created the President's Committee on Farm Tenancy, staffed by, among others, Alexander and Johnson, the co-authors of the Rosenwald/Rockefeller–funded study, and Edwin Nourse of Brookings. Nothing so comprehensive in approach as the committee's report had been fashioned since President Theodore Roosevelt's Country Life Commission in 1909. The underlying objective of the legislation was "protection against the economic, political, social, and personal forces which had conspired to place chronically impoverished farm people in a 'disadvantaged' position as compared with the rest of society."[10]

Roosevelt also met privately with Embree, Alexander, and Frank Tannenbaum of the Rosenwald staff—probably the three people in the country most knowledgeable about southern agricultural conditions, and probably the most influential on federal policy. Alexander managed to persuade the AFL to depart from its policy of restricting its attention to industrial workers and endorse the Bankhead-Jones Act by arguing that it would stabilize marginal farmers and farm laborers on the land, thus reducing the threat that the great reservoir of unskilled labor on southern farms would continue to leave for the cities and take jobs at lower wages than northern workers.[11]

Among the FSA's most successful programs was one that provided improved low-rent housing for displaced farm workers. The Sherwood Eddy Foundation, established by an evangelist minister who was also a YMCA executive, helped finance the initial down payment on one such project, Delmo Homes, in southeastern Missouri, where the government acted as landlord. When the FSA was abolished in 1946, most residents could not afford to purchase their homes, so they were assisted by a group of St. Louis citizens who had not forgotten the roadside demonstrations of 1939; by Marshall Field; and by the Episcopal diocese of Missouri. Eddy was also instrumental earlier in helping thirty black and white families who had been evicted from an Arkansas plantation by supplying part of a down payment for a 2,130-acre property in Mississippi that became a cooperative farming experiment known as the Rochdale Project and continued until the end of World War II.[12] In the late 1930s the FSA also built farm labor camps in California, where John Steinbeck did his research for *The Grapes of Wrath*. The Rosenberg Foundation made grants in 1938–41 for playgrounds in these camps.[13]

At its peak the STFU had enrolled nearly 31,000 members in seven states, but although it preached interracial justice, most of its locals were segregated; by 1941 it had virtually ceased to function. With World War II, rapid farm mechanization, and the huge out-migration of black and white farm workers to war jobs, the diminished STFU became the National Farm Labor Union (1947), affiliated with the AFL, and moved to California to conduct a grape workers' strike. "That," noted one student of southern radicalism, "marked the end of the agricultural union movement in the Deep South."[14] The FSA, housed within the U.S. Department of Agriculture, fell victim not only to assaults by the conservative American Farm Bureau Federation, but also to ideological anxieties over its experimentation in social organization, the decline of the New Deal, shifts in public opinion, and wartime and postwar technological dislocations in agriculture. Twenty years later, about 22 percent of farms in the South were still operated by tenants and sharecroppers, and many black tenant families continued to live at a level unchanged from the days of the Great Depression.[15]

But support for the poorest of farmers did not die. In 1943 Eduard Lindeman and others incorporated the National Sharecroppers Fund, whose first board included educators, church official, and reform leaders.[16] The J. M. Kaplan Fund made several small grants to the affiliated Rural Advancement Fund, but both are now defunct. The Field Foundation was first in the 1960s to stimulate support for the development of black farmer cooperatives as a means for its members to obtain start-up capital, hold on to their land, and provide more control over their own labor. Representatives of twenty-two cooperatives in southern states founded the Federation of Southern Cooperatives in 1967 with funds from the Ford Foundation and the U.S. Office of Economic Opportunity. The federation is still in business.[17]

The California Farm Workers Movement

Unsuccessful attempts to unionize migrant farm workers stretch back to the efforts of the IWW and the AFL in the early 1900s. The AFL Executive Council directed West Coast unions to organize migratory workers after an investigative report described their lot as "in some points worse than slavery,"[18] but the campaigns were halfhearted. Migrant farm workers have always been difficult to organize because of geographic dispersion and movement, the hiring of illegal immigrants as workers or strikebreakers, the lack of an economic margin to support a prolonged strike, and the power of large growers to exert extensive political influence on police and legislators. The hope engendered by the New Deal triggered farm worker strikes in many parts of the country—Cape Cod, the Connecticut Valley, Ohio, Florida, and New Jersey. Several groups obtained better wages and working conditions, but most of their organizations did not last long.[19] A major factor behind the use of braceros (workers imported from Mexico "to relieve labor shortages" but also used as strikebreakers) was the growing political power of large farm owners. Ernesto Galarza received a grant from the Fund for the Republic to write an eighty-page report on the bracero system, "Strangers in Our Fields," "the most damaging bombshell to hit the institution of braceroism up to that time."[20] Published in 1956, it received wide publicity, even in the conservative *Los Angeles Times,* and went through two editions and 10,000 copies, prompting Walter Reuther's AFL-CIO Industrial Union Department to give the National Agricultural Workers Union $12,500 in 1957 for organizing in California. The bracero system was finally outlawed in 1964.[21]

In 1938, Cesar Chavez's family, having lost their homestead in Yuma, Arizona, joined the migrant stream, following crops from the Imperial Valley to Sacramento. Chavez worked for a decade with Fred Ross and the Community Service Organization, a barrio-based self-help group formed in 1947 to serve the 100,000 Mexican Americans then in Los Angeles. Under Ross's low-key, effective persuasion, CSO groups sprouted as far north as San Jose, inspired and trained by the Chicago organizational pioneer Saul Alinsky. The core of Alinsky's philosophy, which he put into practice through the Industrial Areas Foundation (supported by foundations and liberal businessmen), was that social change is more fundamental and longer-lasting if the people affected by problems identify those problems for themselves and band together to deal with them.[22]

Chavez became national director of the CSO but broke with it when it turned down his plea to commit itself to farm worker organizing, founding his own National Farm Workers Association in 1962. Three years later, the NFWA joined in a strike against grape growers in Delano called by the AFL-CIO's Agricultural Workers Organizing Committee (AWOC), whose membership there was mostly Filipino (a dominant worker segment in California agriculture from the 1920s, when laws banned Japanese and other Asian laborers; as an American territory, the Philippines was exempt).[23] In 1966, the AWOC merged with Chavez's NFWA to form the United Farm Workers, an independent union chartered by the AFL-CIO and headed by Chavez. The united union won a landmark contract.

Among early foundation supporters of efforts to organize Mexican American farm workers was the Schwartzhaupt Foundation, which granted $112,000 to the National Council of Churches in 1958 for a three-year citizenship-training project among Mexican American immigrants in California. Run by the council's Migrant Ministry, it led to a close liaison with, and eventual sponsorship of, Chavez's United Farm Workers Union. The grant was an essential element in building linkages to mainstream congregations; it also encouraged several educated, middle-class clergymen to devote themselves to farm worker issues.[24] The Spectamur Agendo Foundation of the radical philanthropist Stewart Mott provided critical support for the first grape boycott. Through a foundation staff member, Ann Israel, other foundations, particularly Rosenberg, joined the action.[25] Although these sources were less critical in the initial campaign, Craig Jenkins observes, "their scale and diversity guaranteed the United Farm Workers independence vis-à-vis any single sponsor and allowed the challenge [to growers] to survive several major disasters."[26]

Boycotts and strikes marked the years following the initial contract as the union sought to win agreement from more growers and to build its membership. Chavez was more a charismatic, nonviolent leader—his activities included fasting and leading religious processions—than a typical union organizer. The union's goals went beyond traditional bread-and-butter demands in seeking social change; the UFW operated clinics, built retirement villages, and opened credit unions, all on a cooperative basis. The union's motivating dynamic—"La Causa"—called for a power struggle involving the church, health and social services, land reform, and community-development projects. This was hard for leaders of the AFL-CIO and the Teamsters, who had moved into the fields in 1966 and made deals with growers at the expense of the UFW, to grasp. "From the outset Chavez steered away from large grants or donations that had any strings attached; he had a feeling that such money would corrupt the learning processes the workers must go through . . . to create a strong union. The struggle itself was important. Any outside helpers would have to join . . . [and] suffer the hardships along with the workers,"[27] noted a historian of the struggle. "Cesar always said that whoever is paying the bills will determine what will happen in the organization," recalls one of his key aides, Dolores Huerta. "So when he started the farm workers' union he made it very clear that the workers themselves would be paying the expenses."[28] Nonetheless, considerable external help went to the farm worker centers that undergirded the union. The UAW, for example, sponsored and paid for a new headquarters building in 1969.

The Field Foundation became embroiled in a dispute between Chavez and a union in Texas that was using Chavez's name in efforts to organize watermelon workers, though he had no knowledge of it. The organization had obtained Field funds. Through Roger Baldwin of the ACLU, Chavez persuaded Field to discontinue these funds and instead support the UFW. Field also funded the Cannery Workers Legal Project in 1977, which took action against the Teamsters Union in San Jose, charging racial discrimination against Mexican, black, and Asian workers.[29]

The UFW lost strength after the 1970s owing to increased mechanization in harvesting, the continuing flood of immigrants, and the resistance of the state's Republican administration. Membership fell from 60,000 to 15,000, and the number of contracts dropped by one third from its high of 100. In addition the union was damaged by dissension centering on Chavez's style, which was perceived as increasingly authoritarian.[30]

By the 1990s the UFW was making a comeback. In 1995 it had the best record of organizing new members—4,000—of any union. Rather than relying on support from liberal donors, the UFW's budget is now 75 percent covered by dues-paying members.[31] In 1996, for the first time in twenty-five years in Washington State, farm workers were permitted to vote to unionize under a voluntary agreement by the state's largest winery, which had tired of pressure from church groups and stockholders. Two-thirds chose the UFW. The union's president, Arturo Rodriguez, is characterized as more pragmatic than his late father-in-law Chavez, and the UFW is seen more like a labor union as opposed to a social cause.[32]

The role of the Rosenberg Foundation in support of California farm workers deserves to be singled out. The foundation was established in 1935 under the will of Max Rosenberg (1871–1931), one of three brothers who founded a successful dried fruit business on the West Coast. Among its purposes, the will cited "the advancement of industrial cooperation" and "the improvement and betterment of living and working conditions of the working classes." The foundation's engagement in union causes was stimulated by a family member, Louise Rosenberg Branston, who was active in radical politics. In the Cox Committee investigation of foundations, Louis Budenz, a former Communist Party official, cited her as "one of the angels of the Communist Party" and accused her husband of being a high party official in New York.[33]

Because of its support of the California Labor School, the California Un-American Activities Committee scrutinized the foundation after World War II. The school, an adult education program, had been sponsored by seventy-five AFL and CIO unions, but after charges that it was Communist-dominated, AFL unions withdrew their funding. Over the next twenty years the award of Rosenberg grants was assumed "to prove that controversial organizations receiving [our] grants were somehow un-American," comments Kirke Wilson, the current director of the foundation.[34]

Since the mid-1950s, the Rosenberg Foundation has been one of the most active supporters of projects assisting Mexican Americans. Its health grants were the model for the federal Migrant Health Program of 1962. Soon after the Delano grape strike began in 1965 organizers from foundation-assisted projects abandoned their work and joined the strike but continued to receive salaries for the jobs they had abandoned; some Rosenberg-funded projects collapsed, with the foundation apparently unaware of the situation, according to Wilson. Some years later, the California Un-American Affairs Committee concluded that the foundation was covertly supporting the strike because the organizers were drawing salaries from projects the foundation supported.[35]

The foundation's knowledge of farm worker issues was enhanced by the backgrounds of two of its trustees. One, Herman Gallegos, had worked with Chavez in the 1950s and 1960s. He went on to become the director of the National Council of La Raza, a Mexican American civil rights organization, a consultant to the Ford Foundation on Hispanic affairs, and a trustee of the Rockefeller Foundation. The other was an agricultural businessman, Robert DiGiorgio, whose company had been struck by the old NFLU in the late

1940s. Ruth Chance, then head of the foundation, recalls that even then Di-Giorgio, who had been educated in eastern schools, "gave the impression of being far more concerned about the lives of farm labor families than the usual absent landlord is."[36] He was on the board when the foundation funded a socioeconomic study of farm workers in Fresno, community development among black agricultural workers, and a program in Tulare County to train farm laborers to do skilled ranch work.

Rosenberg grants to the California Migrant Ministry (whose staff was influenced by the Alinsky approach to organization) raised hackles when some ministry staff joined the grape strike picket lines. Local churches that initially supported the ministry withdrew. "Some sincere people changed their minds and some were influenced by pressures from powerful people or interests," Chance recalls. "Some . . . , after all, were trades people, or businessmen, or professionals, much of whose livelihood depended on the growers. They had a great stake in what happened to the growers, and tensions were high during that transitional period in labor relations." The foundation told the ministry that its grants (for social services) were not to be used for organizing unions, but, says Chance, "we had made a commitment, and the board decided that it was not going to withdraw." Some ministers lost their positions. Wayne Hartmire, head of the Migrant Ministry, later became one of Chavez's closest advisers.[37]

The Ford Foundation's involvement with California's farm workers came later than Rosenberg's but also embroiled it in controversy. Mitchell Sviridoff had once noted that the problem of migrant workers was not high on Ford's agenda since "it eventually will work itself out because there will be very few migrant laborers. The farms are becoming highly industrialized. . . . It doesn't follow that one should not pay attention to the problem, because it is serious . . . but the question is, should the Foundation with its limited resources take on every social problem in the nation? Obviously not. We've had to make choices."[38] Still, substantial Ford Foundation grants were made to the National Farmworkers Service Centers in the 1970s, resulting in threats by groups of growers to boycott Ford Motor Company products. As a buffer of sorts, the grants were made to, and administered by, the Center for Community Change, in Washington, D.C. Although Chavez had developed the service centers, the foundation's staff took care to point out, disingeniously, to its own trustees and to the public that the centers were "a separate and distinct entity [from the union] with different organizational purposes. . . . The Foundation has never contributed to the union and has no intention of doing so."[39] In responding to critics, the foundation also pointed to the separation between the Ford Motor Company and the foundation. Poker-faced, foundation officials also declared that their grants were "not intended to assist or encourage the activities of the United Farmworkers Organizing Committee." In fact, the service centers, as products of Chavez's efforts, were strong advertisements for the union.[40]

The general counsel of the Center for Community Change further assured the world that "no Foundation funds will be used for any union activity including strike and picket line uses. Care . . . will continue to be taken to clearly separate the expenses of any legal proceeding involving union matters and to assure that the legal services and their costs [are] borne by the union." With $50,000 from the AFL-CIO's Industrial Union Department, a network of service centers was built throughout the farming areas of California and Arizona.[41]

Current Farm Worker Programs

One of the country's leading community organizers, Gary Delgado, has observed; "Farmworkers organizations perform a number of functions: they advocate for farmworkers with their employers and state agencies, forge alliances with other constituencies to obtain better working conditions, organize workers, and develop mutual assistance groups." Like worker centers in industries, he points out, they function very much as unions do without the formal designation, and their nonunion status may give them leverage.[42]

A second generation of farm labor organizations, in Florida, Oregon, Washington, New Jersey, and Texas, has attracted substantial foundation support. The thirty-year-old Farm Labor Organizing Committee (FLOC), based in Ohio, has framed a strategy of merging unionization with community support, developing collective bargaining agreements with processors, farmers, and FLOC members—a unique multiparty collective bargaining arrangement—and generating public pressure on corporations in agribusiness (as in an eight-year struggle with Campbell Soup) to bargain in good faith. The Heinz family foundations have supported FLOC organizing and migrant housing efforts. The MacArthur Foundation recognized the leadership of FLOC's president, Baldemar Velasquez, with one of its coveted prize fellowships. Another MacArthur Fellow is Lorna Bourg, co-founder of the Southern Mutual Help Association in Louisiana, which deals with sugar cane workers and is credited with ending their exploitation.[43]

The Rural Development Leadership Network (RDLN) receives foundation support to assist Mexican American women who have organized farm workers. Francisca Cavazos, for example, mediated between labor and management on both sides of the U.S./Mexican border. She also taught labor history and was executive director of the Maricopa County Organizing Project in Arizona, which received grants from the Norman, Field, Shalan, and Bert and Mary Meyer foundations. The Maricopa project helped double workers' wages and obtained agreements with farm operators to improve working conditions and housing.[44]

In New York's Hudson River Valley and in Arizona, Oregon, and Florida, projects funded by the Public Welfare Foundation educate farm workers about pesticide protection and conduct leadership training and organizing. Similarly the Veatch Foundation, sponsored by a Unitarian-Universalist church in Manhasset, New York, has funded a Farmworker Outreach and Pesticide Education Project run by the Convenio de Raíces Mexicanas in Phoenix and Oregon, and a woman's program, Farmworkers Self-Help of Dade City, Florida.[45]

For her colleagues in the National Network of Grantmakers, Ann Bastian of the New World Foundation has analyzed the relation of farm workers to environmentalism. Although they are highly vulnerable to environmental hazards—pesticides in particular—they are virtually invisible in the environmental movement, she concludes. The large, relatively well financed national environmental groups and funders have been slow to recognize farm workers as an at-risk group and central to the dangers of chemical substances. Bastian regards the vulnerability of farm workers as an issue of social justice as much as an environmental one and in turn maintains that environmental protection hinges on achieving rights for laborers.[46]

The Farmworker Justice Fund (FJF) is a dramatic instance of foundation response to a public policy crisis. It was created in 1981 to assume the work of the federally supported Migrant Legal Action Program, a major subsidiary of the Legal Services Corporation, which the Reagan administration tried to dismantle. The Reagan administration opposed the MLAP's support centers as "ideological havens for overly zealous lawyers who brought costly class action suits against the government."[47] The FJF monitors enforcement of the farm labor laws, educates farm workers on chemical exposure, promotes worker rights to housing and education, and provides unions with information and technical assistance. When monitoring and advocacy fail, the FJF resorts to litigation; thus the organization got the Department of Labor to set a prevailing wage for seed cane cutters in Florida, and employers then agreed to pay some five hundred farm workers more than $500,000 in back wages to settle related lawsuits.

Foundations have been the lifeblood of the FJF, but after its principal supporter, the Ford Foundation, discontinued its grants, the fund became a subsidiary of the National Council of La Raza. The advantages were twofold: one, it provided economies in the operation; two, services were more efficiently delivered since most of the farm workers it assists are Latinos.[48]

To forge a common voice in policy debates dealing with pesticide dangers, seven farm worker groups formed the Farmworker Network for Economic and Environmental Justice under the auspices of the New World and Public Welfare foundations. Ann Bastian of the New World Foundation, which has granted more than $600,000 to farm worker projects since 1986, observes: "Farm workers are socio-economically marginalized, making them completely disposable workers. But funders should know that they are the front lines of agricultural issues. They are also connections to core environmental issues. The conditions under which they work correlate with the quality of our food, pesticide contamination, sustainability."[49]

The strongest, most consistent supporters of farm workers and migrant labor over time have been religiously connected philanthropies—the Campaign for Human Development (Catholic), the American Friends Service Committee (Quaker), the Presbyterian Committee for Self Development of People, the Jewish Fund for Justice, and the National Farm Worker Ministry.

The need for further help from foundations remains. Farm workers still lack access to health insurance, adequate occupational safety standards, and protection under the National Labor Relations Act. Since passage of the 1996 welfare legislation, the legal immigrants among them face increasing difficulties.[50] And despite decades of efforts to improve the lot of farm workers, their wages trailed stubbornly behind inflation during the two decades that ended in 1997—7 percent in constant dollars, according to the U.S. Department of Agriculture, as much as 20 percent according to others, such as the California Institute for Rural Studies.[51]

8

Education

For foundations, education has been the major field of investment, and their interests have at times converged with those of organized labor over two major issues: what schools, colleges, and universities teach about the U.S. economic system, particularly about unions, and the condition of public education, a concern that has grown with the expanding strength of teacher unions.

In 1949 foundations funded the creation of the Joint Council on Economic Education (now National Council on Economic Education, NCEE), which provides teaching materials and curricular assistance for public schools. The Joint Council was established by the moderate Committee for Economic Development in reaction to vigorous propagandizing by the National Association of Manufacturers to inculcate free-enterprise ideology in public schools, ranging from Business-Industry-Education Days (schools closed for a day to enable teachers to tour local firms to learn "the story of the enterprise system first hand") to an economics curriculum that schools were pressured to adopt without modification. The Joint Council, contending that NAM-run programs were "too rabid, too extreme, and aroused too much suspicion," had on its board of trustees and as officers representatives of business, labor, and agriculture. With start-up funds from the Ford Foundation, it sponsored university-based summer workshops for teachers, in which all viewpoints were presented, raising the hackles of the NAM, whose own workshops excluded organized labor. The NAM placed pressure on industrialists who supported the Joint Council to withdraw.[1]

For different reasons, business and labor were early supporters of public

113

elementary and secondary education. Corporate interests viewed free public education as a bulwark against radical threats and social disorder. The AFL, on the other hand, advocated free, compulsory education in part as a counterweight to "conditions that educate the student or apprentice to non-union sympathies or prepare him as a skilled worker for scab labor and strike-breaking purposes."[2] For unions, compulsory education was also the best argument against child labor. A union leader wrote in 1902: "Let organized labor make its demand that the school, from the kindergarten to the university, shall cease to be a mere police force for protection of the 'vested interests' of the few and that it shall become the means for the development of all that is best in the life of all."[3]

Business and labor clashed as well over the role of vocational education. The NAM strongly advocated it, while labor feared that more trade schools would produce low-wage, nonunion competitors for union jobs. By the eve of American entry into World War I, however, the AFL and the NAM joined in promoting passage of the historic Smith-Hughes Act (1917), which provided federal support for vocational education—trade and industrial as well as agricultural.[4]

After World War II, foundations, along with business and labor, advocated increased public expenditures for education, though business stopped short of promoting massive federal aid. In 1949, using a grant from Carnegie Corporation, the business-supported Advertising Council joined forces with the National Citizens Committee for the Public Schools in a nationwide campaign to have states and localities increase spending for education. The AFL also supported a proposal by the National Child Labor Committee (a recipient of considerable funds from foundations) to extend federal aid to elementary education, both urban and rural.[5]

Conflict over Control

Unions and foundations have clashed over influence on educational policy. In 1915, labor leaders (along with Tammany Hall and the Hearst press) denounced New York City's mayor, John Purroy Mitchel, for placing officers of two Rockefeller philanthropies—Abraham Flexner of the General Education Board and Raymond D. Fosdick of the Rockefeller Foundation—on the Board of Education. At the time Mitchel was battling with the school administration over introduction of the "Gary Plan," which aimed to model public schools along progressive education lines and save money at the same time. Several labor unions formed their own committee and warned, "If John D. Rockefeller gets another appointment to the Board of Education, this town is going to hear about it." The president of the State Federation of Labor wrote Mitchel, "Commissioners Flexner and Fosdick are trying to secure control of public education for the Rockefeller crowd," and demanded their removal. Mitchel assured labor leaders that the schools would not become captive to private interests, but Fosdick and Flexner resigned in 1917.[6]

The Carnegie Foundation for the Advancement of Teaching was strongly criticized by the National Education Association and Margaret Haley, turn-of-the-century head of the Chicago Teachers Federation, for funding reforms that allegedly centralized management of school systems. An NEA resolution in 1914 declared, "We view with alarm the activity of Carnegie and Rockefeller foundations, agencies not in any way responsible to the people, in their effort to control the policies of our state educational institutions; to fashion after their own conceptions and to standardize after their own notion our courses of study."[7] Haley's strategy reflected the fact that men held the upper hand in educational policy making, in having a monopoly on the vote and in occupying all the seats on the board of the Carnegie Foundation. Determined that teachers not submit quietly to being robbed of a voice in educational decision making by an elite, male-dominated centralized control system, she reasoned that the largely female teaching force needed allies to obtain political power. She therefore forged an alliance between the teachers' union and the Chicago Federation of Labor, which had the voting strength of 200,000 members.[8] Teachers reluctant to affiliate with big labor were won over by a speech by Jane Addams—the sight of aristocratic and respectable "gentle Jane" advocating unionism convinced them to cast their lot with organized labor.[9]

In its efforts to reform the school environment, the Fund for the Advancement of Education, an autonomous spin-off of the Ford Foundation, managed to raise the hackles of teacher organizations. Teacher aides were a point of contention when the fund introduced them on an experimental basis in Bay City, Michigan, in 1952. Under the plan, supervised nonteaching aides took over various tasks—preparing classroom equipment, collecting lunch money, and so forth. Teacher organizations balked, refusing to accept the fund's analogy to nurses' aides. "Some of them," said a historian of the fund, "insisted that no one except a fully certified teacher should be allowed to work with school children in any capacity—some even opposed letting aides supervise playgrounds and lunchrooms." The fund claimed that the use of teacher aides would reduce the number of teachers required, an argument that in retrospect the fund regretted. Teacher aides are now common in classrooms, yet they have not diminished the role of the teacher.[10]

The fund also clashed with the American Federation of Teachers on the issue of class size when fund-supported research challenged the axiom that, regardless of circumstances, small classes are essential to good teaching. Alvin C. Eurich, an officer of the fund, argued that class size should vary according to subject and teaching techniques used; team teaching could offer effective instruction to groups ranging in size from ten to as many as one hundred. The fund's grants to reform teacher education were criticized as well, but in time the NEA acknowledged their value. One of its officials, T. M. Stinnett, observed, "The Fund has had great influence on securing a breakaway from the extreme concentration upon methodology which most teacher education institutions and state departments of education inherited from the normal schools and teachers colleges."[11]

Similarly, the NEA challenged the National Assessment of Educational Progress, a series of standardized tests inaugurated in 1967 with a grant from the Fund for the Advancement of Education and later supported by substantial federal funds. After thirty years, the idea of national education standards no longer raises hackles in teacher unions.[12] Various Carnegie foundations had funded research to improve educational testing for many years, but according to Frederick Mosher, a Carnegie official, "The NEA really didn't understand it and they were not much help; the AFT [American Federation of Teachers] was more sophisticated." Both the AFT and the NEA supported the National Board for Professional Teaching Standards when it was established in 1987, mainly with Carnegie Corporation funds. "The NEA more or less had to be dragged into it, whereas Shanker was a key ally," Mosher notes.[13] This pattern of fear and of resistance to change explains much of the present view of teacher unions as barriers to educational reform.

The Ford Foundation and School Decentralization in New York City

In the late 1960s the United Federation of Teachers (UFT), the New York City affiliate of the AFT, clashed bitterly with the Ford Foundation over the issue of decentralization of the public school system. Ironically, that dispute occurred at a time when the foundation, which had had only sporadic contact with organized labor through most of its fifteen years as a national institution, had recently taken a deep interest in becoming involved in labor union issues. Henry Ford, founder of the Ford Motor Company and the foundation, was notorious for his opposition to unions. His grandson, Henry Ford II, who took the reins of the company and the foundation after his grandfather's death in 1947, differed radically, regarding unions as a fact of industrial life, to be bargained with rather than fought.[14] In 1948, a blue-ribbon committee charted the transformation of the foundation from a local philanthropy typical of hundreds of family foundations to a vastly enlarged organization operating nationally.[15] Although industrial relations was one of many subjects recommended for attention by the foundation, a sustained involvement with the labor movement began only in the late 1960s, the result of several factors: deteriorating inner cities, the decline of industrial jobs, the black civil rights movement, and the women's movement. A unique insight into union/foundation relations was afforded by the appointment in 1967 of a labor movement veteran, Mitchell Sviridoff, as vice president of the foundation's National Affairs Division. A former sheet metal worker, he had been president of the Connecticut AFL-CIO Council. About foundations' relationship to labor, he asked, "Is it wise for foundations to be so isolated from such a major force in American society? Are the foundations sensitive to the concerns of organized labor? Do they consider and involve labor leaders in their work as they do the representatives of business, the professions, minorities, and academia? Are they forfeiting a potential for significant collaboration and support? Or missing an opportunity to inform their judgment with an important perspective?"[16]

Another impetus for Ford's growing involvement with labor was the foundation's concern with the increasing discontent and alienation of the white, especially blue-collar, ethnic worker. The malaise manifested itself in white lower-middle-class support for the presidential bid of Governor George Wallace of Alabama in 1964, white "backlash" riots in some northern cities against school and neighborhood integration, and "hard hat" clashes with anti-Vietnam protesters. In the workplace, a major internal analysis noted, "absenteeism, lateness, and poor quality workmanship were becoming serious problems, particularly in the automobile industry. . . . Union members, especially the younger ones, increasingly rejected contract settlements negotiated by older union leaders." A major factor was alienation from work— "resentment against being locked into dull, dirty, sometimes dangerous, uninteresting, low-status jobs." Underlying resentment also was based on a feeling that "the rules have changed"—that blacks and antiwar protesters were getting away with actions that should be punished or were receiving public benefits that they did not merit.[17]

Basil Whiting, the Ford program officer chiefly responsible for programs in this area from 1968 to 1977, recalls "trying fairly hard to interest a few other foundations and find partners for some of what we were doing, without success."[18] "We're not going to deal with white ethnics," Whiting quoted one foundation officer as saying. Among some foundations there was great antipathy toward the labor movement on grounds that it had turned conservative, that it was antiminority, that the Teamsters not only were corrupt but had supported Richard Nixon's campaign for the presidency.

Beginning in the fall of 1970, and for several years thereafter, the foundation made an extensive series of grants focusing on white worker discontent, many of them touching on the labor movement. Recipients in the first round, totaling $1 million, included the American Jewish Committee, which had already begun to frame programs of conferences, training, research, publications, and liaison with the mass media and the intellectual community; the National Opinion Research Center at the University of Chicago, to establish a Center for the Study of Ethnic Pluralism; and the U.S. Catholic Conference, for a Center for White Ethnic Community Development, headed by Msgr. Geno Baroni, to help working-class white ethnic groups develop community structures and leadership and to lay the groundwork for possible cooperative efforts with blacks.

The foundation also supported research and experiments on the quality of working life, such as an evaluation of a coal-mine shift reorganization involving the Rushton Mining Company and the United Mine Workers, and sponsorship of a delegation of six American auto workers who worked for four weeks in a Saab truck engine assembly plant in Sweden which had largely reorganized its work force into production groups of ten to twelve members to afford workers more participation. The American workers' reactions were mixed—negative about some features of the Saab plan, positive about others.[19]

That the foundation's bitter clash with the teachers' union occurred at the same time that its affirmative interest in the labor movement was at a high point was an artifact of the foundation's organizational structure. The latter engagement was the bailiwick of Sviridoff's National Affairs Division, the former of the Education Division; the twain hardly met.

The swollen bureaucracy at New York City's school headquarters, which included many former teachers waiting to retire, was widely regarded as being out of touch with the needs of the system's million pupils. The foundation, long involved in efforts to improve urban education and convinced that greater parental participation would enhance educational progress, made planning grants to three experimental school districts that the state legislature had authorized with the aim of giving greater voice to parents in school decisions. Mayor John Lindsay, charged with preparing a blueprint for decentralization, appointed McGeorge Bundy, president of the Ford Foundation, to head a commission to plan the change. The study director was the foundation program officer who first brought the foundation into the decentralization maelstrom.

The UFT initially supported the concept of decentralization, but the Bundy plan pitted the union and community groups against each other. The union accused these groups, mainly composed of minorities, of seizing power and arbitrarily firing and reassigning teachers without due process. Not surprisingly, opposition was also strong among school administrators. Although the plan recommended that labor negotiations remain centralized, union leaders argued that the "breakup" of the system would make it more difficult to bargain forcefully. At the time the union's self-confidence was at an all-time high as a result of a recent two-week strike and a strong new contract.

A critic of the foundation's role, the historian Diane Ravitch, concludes that "the Foundation had funded the [experimental districts] without concern for the adequacy of the plans and without regard to the consequences for the participants. Ford used its weighty influence to contribute to the districts' unreal aspirations."[20] Sviridoff recalls, "We were right to stay with them [the districts], but once they got so committed to such an extremely political and ideological position, we should have found a way to get out, though it was extremely difficult to do so." The Bundy plan itself, he goes on, was not a recommendation for community control of the schools; rather, "it was . . . middle-of-the-road . . . administrative . . . with a significant degree of participation."[21]

The issue boiled over in the fall of 1968 with a thirty-six day strike by the UFT. Many parents accused teachers of abandoning their pupils for self-interest, and teachers accused parents of serving as scabs (some ghetto schools remained open, using mostly parents and a bloc of black and white teachers who crossed picket lines).[22] The controversy fanned black-Jewish tensions, since most teachers and school administrators were Jewish, and blacks were the main advocates of a greater parental voice. The UFT president, Albert Shanker, declared, "Without a strong central authority [and safeguards] decentralization will be a movement toward apartheid, bringing forth extremists, black and white, and the creation of a huge community pork-barrel." Vehemently critical of the Ford Foundation's role, Shanker went on a nation-wide speaking tour to warn other teachers' organizations of the threat posed by the "irresponsible intervention" of philanthropic organizations.[23]

The struggle over the shape of decentralization continued for more than two years, culminating in the defeat of many key elements of the Bundy plan in the state legislature, and the strike nearly cost John Lindsay his second term as mayor. A group called the Urban Coalition Education Task Force attempted to mediate. Headed by Alan Pifer, president of Carnegie Corporation, and composed largely of lawyers and businessmen, the task force "found the bureaucratic self-protective reflexes of the civil service system and the unions as reprehensible as the militant blacks and Puerto Ricans did," Ravitch observed.[24]

Animosity toward the Ford Foundation has not abated. In an interview more than twenty-five years later, Shanker, then president of the American

Federation of Teachers, said, "The Foundation tried to destroy us. I told Bundy, 'If you have the same kids, same textbooks, and the same teachers, what makes you think breaking up the system into 120 districts is going to change anything?' . . . It was a Vietnam thing—'turn the ghetto over to the people.' Remember, after the Watts riot [1967], Lindsay was given a lot of credit for keeping New York cool. So decentralization was essentially a pay-off. A lot of people were threatening to burn the place down."[25]

Reform through Mediation

In 1977, a few years after the New York confrontation over decentralization, the Ford Foundation, in a grant aimed at combating the growing power of teacher unions, provided funds for the development of the Florida School Labor Relations Service, an organization run in tandem with associations of school boards and district school superintendents. An internal Ford paper noted, "The growth of teachers' organizations has pushed local school boards and the public at large to a confused and often defensive posture."[26] After two years, the service was credited by an independent evaluator with improving the climate of labor-management relations in Florida. The concept was replicated on the West Coast and marked the emergence of an ideology of "professional unionism" in the field of education. Since the 1980s, teacher unions have been discarding the inherent separateness of labor and management, of teaching and administration, and the habit of adversarial relations. Unions and school administrators are aware that the quality and integrity of teaching, as well as the due process rights of teachers, need protection, and administrators recognize that evaluation and assessment are not their exclusive prerogative, that unions have a legitimate role.[27]

Such reforms have been assisted by foundations across the country. Partly in response to Shanker's criticism of its role in school decentralization, Carnegie Corporation assisted several union-run teacher centers. "We wanted to show an extra willingness to work constructively with teacher unions," said Frederick Mosher. "You have to find ways of taking teachers' interests into account, and unions are an honest mechanism for doing that. They're constructive and [the leadership] is often better than the members."[28] At the teacher-training level, the Hewlett Foundation funded the American Federation of Teachers Distinguished Visiting Practitioner Program at Stanford University. Stanford students and faculty welcomed the presence of a practicing public school teacher, and according to the foundation, the program strengthened the AFT's motivation to manage sixteen additional teacher-training workshops in California. Foundations continued to find mediating between unions and school management frustrating, however. In Los Angeles, "they have a long history of acrimonious relations," observed Eugene R. Wilson, former president of the Arco Foundation, "and trying to keep them at the table to hammer out a restructured school system while they are suing each other has tested our capacity to conciliate."[29] The Hewlett Foundation and the Stuart Foundations have funded the California Foundation for Improvement of Employer-Employees Relations, a coalition of unions and school boards, to run workshops for key labor and management personnel in some one hundred California school districts. Begun in 1987 and termed "an enormous success" by the foundations, the process goes beyond the resolution of contract disputes to address staff reorganization and the full array of issues confronting public schools. Participating districts experienced a 93 percent reduction in charges of unfair labor practices.[30]

In contrast, several conservative foundations (the Lynde and Harry Bradley, John H. Olin, Scaife Family, and Sarah Scaife foundations) support the Los Angeles–based Center for the Study of Popular Culture, an organization that attacks teacher unions as barriers to reform. "Whatever the school reform is," a Center officer said, "you name it, there are usually the same opponents, the school unions." To "expose and ridicule the opponents of school reform, and promote proponents," it publishes a newsletter, *The Report Card*.[31] The Olin Foundation also funds the work of a well-known critic of teacher unions, Myron Lieberman of the Social Philosophy and Policy Center at Bowling Green State University in Ohio. Lieberman has accused teacher unions of maintaining a public school monopoly, resisting improvements and the acquisition of labor-saving technology, in order to increase their salaries and fringe benefits. He urged participants in an education summit at the 1996 National Governors Conference to challenge Louis Gerstner, chairman of the summit meeting, as to "what there is to show for the millions of dollars RJR [the corporation Gerstner formerly headed] and its foundation have spent on education reform. The answer may explain why Gerstner is an appropriate choice to lead the parade of futilitarians at [the education summit]."[32]

Nonetheless, corporate foundations have also funded direct experiments in school reform. In 1989 the Exxon Education Foundation granted the AFT Education Foundation $639,500 to test professional practice schools for beginning teachers in two school systems, later extended to several. The Panasonic Foundation, which funds multiyear reform efforts in six school districts, has run retreats and bargaining workshops for teacher unions and management: "We are generally quite insistent with the boards and administrations in our sites that they include the union in as many discussions as possible," says Sophie Sa, president of the foundation.[33]

In an earlier cooperative development, the Boston Compact of the 1980s, unions joined foundations, businesses, and universities in a successful program that guaranteed low-income youth part-time jobs if they remained in school, and that had a substantial impact on education. Agreements between business leaders and the school system evolved into summer jobs and entry-level jobs for graduates and business funding for innovative teaching, counseling, and financial aid for prospective college students. A Boston Area Building Trades Unions' agreement with the school system increased the number of high school graduates admitted into apprenticeships. At its peak the Compact involved some nine hundred Boston-area businesses committed to building a bridge from school to work. As the New England economy collapsed in the late 1980s, companies found it increasingly difficult to honor their pledges. Even so, as late as 1992, the Compact was able to arrange some 2,700 summer jobs, at an average wage of more than $5 an hour.[34]

Yet another slant to union efforts toward school reform is embodied in the National Foundation for the Improvement of Education (NFIE), established by a labor union, the National Education Association, and benefiting from funding from private foundations. The largest and most ambitious labor-based foundation, it is also closest in operating style to private foundations. When the NEA formally became a union in 1969, it created the NFIE to enable members "to assume a leadership role in the national fight against high school failure."[35] The NFIE receives $500,000 annually from the NEA for general support, and for several years was almost entirely dependent on foundations and other outside sources for project funds. In turn, the NFIE itself makes grants; its first major initiative was a dropout prevention program. In order to reduce its heavy reliance on external funds, the organization has now converted itself into a self-sufficient, endowed grant-making foundation, assessing each NEA member $1 for an endowment, which it is estimated will reach between $30 million and $35 million by the year 2003.

Donna C. Rhodes, executive director of the NFIE from its inception until 1994, describes the organization as "an alternative to the 1960s and 1970s model of confrontation between unions and school systems. In the zeal to improve working conditions, unions sometimes built restrictions that people found unmovable. We promoted a collaborative effort for constructive change in education."[36] A dozen NFIE state affiliates have set up their own foundations.

School Decentralization in Chicago

A remarkable instance of union-foundation collaboration in education grew out of the Chicago School Reform Act of 1988, which mandated a decentralized school system, through which elected councils in each of the system's six hundred local schools have a major role in school governance. Stimulated in part by reaction to a nineteen-day teachers' strike in 1987, the act has been described as "one of the most aggressive school reform laws" of the twentieth century.[37]

The process contrasts sharply with New York City's tumultuous attempt at school decentralization. Initially in Chicago, a group of foundations backed school reform initiatives to the tune of $2.7 million in the two years before passage of the act. During the legislative process, twenty-one funders signed a joint letter to the governor and legislature urging its adoption.

Peter Martinez, a MacArthur Foundation program officer and former community organizer, credits the business community as a mainspring of reform. "Chicago business felt a deep self-interest in educational failure because of the great costs of recruiting and training qualified minority staff," he says. "At the same time the costs of education were rising without comparable result."[38] Business raised $500,000 for a lobbying campaign in the state legislature that overcame union opposition to the reform bill.

After the act passed, foundations more than doubled their school reform grants over the next five years, to $10 million. Most Chicago foundations were reluctant to provide direct funding to local schools, but twenty funders formed a citywide Fund for Educational Reform, which distributed small sums to schools. In addition, the Chicago Community Trust and the Joyce Foundation focused on improved teacher training and selection. Following their lead, the John D. and Catherine T. MacArthur Foundation made a three-year, $1 million grant in 1991 to the Chicago Teachers Union (since supplemented by $125,000) for the Quest Center, which offers competitive incentive grants to schools; 110 schools applied for the first round of 20 awards. At the end of a three-year period a Quest team in each school that demonstrates progress in student achievement receives a cash award, usually $5,000. Since very few foundation grants are made directly to unions, the MacArthur grant was dramatic and unprecedented in scope.

The Quest Center was born of discussions between Martinez and the late John Kotsakis, the union's issue coordinator. "I became convinced he was an enlightened leader, capable of interpreting the union's interests in non-stereotypical ways," Martinez says. The union agreed to an independent board to govern the Quest program, to a national advisory committee, and to foundation review of the candidate for director. Foundation officers met with Albert Shanker to ensure his backing. The only opposition to the MacArthur grant came from some community organizations that regarded the union as an enemy of reform.

Deborah Walsh, director of the Quest Center, says the project "represents a maturation of the union. Because the schools were losing or failing so many students, our work to strengthen the professional arena is the ultimate in worker protection. The MacArthur grant was a major factor in supporting the union's credibility, and Martinez engaged us with other grant recipients in the school reform efforts."[39] But despite the apparent success of the Quest program, Martinez believes that the union is missing the boat by failing to change its overall negotiation approach to one along the lines of the union-management collaboration in General Motors' Saturn plant.

Another major legislative change in the governance of the Chicago public schools in 1995—which turned control of the central school administration over to the mayor—left the local school structure intact, but with diminished authority and more requirements for accountability to system-wide standards. The new central school board and administration are credited with gains in a short period of time, including a four-year agreement with the teachers' union.[40] On the eve of the new law's implementation, however, many local and state groups "were increasingly frustrated with the decentralization experiment," according to researchers for the University of Chicago. Students were reported to be performing poorly, and the Local Schools Council "failed to develop into an institution that broadened parental involvement in school affairs, as measured by local voter turnout."[41] At the same time a budgetary crisis contributed to diminished confidence in the school system.

In 1995 Chicago school reform was given a major stimulus with a $49.2 million, five-year matching challenge grant from the Walter K. Annenberg Foundation. A $50 million Annenberg grant for school innovation in New York City was facilitated when the teachers' union waived seniority requirements in the affected experimental schools. The Annenberg gift requires two-to-one matching by public and private funds and, as of April 1998, $22 million had been raised from New York City foundations and corporations. Among some fifty small public schools organized around a variety of themes and pedagogies which have opened in New York City is the School for Social Change, established by Local 1199 of the hospital workers' union with help from a dozen foundations.[42]

Chicago's school decentralization went more smoothly than New York's because Chicago learned from New York's experience. Authority was carried to the local school level instead of to large districts governed by boards that were susceptible to political corruption; many foundations were engaged instead of just one; and corporate support weighed in. Also, the national climate had changed—in the intervening twenty years, discussion of educational "crisis" had broadened to include national, state, and local leaders, and both locally and nationally foundations were focusing on school reform.

Adversarial relations will probably continue among teacher unions, school boards, and communities as public schools continue to be financially pressed.

Furthermore, political pressure is growing for tax-assisted privatization and "choice" in the form of charter schools, which are publicly financed but independently run. In both cases unions fear that teachers will suffer reductions in salaries and benefits. Because unions have lobbied against some of these efforts, they have been tarred again as barriers to reform, most prominently by Robert Dole in his campaign for the presidency in 1996. But teacher unions have been in the vanguard of school reform in the past, not least in pushing for the improvement of working conditions in order to attract better teachers. Recent initiatives include the NFIE and a $1 million program to help teachers set up charter schools in a union setting.[43] Teacher union officials and members are also involved in two foundation-assisted independent reform initiatives—the Cross City Campaign for Urban Schools, a network of large-city educators organized in 1993 by Anne Hallett (former executive director of the Wieboldt Foundation), who are "rethinking from scratch the role of large bureaucracies," and the National Coalition of Education Activists, composed of teachers who want their unions to deal with educational issues as well as member benefits.[44] Whether teacher unions remain on the defensive, however, depends not only on whether they reach beyond traditional goals of job security, but also on public attitudes toward increased investment in education and toward organized labor generally.

9

Labor Education

Education for union members and officials has ranged from radical programs to arouse workers' consciousness to university courses with sophisticated economic and managerial content. Although the foundation role in labor education has been limited (contrasting sharply in scale with foundation-supported engineering and business education, through which colleges and universities serve the needs of corporate America), in some cases it has been significant.

Schools for Workers

Union schools were advocated by the AFL early on to counteract negative public attitudes toward organized labor by enabling union members to "defend themselves." These schools, said an AFL resolution in 1905, should teach "at least the elementary principles of the trade union movement, demonstrate a correct understanding of trade union history, struggles and achievements," and instill knowledge of "what marvelous changes and improvements have been wrought in the life of labor."[1] In 1919, the AFL voted to sponsor workers' education where public school authorities refused to offer classes for workers.

Summer extension courses in worker education grew rapidly in the 1920s and 1930s—for example, at Bryn Mawr College, the University of Chicago, and the University of Wisconsin—to teach workers the rudiments of the economic system and provide political and cultural enrichment. During this period, a handful of foundations supported some union-centered institutions and coordinating organizations. (Foundation funding of summer schools for women workers is discussed in Chapter 6.)

In those decades the impetus for workers' education came largely from labor intellectuals and educators, such as James H. Maurer and the historians Charles Beard and Mary Beard, who founded the Workers' Education Bureau in 1921. (Maurer, the bureau's president for many years, was a vice presidential candidate of the Socialist Party and a Socialist city councilman in Reading, Pennsylvania). The WEB's purposes were "to collect and to disseminate information relative to efforts at education on any part of organized labor; to co-ordinate and assist in every possible manner the educational work now carried on by the organized Workers; and to stimulate the creation of additional enterprises in labor education." The organization published a "Worker's Bookshelf" on politics and economics and promoted lectures, courses, and radio programs—in effect becoming the educational arm of the AFL while maintaining formal autonomy. By 1928, however, the AFL was distancing itself from the WEB; the Executive Council declared that the workers' education movement posed a threat to unions because, by its very nature, it encouraged workers to question cherished federation policies.[2]

By the early 1920s the Amalgamated Clothing Workers Union (ACWA) labor schools (not affiliated with the WEB) were deeply committed to large-scale, uplifting education for the masses. Classes ranged from the basics of trade unionism, parliamentary procedure, and English composition (the ACWA encouraged the use of English to weaken old ethnic ties and reinforce Americanism) to lectures by distinguished academics on American and European culture. The range of classes was extraordinarily wide for a labor school, encompassing music, psychology, and artistic and literary subjects, from Mozart and Dickens to Goya and Tolstoy.[3]

Most labor schools avoided overt propaganda, asserting that if workers received the facts, correct understanding and action would follow. Their mission was to raise workers' consciousness through analyses of the history of the labor movement, from a progressive viewpoint.[4] The Garland Fund provided most foundation funding for workers education in the 1920s. At least ninety-three labor schools already existed when the fund began its support. Garland made grants for classes given by UMW Districts 2 and 12, to labor schools in several cities (including the Philadelphia Labor College and the Rand School in New York), and the Southern Summer School for Women Workers.[5] The fund rejected an application from the Bryn Mawr Summer School for Women Workers because the college, not the workers, controlled it, it promoted gradualism, and it received funds from John D. Rockefeller Jr. and Carnegie Corporation, the latter's policy being that American workers' education should differ from the European because "there are no economic classes in the United States."[6]

The recipients of the Garland Fund's largest worker education grants were the Commonwealth College in Arkansas and the Brookwood Labor College in Katonah, New York. Commonwealth was charged by the American Legion with fomenting radicalism and attacked by local landowners who resented its work with sharecroppers. At the same time, it was torn internally by ideological differences. By 1936 most of the students and faculty were Communists or Communist sympathizers, and the college even turned its back on the Southern Tenant Farmers Union because the STFU had Socialist Party backing. Commonwealth closed in 1941.[7]

Brookwood, the school most favored by the Garland Fund, received $200,000 in grants. Other important contributors were Evelyn Preston ($10,000 from 1932 to 1935) and the Elmhirst Fund ($5,500), whose money came from Dorothy Whitney Elmhirst, later the founder of the William C. Whitney Foundation, which became the second largest contributor to Brookwood. Eduard Lindeman, an adviser to the Whitney Foundation, chaired Brookwood's fifteenth anniversary celebration in January 1936 and helped raise funds, as did the progressive educators George Counts and John Dewey.[8] The college offered a year-long residential course, and its staff included Mark Starr, education director of the International Ladies Garment Workers Union, his wife Helen, a labor journalist, and the distinguished historians Joel Seidman and David Saposs. In 1928, an AFL-commissioned report charged that the school's curriculum was "propagandistic and communistic" and a threat to the federation's principles because it supported "dual unionism."[9] Suffering in its later years from high staff turnover and ideological struggles, Brookwood closed in 1938.

Although some critics termed the residential workers' education movement of the 1920s an idealistic failure or oddity, others differed. The schools provided a deeper study of social issues than did the later courses that emphasized such "tools" as collective bargaining and union office management. Many former students became labor leaders and imbued their unions with a broad social vision, and the schools were forums for discussion of union policy and challenges to the official position of the AFL on many issues.[10]

The leading educational center for southern labor leaders through the Depression was the Highlander Folk School in Tennessee. Hundreds of union members from more than twenty international unions attended Highlander programs, and the school's staff participated in organizing drives and strikes.[11] Highlander declared in 1940 that it would not run worker education programs for unions that discriminated against blacks, and would enroll workers

The Highlander Folk School in Tennessee was the leading center for southern labor leaders during the Depression. Because it enrolled workers regardless of race, it was harassed. Support came from the Rosenwald Fund and other foundations. (Southern Historical Collection, Wilson Library, The University of North Carolina at Chapel Hill)

regardless of race or sex. The dreams of Myles Horton, its co-founder, of militant unionism in the South were shattered by several factors, but, as Horton wrote later, "the decisive barrier . . . was racism, pure and naked." Responding to complaints from a local vigilante group to Representative Martin Dies of the House Un-American Activities Committee, FBI agents, beginning in 1940, made frequent visits to Grundy County, Highlander's location, asking about blacks and Communists.[12]

Highlander's finances were troubled from the outset. Reinhold Niebuhr, the theologian under whom Horton had studied, used his influence to secure scarce funds and urged Horton to seek foundation grants. Support came from the Schwartzhaupt, Rosenwald, and Field foundations, with Rosenwald Fund grants for educational programs targeting industrial and farm workers and for personnel development in southern labor unions through grants-in-aid to individuals. Foundation grants reached a postwar high of $14,303 in 1948, but support for the school from organized labor was half-hearted, rising to a peak of $6,600 in 1946 and then dropping sharply. Four-fifths of the school's funds came from individual contributions. Fund-raising was hampered by the Internal Revenue Service, which tried to revoke the school's tax-exempt status three times between 1957 and 1971, though those efforts were ultimately unsuccessful.[13]

Early on, Highlander sought unsuccessfully to work with the AFL, as it did later with the CIO, and still cooperate with the Communists. In the late 1940s the CIO demanded conformity to its anti-Communist policies and asked unions to end relations with Highlander when the school did not comply. Horton's wife, Zilphia, declared in 1952, "The unions have become so reactionary and so complacent that they've lost their ideals."[14] Although some labor union activity continued, Highlander turned increasingly to issues raised by the Supreme Court decision on school desegregation. Among those who attended its desegregation workshops was Rosa Parks, who made history later by her refusal to move to the back of a segregated bus, setting off the Montgomery, Alabama, bus boycott in 1955 and changing the course of the civil rights struggle. Reorganized in 1961 as the Highlander Research and Educational Center, the institution emphasizes programs dealing with civic leadership training, and it enjoys considerable foundation support. Highlander again became the scene of labor education in 1993, under a program of the New Directions Worker Education Center, which sponsors workshops at which union activists rethink union strategies and seek to develop a new vision for the labor movement.[15]

Worker Education Resources

The American Labor Education Service was also an outgrowth of the progressive education and women's movements. Funded by unions, foundations, and individuals in the 1930s, the ALES took on a life of its own as an educational service agency, organizing conferences, publishing, conducting special projects (for example, the Summer School for Office Workers), and working with residential workers' schools, of which there were six in 1941. The residential schools of the 1930s and 1940s operated without racial prejudice in the classroom or in living arrangements; indeed, the ALES sponsored conferences that dealt with minority groups and workers' prejudices, attempting to eliminate bias from unions. In applying for a Rosenwald Fund grant in 1945, Eleanor G. Coit, director of the Service said, "the prime [postwar] tension anticipated in the competitive struggle for a lessening number of jobs is the interracial one."[16]

Rockefeller's General Education Board made grants for three years beginning in 1934 to enable both the ALES and the AFL's Workers' Education

Bureau of America to assist the federal government's Workers' Education Project, which ran fourteen demonstration centers that conducted in-service training for teachers in workers' education methods. The ALES postwar programs involved state and local labor groups, city councils, human relations panels, universities, YMCAs and YWCAs, the National Urban League, the NAACP, and other agencies. The Rosenwald Fund financed ALES experiments in Trenton and Camden, New Jersey, and St. Louis, to encourage more workers to participate in discrimination-free union and community affairs and programs in southern states run through the School for Southern Workers, the Georgia Workers Education Service, and Highlander.[17] After stimulating liberal education for workers in urban centers and small communities for thirty-five years, the ALES closed in 1962.[18]

The coupling of worker education with general adult education began after World War I under foundation auspices when Carnegie Corporation embarked on a program to promote "further understanding of that deeper stratum of knowledge and feeling which involves philosophy, art, and the comprehension of human relations."[19] The Carnegie program was influenced by *The Way Out*, a publication of the British Workers' Education Association, established by Albert Mansbridge in 1903. At a time of increasing trade union militancy, proponents thought confrontation could be tamped down through nonvocational adult education, education in which all social classes would participate under joint worker-university sponsorship: the radical notion of offering advanced study to working people was justified by the conservative goal of social stability. Carnegie's president, Frederick P. Keppel, saw this idea as a model of what his foundation might do. In 1926, the foundation formed the American Association for Adult Education (AAAE), which operated until 1941. Viscount Haldane (a leader of the British Workers' Education Association, to whom Keppel sent a staff member for advice before launching Carnegie Corporation's own program) warned Keppel to beware of "special interest groups like the labor movement, the social workers movement, and the public schools," which "would attempt to swallow the adult education movement for the gain that might be in it for themselves." To populists the AAAE overemphasized liberal education and classical high culture, though they approved of the AFL's Workers' Education Bureau, which received continuing Carnegie grants between 1926 and 1940 ($140,250). When Carnegie terminated funding, the AAAE was forced to merge with the NEA's Department of Adult Education to form the Adult Education Association of the United States.[20]

The major post–World War II resource for adult education, which included workers as a main target group, was the Fund for Adult Education, an independent spin-off of the Ford Foundation. The FAE made a grant to the

Inter-University Labor Education Committee for a fresh look at labor education. To direct the study, the fund hired Joseph Mire, a former official of the AFSCME. His criticisms were sharp: "Workers' education doesn't try to appeal to the worker's desire to 'get ahead' or leave the factory for some higher occupational status. Instead it appeals to his sense of group responsibility . . . to improve the lot of all workers." He perceived a shortage of good teachers, especially in middle- and small-sized towns. Union leaders were handicapped in dealing with racial and religious discrimination, he said, by a lack of experience and fear of divorcing themselves from their own members. "Many difficulties in industrial relations arose from inadequate schooling," Mire wrote. "Every so often our school system continues to function as though we still lived in an era of economic individualism rather than in an era of mutual interdependence." He called for future leaders of labor to be trained through schools whose curricula are tailored to meet the needs of workers. "Education could reduce industrial strife," Mire said, "and enhance American labor's role in resisting Fascist and Communist totalitarianism."[21]

Unions and foundations are currently collaborating in programs ranging from adult literacy to training displaced workers. The New World and several other foundations support the Labor Institute in New York, which produces curricula that combine teaching about economic issues with material on concrete workplace matters—occupational health and safety, sexual harassment, technology, plant closings, and so on. Although the institute was established in the mid-1970s by radical economists, its programs now draw participation from mainstream local, regional, and international unions.[22]

Education through the Arts

Unions have used cultural approaches to educate their own members and the public about the labor movement, with occasional foundation support. One notable effort is the Bread and Roses Project of District 1199 of the Drug and Hospital Employees Union in New York (the title comes from the chant of striking women textile workers in Lawrence, Massachusetts, in 1912, "We want bread, and roses too," derived from a poem). Founded in 1979, the project has included professional theater productions for staff and patients in hospitals and nursing homes, evenings with theater artists, videotapes and film showings, conferences on patient care and on the role of labor in the arts and humanities, and a musical revue, *Take Care*, about hospital life. The union also received a grant from the W. Alton Jones Foundation for an eleven-city tour of an art exhibition titled "Disarming Images: Art for Nuclear Disarmament" (1984). The AFL-CIO's Labor Heritage Foundation (LHF) re-

ceived a grant from the Nathan Cummings Foundation for exhibit throughout the country of Ralph Fasanella's paintings on working-class themes, and
the hanging of his noted "Great Strike" in the Capitol Rotunda in Washington.[23]

Foundations have funded films on labor issues—for example, *The Uprising
of '34*, dealing with the general textile strike of a half-million workers. A tele-
vision documentary on the United Mine Workers' strike against the Pittston
Coal Company in Virginia was supported through a grant to Appalshop, a
nonprofit media center in Kentucky, from the J. Roderick MacArthur Foundation, which also funded a film documentary on Harry Bridges, the fiery
head of the International Longshoremen's and Warehousemen's Union. One
of the most notable films was *With Babies and Banners*, dealing with the
Women's Brigade in the sit-down strike against General Motors in Flint,
Michigan, in 1937. Although several foundations made grants to the film-
makers, the Charles Stewart Mott Foundation, whose endowment comes
from a General Motors founder, declined, its board of trustees narrowly divided between old-timers and newer members.[24]

Higher Education

During the first part of the twentieth century, organized labor viewed colleges and universities warily, perceiving threats from business efforts to
shape the political climate on campus and create among educators feelings
of obligation and indebtedness. Thus in 1948, the Foundation for Economic
Education began a College-Business Exchange Fellowship program, targeting young faculty members "when they are open-minded." Sponsored by
more than 100 major firms, it was complemented by business-sponsored
speakers' bureaus.[25] The American Council on Education (ACE), an influential higher education association and frequent recipient of foundation
grants, has been characterized by David Montgomery as "the General Staff
organization of education." Its challenge, the council's director, Charles R.
Mann, had declared in 1927, was to "decide how education can be organized
to meet industrial specifications."[26]

In the 1920s, however, some thirty major universities (including Yale,
Berkeley, the University of Chicago, and Cornell) began to run labor-
management centers funded in part by foundations; several are still active.
Typical is the Industrial Research Unit of the Wharton School at the University of Pennsylvania, a publisher of books and monographs on employee
relations, manpower, and human resources, through its extensive Labor Relations and Public Policy Series, funded by the Pew Charitable Trusts.

In the 1960s the Ford Foundation and Carnegie Corporation sponsored an overhaul of American business education. Ford granted $35 million to business schools to improve faculty training and research and expand the use of quantitative analysis and the behavioral sciences. Carnegie sponsored a major report, "The Education of American Businessmen: A Study of University-College Programs in Business Administration."[27]

The country's most prestigious university program for labor leaders, the Harvard Trade Union Program, embodies an irony of sorts. It was established in 1942, four decades after Harvard president Charles W. Eliot, a favorite adviser of foundations, referred to scabs as "19th century heroes." Invited to address the Boston Central Labor Union in 1904, Eliot warned that labor and capital, "both fighting organizations," abridged individual liberty. Although speaking approvingly of increased wages, pension plans, and improved working conditions, he argued a libertarian viewpoint: "Democracy believes that all should have a chance to move up. Democracy must distrust labor's effort to restrict efficiency and output. The objection is moral."[28]

Harvard's ten-week residential labor leadership program, which some 1,800 labor leaders have attended, has received substantial support from foundations. Thomas Donahue, former secretary-treasurer of the AFL-CIO, terms it "the graduate school of the American labor movement." Richard Trumka, Donahue's successor (former president of the United Mine Workers of America), remarked, "I have sent our staff to the Program because the people we deal with have expertise in areas that unions traditionally don't. . . . I believe that union leaders need to be as well educated as their corporate and political counterparts." The program was first housed at the Harvard Business School, which decided in the early 1980s to discontinue it. "Many of the senior professors with interests in industrial relations had retired," said Elaine Bernard, executive director of the program, "[and], reflecting the overall decline in the U.S. labor movement, the new generation of scholars tended to see unions as dated organizations and industrial relations as a discipline destined to disappear."[29] Under the driving force of Professor John T. Dunlop, former secretary of labor, the Program was reorganized as a university-wide effort. The labor movement has since contributed funds for an endowed chair named after Dunlop. The Program's union advisory committee is chaired by Gerald McEntee, president of the AFSCME.

Market-oriented foundations have funded "free-enterprise" chairs at several universities, but some conservatives criticize the practice. Milton Friedman, formerly of the University of Chicago, says, "I am as opposed to [them] as I am to chairs of Marxism-Leninism or socialism." Martin M. Wooster, Washington editor of *Reason* magazine, says "the ideological nature of free-enterprise chairs makes it difficult to find qualified people to occupy them, and few holders of such chairs conduct serious scholarship."[30] On this, Montgomery observes, "The drive . . . by corporations and foundations to establish professorial chairs of 'private enterprise' is really gilding the lily. . . . Academic and industrial systems have been inseparable for half a century."[31]

As interest in labor-management centers at private colleges and universities leveled off, labor education programs expanded in state colleges and universities, spurred by the influence of organized labor in state legislatures. Labor education programs in publicly supported institutions of higher education were justified as comparable to public support of similar training for farmers and businessmen through colleges of agriculture and commerce. In addition, across the country several union contracts provide reimbursement to workers for tuition in traditional and nontraditional college and university programs.

Organized labor strengthened its ties to the higher education establishment in 1983 by founding a Labor/Higher Education Council composed of AFL-CIO officers and ACE university presidents. As intellectuals have drawn closer to the labor movement since the election of John Sweeney, unions and higher education may grow nearer to the ideal expressed by Lane Kirkland: "Universities need labor if they are not to be reduced, morally and intellectually, to elitist enclaves insulated from the needs and aspirations of ordinary people. . . . And labor needs [universities] to help refresh our thinking as we explore new ways of fulfilling our unending mission . . . to humanize economic and social life, and to provide the incentive and the means for every man and woman to rise to their full potential."[32]

Some thirty universities now house labor archives, notably the Archives of Labor History and Urban Affairs in the Walter P. Reuther Library at Wayne State University in Detroit and the labor collections of Catholic University in Washington, D.C. Foundations provide a small portion of the funds for these centers. An exception is the Tamiment Institute Library at New York University, which originated as the library of the Rand School of Social Science, a Socialist center. After the school closed in the 1950s, the library was transferred to NYU, where it receives support from the Tamiment Institute, a foundation established with the proceeds of the sale of a mountain resort owned by the Rand School. The institute also supports the journal *Labor History*.

10

Health, Safety, Environment

Public health, a major area of engagement for foundations from the earliest days, and medical care, a need ranking close to food and shelter, should logically tie foundations and unions together in joint efforts, yet such links have been limited. A significant reason has been the cyclical fortunes of the labor movement. When, for example, in the late 1920s unions were a marginal element in the most extensive foundation effort to rein in medical costs—the Committee on the Costs of Medical Care (CCMC)—union membership was low. When union strength was at an all-time high after World War II, organized labor's interest in health plans that foundations were advancing was limited, since the unions were by then obtaining generous benefits through collective bargaining.

Throughout the twentieth century great advances in medical science enhanced the capability of doctors and hospitals to combat disease. Vastly improved health practices also escalated medical costs. At the same time progress in medicine and public health (widely heralded in the media) led more people to expect more. Now at the century's end, medical care, treatment, and services have developed a complex weave: employers, unions, insurers, hospitals, the medical profession, and government are involved in the financing, administration, and scope of services. Political, economic, and social conflict swirl around health care issues.

Foundations have supported the practice of medicine through individual research grants and programs in community health and hospital utilization. The most richly endowed research center in the world, the Rockefeller Institute for Medical Research (now Rockefeller University), was established in 1902. The Rockefeller Foundation's Sanitary Commission was instrumental in ridding the South of endemic hookworm disease, which debilitated large parts of the population. Apart from labor's general antipathy toward any activities associated with the Rockefeller name, there is no evidence of any particular union attitude one way or another to these early enterprises in public health. After World War II, groundbreaking federal outlays flowed from the newly established National Science Foundation and the National Institutes of Health. The National Research Council initiated a group of grants for training scientists and for graduate research fellowships.[1] The founding of the National Cancer Institute was chiefly spurred by the Albert and Mary Lasker Foundation, well known for awards to medical researchers.

Early health benefit structures took the form of mutual aid societies and insurance programs that union members paid for through dues and assessments.[2] Contract practice—payment to a physician by a fraternal lodge for service to its members—spread through immigrant communities. Ironically, medical societies that opposed doctors' affiliations with lodges (on the grounds of loss of control over fees) invoked a union theme, as shown in a complaint voiced in the *West Virginia Medical Journal:* "Working men . . . should decline to enter into an arrangement that compels men of education to engage in the very thing that the labor unions so bitterly denounced, namely, the cutting in the price of labor."[3] On the other hand, a lumber company physician said in 1914: "It was not surprising that workingmen who have learned to organize themselves in trade unions, should also unite for mutual protection against accident and illness. . . . There are many indications that government insurance similar to the social legislation in various European countries will be adopted in the United States."[4]

The intransigence of the medical profession is legendary. As Paul Starr notes: "[It] has been worried about both competition and control. Private physicians have sought to keep government from competing with them, regulating their practice or . . . incorporating medical care into the state as a public service like education. Their struggle to limit the boundaries of public health, to confine public services to the poor, and to prevent the passage of compulsory health insurance all exemplify these concerns."[5]

With the emergence of the germ theory and the subsequent drive to conquer infectious diseases, the early twentieth century was marked by a series of aggressive health initiatives on national and local levels that involved the public. Although such groups included laymen along with physicians, organized medicine, as represented by the American Medical Association (AMA), opposed "non-medical intervention."[6]

After successfully passing workers' compensation laws in thirty states by 1915, Progressive-era reformers turned their attention to the financial toll

that illness took on both middle-class and working-class families, and advocated mandated health insurance. Plans called for using the American Association for Labor Legislation (AALL) as the fulcrum of a state-by-state campaign. Foundations, Progressive politicians, and university professors involved
in the AALL reasoned that state laws on health would more likely be immune to constitutional challenge than federal, that the states as well as workers would benefit by effectively limiting medical costs to their obligations
under a plan, and that employers would benefit through stabilized labor relations and increased productivity. As one social scientist put it, "Doctors
were forced to recognize that rapid advances . . . were putting high-quality
medical care beyond the financial each of a whole class of industrial employees," and the AMA in 1917 actually endorsed a version of compulsory health
insurance compatible with the AALL model bill. State and local federations
of labor and some national labor leaders also approved.[7]

Optimistic expectations, however, were dashed by the opposition of a
broad range of groups—employers who thought they were unfair targets,
insurance companies, taxpayer associations, Christian Scientists, and drug-
gists; the National Civic Federation split on the issue. The linchpin of opposition was the commercial insurance industry, which strongly influenced
the position of the medical and dental professions (Frederick L. Hoffman,
the industry's chief spokesman, resigned from the AALL over the issue). By
1917 many state medical societies were in open revolt against physicians and
scientists who supported the AALL bill, and in the end the AMA urged caution even on voluntary plans.[8]

Another severe blow came from the AFL. Gompers worried (and so testified vigorously in Congress) that a government insurance system would
weaken unions by usurping their role in providing benefits. In Paul Starr's
words, he "repeatedly denounced compulsory health insurance as an unnecessary, paternalistic reform that would create a system of state supervision of
people's health." Labor leaders feared that enactment of a plan would reduce
the need for workers to join and support unions and would provide employers with an excuse to avoid raising wages. "Neither unions nor big business
at that time wanted any competition from government in social welfare programs that could potentially decrease workers' loyalty to either side; thus
health insurance, rather than pitting unions against capital, pitted both of
them against the reformers."[9] Finally, America's entry into World War I dis-
tracted attention from the issue, at the same time leading to jingoistic
charges that such proposals were "foreign" and "radical."[10]

Industrial medicine, an element of "welfare capitalism," evolved as a
means of ensuring both a healthy workforce and worker loyalty to employers. Organized medical departments with full-time physicians were common

in the largest companies by the mid-1920s, but unions, distrusting company doctors, pressed for cash benefits instead of company medicine. Opposition also surfaced from medical societies to such services, except for routine examinations and oversight of sanitary conditions and hygienic practices.

Foundations and unions largely passed one another like ships in the night on health issues. One exception was a radical health organization—the Workers' Health Bureau (WHB), organized in 1921 by three Marxist-oriented women who believed that "only workers and their unions could improve working conditions by agitating to eliminate the numerous health and safety hazards endemic in almost every industry." The WHB received funds from the Garland Fund and a few union locals.[11] Viewing mainstream science as an adversary, supporters of the WHB argued that the labor movement required assistance from an independent staff of experts in industrial hygiene to counter the industrial physicians sponsored by the National Industrial Conference Board, as well as scientists sponsored by the Rockefeller Foundation. Angela Nugent writes: "Contemptuous of [the Rockefeller Foundation] for being 'endowed with profits gained through the very exploitation of workers' bodies,' the Bureau's directors nonetheless recognized that its standards prevailed as the contemporary yardstick for respectable medicine. . . . The Bureau's research goals, it insisted, made it comparable to the Rockefeller Foundation but in the interests of, and controlled by, workers."[12] With the cooperation of a few health professionals, the WHB managed to provide limited health services and health education programs for hundreds of workers in some 180 locals. The bureau even conducted labor-organizing drives, and the AFL, aroused by its activism and radicalism, accused it of dual unionism and pressured local and state federations to withdraw support; the WHB went out of business in 1928.[13]

The Committee on the Costs of Medical Care (1928–32) grew out of concern, especially among the middle class and hospitals, that rising costs were denying a large proportion of the population adequate medical care. As the chairman of the committee, Dr. Ray Lyman Wilbur, an outstanding physician, president of Stanford University, a past president of the AMA, and later Hoover's secretary of the interior, put it, "Something must be done to devise financial plans for the provision of adequate medical service to all elements of the population."[14] Other issues that spurred the formation of the CCMC were the expanding role of the hospital, the large number of defects observed in examination of draftees in World War I, and perhaps most important, the lack of any data from which to draw conclusions and make recommendations for organizing medical care more efficiently and rationally. Wilbur obtained a total of over $1 million from eight foundations: Carnegie, Josiah Macy, Milbank, New York Foundation, Russell Sage, Rosenwald, Rockefeller, and the Twentieth Century Fund. In addition, foundation officers from the Commonwealth Fund and the Duke Endowment were active participants.[15] It was probably the most distinguished gathering of foundations ever to coalesce around an issue.

The forty-eight members of the CCMC took care to enlist the cooperation of the AMA and insurance industry interests. In twenty-seven reports filed over a five-year period (1928–33), the committee's research staff compiled data on national health expenditures, their distribution through income groups, the impact of workmen's compensation laws, and benefits at some of the largest companies (discovering, among other facts, that some one million employees in the railroad, mining, and lumber industries were receiving fee-based company care, "not all of good quality").[16] The CCMC's attempt to delineate "a picture of the whole" extended to including two union executives on the committee as "public representatives." They were John Frey, secretary-treasurer of the AFL, and Matthew Woll, vice president; Woll resigned before the study was completed. The current president of the Milbank Memorial Fund believes that the failure to reach out to organized labor "was part of the dreadful political acumen that led foundation leaders to think it would be easy to redistribute payment for care and, incidentally, challenge the autonomy of physicians."[17]

The committee's final report endorsed community-based medical centers, hospital-based group practice, and group payment, recommending that the U.S. health system reorganize around community hospitals. It opposed compulsory health insurance, which did not stop the *New York Times* from using the term "socialized medicine" in its front-page headline.[18] The AMA denounced the proposals as "incitement to revolution," and an editorial in its *Journal* attacking the CCMC said: "The rendering of all medical care by groups or guilds or medical soviets has been one of the pet schemes of E. A. Filene [founder of the Twentieth Century Fund], who probably was chiefly responsible for establishing the committee and developing funds for its promotion."[19] Later studies and demonstration programs funded by the Rosenwald Foundation and the Twentieth Century and Milbank funds were similarly condemned by organized medicine. In fact, some members of the AMA went so far as to boycott the Borden Milk Company, source of the Milbank Memorial Fund endowment, which led the fund to abandon its interest in health insurance.[20]

Negative reaction to the CCMC plan led New Deal planners to be extremely cautious on the health issue; health insurance was never incorporated into the original Social Security legislation. Still, the committee's findings had a long-term influence, and government officials persuaded President Roosevelt to call a national health conference in 1938 to consider a national health program. Of the two hundred invited participants, several were consultants, officers, or trustees of foundations, and this time at least a dozen were union representatives. The conference, while not recommending specific legislation, did identify medical insurance as a national issue that would not go away, but Roosevelt, reacting to a conservative tide, dropped it from his agenda.[21]

A major advance in health care arose from labor conditions during World War II. Demands for vastly increased production required round-the-clock shifts in many plants, and absenteeism was high. With wage increases proscribed under wartime controls, employers sought other incentives to forestall absenteeism due to illness. Henry J. Kaiser Jr. had set up a limited medical plan for workers he employed in construction of the Grand Coulee Dam in the 1930s, and the mining, lumbering, and railroad industries took limited responsibility for employees' health care. Now Kaiser, recognizing the relationship between health care and productivity, joined with the United Steelworkers to provide medical care for his workers on an unprecedented scale. He built medical clinics, financed under government contracts and strongly supported by unions. After the war, Kaiser established a complex set of organizations, the end result being the Kaiser Foundation Health Plan, which contracted with Kaiser Foundation Hospitals for services from hospitals and medical centers, and with Permanente Medical Groups for services from physicians organized in independent doctor partnerships.[22] The arrangement was actually the country's first large-scale prepaid group practice or, in today's terms, health maintenance organization. This form of coverage grew slowly on the national level until the mid-1980s. In providing group competition to solo practitioners and conventional health insurance, Kaiser-Permanente eventually became the world's largest private health care system, enrolling 6.5 million by 1990. The AFL-CIO gave its highest award to Henry Kaiser in 1965, honoring his lifelong appreciation of "the worker as a human being."[23]

In contrast to Kaiser's approach, health benefits for workers grew rapidly after World War II because the wartime anti-inflation wage freeze allowed employers to offer fringe benefits such as health care to employees as a substitute. The major industrial unions eagerly enfolded these benefits in their postwar collective bargaining packages, but the many unions whose members lacked health benefits strongly supported national health insurance.[24] In 1944, a broad-based conference to set the stage for a national program brought together the research directors of the AFL and the CIO as part of a twenty-nine-member group that included Alan Gregg of the Rockefeller Foundation, Will Alexander of the Rosenwald Foundation, and several of the country's most eminent physicians. Although the plan advanced by this conference was less centralized and more voluntary than the Wagner-Murray-

Dingell health insurance bill then before Congress, it won no allies.[25] Wagner-Murray-Dingell went down, and Truman's strong initiative for health insurance under Social Security was stonewalled by a massive AMA public relations campaign portraying it as an opening wedge to Nazism and socialism.[26]

Foundations and unions played key roles together in establishing the Health Insurance Plan of Greater New York (HIP). Promoted by Mayor Fiorello LaGuardia in 1944, the scheme was based on studies financed by the New York and Josiah Macy foundations. Responding to the fact that many city employees were in debt because of health bills, HIP provided prepaid medical service for employed New Yorkers and their dependents whereby enrollees paid an annual fee and chose a medical group organized by HIP. Costs of the initial administrative staff and facilities were met through loans (all of which were repaid) from the New York, Rockefeller, and Lasker foundations. Start-up funds also came from the CIO and the Union Health Center of the ILGWU, and the original HIP board of eight included four union representatives. Besides unions, HIP members included United Nations staff, teachers at the city colleges, and business employees. By 1957, 506,000 men, women, and children—one of every sixteen New Yorkers—were in the program. The Rockefeller Foundation made an interest-free loan of $250,000 to HIP in 1947 as working capital for the program's expansion.[27]

What unions were unable to obtain legislatively was won to a great extent through what John R. Commons called the "private legislation" of the collective bargaining process.[28] But though labor and management have played major roles in fueling the growth of the health care industry, neither sector seems to have substantive control of health care policy.[29] Private foundations, however, continue as engines of research and reform. Of the vast (three quarters of a trillion dollar) national health industry, only 20 percent is devoted to the development of new knowledge and capability. Foundations, on the other hand, devote about 90 percent of their health and medical expenditures to the improvement of the knowledge base and the organizational and financing structures of health and medical care.[30] Among the achievements of the last two decades are:

- advancing the concept of mid-level health professionals (nurse practitioners and physician assistants), with support from Macy, Commonwealth, and Robert Wood Johnson;
- advancing more sophisticated models of the concept of health maintenance organizations as an alternative to fee-for-service medical care, with support from the Kaiser Family Foundation, Carnegie, and Robert Wood Johnson;
- developing the economics of medical care into an academic research

specialty. The Twentieth Century Fund, which delved early on into the affordability of voluntary health insurance plans, and the Commonwealth Fund, after decades of emphasizing programs for hospital expansion, supplied seed money for pioneering research by the National Bureau of Economic Research.[31]

An extensive experiment in cost containment was conducted in the 1980s by the Robert Wood Johnson Foundation. The $15 million program—Community Programs for Affordable Health Care (CPAHC)—distributed planning grants to sixteen communities and four-year implementation awards to eleven sites (large and small cities, counties, and the state of Iowa) to demonstrate that community-based groups—private insurers, professionals, unions, business, and local citizens—could collaborate to contain health costs. A national advisory committee was headed by John Dunlop of Harvard and included John Sweeney, then president of the Service Employees International Union. Some of these coalitions did influence hospital use (in such areas as ambulatory care) and benefit arrangements; a few organized HMOs or PPOs (Preferred Provider Organizations), but according to an independent evaluation, the demonstration communities fared no better or worse than others in constraining rising costs: "An unrealistic expectation harbored by the foundation and the program's co-sponsors (the American Hospital Association and Blue Cross/Blue Shield Association)" was "the misguided assumption that cost containment could be achieved [locally] when the true levers of power and control existed at the national and state levels."[32]

Another elaborate experiment on cost containment was carried out by the John A. Hartford Foundation in the 1990s, with union involvement at state and city levels. It consisted of a community health reform initiative (CHR), for which the foundation granted $9 million, and a Community Health Management Information System (CHMIS). Using a market incentive approach, the CHR encourages employers to act cooperatively by using their buying power to keep down health insurance costs and to monitor the quality of health care (this concept also surfaced in the Clinton administration health plan). Hartford also funded the National Business Coalition on Health, whose members measure and control costs. By 1993, the coalition numbered more than seventy groups representing some five thousand employers responsible for over twenty-five million workers and their families. Unions, along with the American Association of Retired Persons and the American Farm Bureau Federation, help sign employers into the system.[33]

The National Committee for Quality Assurance (a nonprofit agency concerned with health care costs) has instituted new industry-wide standards for HMO information disclosure. The committee receives funding and advice from foundations (the Kaiser Family Foundation, for example), and its work has been welcomed by union health-benefits specialists; unions and employers as well as foundations contribute support.[34]

The Robert Wood Johnson Foundation (RWJ) has sponsored several broad efforts to reduce tobacco use since 1993. Its $5 million Tobacco Policy Research and Evaluation Program focuses particularly on unions.[35] Under an RWJ grant, Dr. Glorian Sorensen, a researcher at the Dana-Farber Cancer Institute in Boston and a faculty member at the Harvard School of Public Health, has surveyed all national unions and a sampling of union locals on smoking in the workplace. She finds that 43 percent of national unions and 48 percent of local union leaders support either a complete ban or restrictions at the work site. The controversial nature of the issue was indicated by a call by the Bakery, Confectionery and Tobacco Workers International Union for a boycott of a conference of unions she ran on the subject. The issue for BCT is job loss, while other unions, such as the Flight Attendants and the Restaurant Workers, want to protect their members from exposure to environmental tobacco smoke. The Dana-Farber research has revealed other volatile issues: whether unilateral employer imposition of smoking bans should be addressed in collective bargaining; where smoking stands in relation to other environmental issues; whether the smoking issue endangers union solidarity by pitting smokers against nonsmokers; and whether the public health community is too close to management at the expense of labor.[36]

Unions also belong to coalitions in states (including tobacco-producing Kentucky) participating in RWJ's $10 million Smokeless States Program and have been enlisted in the foundation's Smoke-Free Families: Innovations to Stop Smoking During and Beyond Pregnancy, and a Substance Abuse Policy Research Program that collects data on which to base public and private policies to reduce the damage from use of alcohol and illegal drugs.[37] Union-run, member-assisted peer counseling and referral programs have proved more effective in prevention and treatment of substance abuse than management efforts, according to researchers.[38] Finally, RWJ made a grant to the Service Employees International Union for development and implementation of an AIDS-in-the-Workplace Program in conjunction with the Centers for Disease Control.[39]

Conversion Revolution

In the 1990s both hospital unions and consumers have faced a massive upheaval in the multi-billion-dollar conversion of nonprofit hospitals (including some public hospitals) and HMOs to for-profit status. Such conversions are the product of dramatic changes in the health care industry, particularly the penetration and regionalization of managed care (including financial pressure on hospitals for operational efficiencies such as shorter patient stays), expansion of integrated health care delivery systems, competition from for-profit providers and insurers, and the dynamics of the capital markets. In 1994 and 1995, at least sixty-four hospitals were sold to huge health-care companies for an estimated total of $3.3 billion.[40]

"For hospital unions," says Carol Regan of the SEIU, "one issue is not only whether converted hospitals that have contracts with unions will honor them, but also whether, when contracts are up for renegotiations, the health-care corporations will bargain in good faith or attempt to break the unions." Also, for union members as well as the general public, other major issues are the quality and coverage under these new arrangements. Bill Roush, an economist with the AFSCME, denounced Columbia/HCA, the largest for-profit company in the field in the 1990s, as antiunion and paternalistic: "Columbia has recognized bargaining units in new acquisitions where they exist, but they resist unionization attempts in units which do not now have them."[41]

The foundation community has a major stake in the integrity of the huge conversion deals. Under federal law, an organization that gives up its tax-exempt status must donate an amount equal to the value of its assets to a charity or foundation that will use the money for good works. In hospital conversions, large-scale controversy has arisen over the valuation of these assets. Some regulators believe that the law is being flouted and that "hundreds of millions of dollars that were supposed to be used for charitable purposes are wrongly slipping into corporate coffers."[42] Questions have been raised about board members and executives of nonprofit health groups being courted with plum corporate jobs, stock options, and other incentives from corporate suitors to persuade them agree to conversions. Conversions are subject to approval by state agencies, whose enforcement energies vary. In California, the state insurance commissioner withheld approval for a Blue Cross conversion until the charitable donation was increased from $1 billion to $3 billion, with which two linked foundations were established—together the sixth largest in the country. But many state officials are unfamiliar with the issues or appear not to care, so authoritative information and legal and policy analyses for officials, community organizations, and unions are coming from watchdog groups.[43]

Three foundations (Public Welfare, Kellogg, and Ford) support a conversions watchdog group, Community Catalyst. "We are concerned that the boards of foundations established with the assets derived from the conversions are independent and representative of the community," says Susan Sherry, director, "not playthings of directors and former officials of the converted hospitals."[44] After the opening of a federal investigation into alleged fraud by Columbia/HCA, Consumers Union and Community Catalyst petitioned attorneys general in all fifty states to withhold approval of any conversion plans by Columbia or Tenet Healthcare, the second largest nonprofit chain.[45] Surveying forty of an estimated one hundred foundations created from conversions, Grantmakers in Health, a national association of health philanthropies, found that many of their boards were not community-based but made up of people related to the health organization that spawned them.[46] It followed up by creating a Support Center for New Health Foundations, which provides information, training, and networking on grantmaking, governance, and other issues. One major question is whether new, conversion-based foundations should devote their funds entirely to improving health care, rather than social services or other causes.[47]

Workplace Health and Safety

The roots of occupational hazards have been described as follows: "Speed-ups, monotonous tasks, exposure to chemical toxins, metallic and organic dusts, and unprotected machinery have made the American workplace among the most dangerous in the world."[48] Among the earliest union campaigns was a strike of the New York local of the International Union of Bakers and Confectionery Workers in 1910 to demand sanitary conditions.[49] Workers sometimes appealed to consumers by using fears of disease from tainted goods. In contrast, industry's "Safety First" campaign and the National Safety Council (organized in 1911) blamed industrial accidents and disease on workers' carelessness or ignorance.

Moreover, by the 1920s the germ theory of disease was widely accepted, and germs were seen as the primary agents of medical problems. Workers gave short shrift to alternative causes, such as materials and processes used in the workplace. "What is so pernicious about labor's dependence on the good will of the scientists," as some analysts have observed," is that close economic and class ties link the university to industry."[50] Thus in the early 1930s, the Charles F. Kettering Foundation, in Dayton, Ohio, was implicated in a threat to environmental health through its support of the Kettering Laboratory of Applied Physiology, an influential participant in the lead industry's virtual monopoly of research and information dissemination on the toxicity of lead. Oil and automobile interests feared that if lead poisoning were defined as an environmental problem, tetraethyl lead—an important component of gasoline—would be banned. Industry strategy was to portray the hazards of inhaling lead additive as "a limited refinery problem" rather than one affecting not only gas station attendants but also the public. The Kettering Foundation, Kettering Laboratory, General Motors, and the Ethyl Corporation joined hands in advancing the view that "industrialization . . . was not responsible for lead in the body; that even if it were, it was not harmful; and that even if it were harmful, a cause/effect relationship was impossible to establish."[51] Well-connected scientific and medical professionals who could have reasonably been expected to provide an alternative perspective on emissions and lead toxicology did not do so. They were, in fact, part of the problem, according to William Graebner, and the result was "the suppression of genuine pluralism within the scientific community." Not until 1973 did the Environmental Protection Agency issue a regulation on leaded gasoline. In one of the most widely hailed public health accomplishments of the past quarter century, the EPA completed its total phase-out of lead from gasoline in 1996.[52]

When the Ford Foundation entered the occupational health and safety field in the early 1970s, an internal Ford document noted: "Over 14,000 Americans are killed each year on the job [and] roughly 10,000 chemicals of known toxicity are now in the American workplace, but threshold standards for exposure exist for only five-hundred." Other advanced nations were far ahead of the United States, applying ten to twenty times the resources per capita to training, materials development, health hazard identification, and alleviation procedures.[53] The foundation supported the National Legal Center for Occupational Health (which brought a number of suits concerning mine safety), and the Occupational Health and Safety Project of the Center for Labor Research and Education at the University of California, Berkeley, and funded a principal policy work on the issue, by Nicholas Ashford of the MIT Center for Policy Alternatives.[54]

Among the occupational diseases that foundations sought to combat was byssinosis (brown lung). Although byssinosis was an acute problem for southern textile workers after World War II, occupational health questions were swept aside by unions as their membership declined under the pressures of strong industry opposition and a hostile political climate. The disease was finally placed on the public agenda not by the resurgence of the textile unions, but rather by social empowerment movements that enlisted modest foundation support to challenge company medical practice and state decision makers and their statistics.

Among the agencies active in the struggle to recognize brown lung disease was the Youth Project, a public foundation that provided grassroots organizations with financial and technical assistance. With funding from the Campaign for Human Development (CHD), Joint Foundation Support, the Norman Foundation, the John Hay Whitney Foundation, and others, it collaborated with the Textile Workers Union to build up the Carolina Brown

Lung Association.[55] The latter's efforts resulted in payments of more than $2 million in compensation to brown lung victims and in state requirements that the industry clean the textile mills of the cotton dust that causes byssinosis.[56] Brown lung became a national rallying issue and was finally recognized as an irreversible disease when, with help from the Youth Project and the Industrial Union Department of the AFL-CIO, the National Brown Lung Association (NBLA) was established in 1976. The Occupational Safety and Health Act (OSHA), passed in 1970, set standards for exposure to cotton dust in 1978; these were upheld by the U.S. Supreme Court in 1981. With 7,500 members at its peak, the NBLA forged links between disabled workers and environmental scientists, but by 1985 it had all but disappeared. Foundation interest waned; the Reagan administration cut off federally assisted outreach mechanisms; lawyers took a third or more of the financial awards, while members who won compensation were not required to contribute to the association.[57]

Among other occupational and environmental health projects on which the Youth Project focused was the Bailly Alliance, which rallied organized labor opposition to the construction of a nuclear power plant in Gary, Indiana; the Uranium Research Project, which educated workers and residents on mining and drilling, the two most hazardous parts of the nuclear cycle; and the New Jersey Toxics Project, which through monitoring sought to hold corporations and government accountable for decisions on toxic waste management.

At the grass-roots level, some twenty Councils on Occupational Safety and Health (COSHs) were formed across the country in the 1970s and 1980s, some with foundation assistance and, after 1977, some with OSHA funds. Illustrative is the experience of the Rochester (N.Y.) Council on Occupational Safety and Health: unions pay a yearly fee for membership, and individual union members may belong as well. ROCOSH receives support from union donations through the local United Way donor option program, but most funds come from the State Department of Labor, supplemented by local foundations.[58]

In the late 1980s and 1990s foundations have funded occupational health programs for Asian immigrant workers at centers in New York and California, the Helping Hands Center for poultry workers in North Carolina, and the Louisiana Injured Workers Union Education Fund. The last, founded in 1990, has a thousand members and deals with enforcement of workmen's compensation laws, defense of whistleblowers, and company compliance with environmental regulations. It has criticized union emphasis on prevention as resulting in inadequate attention to workers after they are injured. Nonetheless, "the unions today are beginning to see how important the organizing of injured workers really is to the labor movement as a whole," Allen Bernard, the fund's president, declared in 1996.[59]

Since 1986 the Massachusetts Coalition on New Office Technology has worked on problems of office workers, beginning with the arrival of video display terminals and personal computers whose users developed hand, neck, back, and vision problems attributed to the devices. The coalition sponsors labor-management safety committees, conducts training, and stimulates workers to push for better workplace conditions; it receives support from foundations, membership dues, and the Massachusetts Department of Public Health.[60] Because of the importance of protecting workers who speak out about safety and health dangers from retribution, the J. Roderick MacArthur Foundation has made several grants to the National Safe Workplace Institute for litigation costs in such cases.

Environmental Cooperation

As the environmental movement gathered strength through the 1970s, unions were ambivalent—caring about pollution but viewing industrial cleanups or bans on certain materials and processes as threats to their jobs. Such fears were sometimes fanned by industries seeking to avoid regulation.[61] Among the most active foundations currently working to reconcile differences between unions and the environmental movement is the Bauman Foundation of Washington, D.C. The foundation funded a "Jobs and the Environment" curriculum prepared by the Labor Institute, which is closely connected with the Oil, Chemical, and Atomic Workers International Union. "Tensions between workers and environmentalists arise when industry foments trouble, using the environment as bogeyman," says Patricia Bauman, president of the foundation. "During an early debate on the Clean Air Act, the Steelworkers Union prepared a thoughtful paper on why environment should be a labor issue, but companies then trucked in rank-and-file workers to testify against the Act."[62] Jack Sheehan, a former assistant to the president of the Steelworkers Union, recalls that unions began to pay attention to environmental issues when it became apparent that industrial processes were causing illness inside and outside plants. "The terms were all new to us—epidemiology, for example—but I. W. Abel [then president of the Steelworkers] resolved that the union should be a bridge to, not a buffer against, cleanup efforts. But industry started a campaign of environmental blackmail, warning that environmental protection measures would threaten jobs." By the 1980s, Sheehan and officials of other unions opposed modifications that would weaken the Clean Air Act; their lobbying efforts included visits to Speaker of the House

Tip O'Neill. In the course of his work, Sheehan chaired an American Lung Association commission on clean air and served on the board of the Natural Resources Defense Council, a major environmental group.[63] Another union leader, William Winpisinger, president of the machinists, led a campaign against industry efforts to divide organized labor and the environmental movement.

Several actions by the Bauman, Charles Stewart Mott, and Jessie Smith Noyes foundations aimed to empower local groups and unions to negotiate on a par with industry in resolving environment issues. The Work and Environmental Council (the tax-exempt arm of the Industrial Union Council of New Jersey), conducts a Right-to-Act program that supports community and union plant inspections, health examinations for employees, and other interventions usually thought of as management prerogatives. New coalitions such as Environmentalists for Full Employment, the National Committee for Full Employment, and the Labor Committee for Safe Energy and Full Employment, with support from foundations and organized labor, promote the concept that there need not be a conflict between providing healthy, socially useful jobs and safe, clean workplaces and community environments. Grants have also gone to the Clear Water Fund of North Carolina, which seeks to defuse environmental conflict between unions and communities, and the Center for the Study of Public Policy in Boston, for preparation of a handbook and instruction on community-level "neighbor-labor" negotiation on environmental problems.

In Los Angeles, the Labor/Community Strategy Center, which originated as a protest against plant closings, now engages in extensive environmental work. A regional coalition that includes unions, it sees itself as "perhaps the only multi-racial think tank on social policy in the country," focusing on a variety of occupational health and safety and pollution issues that are especially acute in black and Hispanic neighborhoods.[64]

To the extent that foundations and unions, together or separately, have sought to improve the health and safety of America's workers and their neighbors, they exemplify a concept articulated in 1936 by the Round Table of the Milbank Memorial Fund: "A health problem becomes a public health responsibility when, because of its nature and extent, it is amenable to solution only through organized group action."[65]

11

Economic Development

Foundations and unions have joined together in aid of communities beset by a variety of crises—from race riots to plant closings. For example, the Ford Foundation's most extensive and longest-lasting alliance with the labor movement involved community development corporations (sometimes termed "community unions"), principally in the predominantly black Watts section of Los Angeles and the largely Latino community of East Los Angeles. The Watts Labor Community Action Committee (WLCAC) grew out of a study by the Institute of Industrial Relations at the University of California, which was financed under the 1961 Federal Area Redevelopment Act. To implement their study, the academic planners turned to union men with whom they had developed close relationships. The UAW and Teamsters Joint Council 42 helped organize the WLCAC, together with local teenagers. A dozen other unions, from longshoremen to meat cutters, have since joined in. The WLCAC's activities accelerated after the disastrous six-day riot in Watts in 1967, with emphasis on job training and other skills, housing programs, vest pocket parks, commuter buses, a community newspaper, and a hospital. Through most of its history the organization was run by a former UAW shop steward. Although Ford has been the major foundation supporter ($8.5 million) the WLCAC has also received funds from the Los Angeles city and county governments, the Rockefeller Foundation, and others.

Responding to Plant Closings

Since the 1970s, many communities have been ravaged by the decline, cutting back, or outright closure of manufacturing plants, owing to corporate mergers, technological obsolescence, or moves to lower-wage regions abroad or elsewhere in the United States. Although foundations have been slow to focus on these events, since the mid-1980s they have sponsored groups that work with unions and community organizations on economic revitalization, help for displaced workers, conversion of military bases to commercial and industrial uses, and worker ownership of threatened plants.[1]

Plant closures are the principal focus of the Chicago-based Federation for Industrial Retention and Renewal (FIRR), an umbrella group that embraces some thirty-five organizations around the country, from the Naugatuck Valley Project in Waterbury, Connecticut, to the Tennessee Industrial Renewal Network and the Plant Closures Project in Oakland, California.[2] The most advanced affiliate is the Midwest Center for Labor Research in Chicago, founded in 1982 with a grant from the Stern Family Fund to fight plant closings in the steel industry; it has since received additional funds from a dozen foundations.[3] Combining sophisticated research with technical assistance, the center assists unions in their contract negotiations, promotes employee ownership, and helps local entrepreneurs buy out absentee-owned companies whose aging owners made no plans for succession. The center also documents and corrects the abuse of low-interest loans by cities to companies.[4] Deindustrialization and capital flight call for "a fundamental shift in the development paradigm," says Dan Swinney, executive director of the center, "replacing it with a model [in which] the costs and role of labor, democratic management, corporate obligations to the community, and environmentally-productive technology are not seen as restraints on development, but as dynamic benefits that can drive and develop our productive capacity."[5]

One of the most strenuous, but ultimately failed, efforts to prevent a plant closing was waged in Los Angeles by the Labor/Community Strategy Center, supported by a half-dozen national foundations. The center opposed General Motors' decision to close its Van Nuys plant, which employed five thousand workers, including substantial numbers of blacks and Latinos. According to Eric Mann, director of the center, the issue brought the plant's UAW local into conflict with the international UAW. "The International, advocating a labor-management cooperative model, opposed our efforts," he recalls.[6] The plant eventually closed, but the center has gone on to other projects involving low-income minority workers. With the NAACP Legal Defense Fund, it brought a suit to prevent a bus fare increase, charging that Los Angeles was operating a two-tier system—a limited light-rail network for affluent riders in the suburbs, and a dilapidated, inadequate bus system for low-income, close-in riders.

The ICA Group (Industrial Cooperative Association), based in Boston, advises unions, churches, state and local governments, and community-based organizations on the mechanics of instituting employee ownership to save jobs. Some 15 million American workers were employed by firms with varying degrees of employee ownership in 1995. Since 1978, ICA has been the leading source of technical assistance to firms owned by low-income and minority workers, providing business consulting (for employee stock ownership plans and feasibility studies for employee buyouts); financial packaging through a loan fund, combining with other lenders; and legal assistance (on legislative and administrative precedents that facilitate formation of employee-owned firms). ICA has received fourteen labor-related foundation grants, with additional support from unions and government programs. In Pittsfield, Massachusetts, for example, the electrical workers' union decided to buy out a plant that was scheduled for closing; more than a dozen public, private, and community organizations collaborated in a worker buyout. ICA's sister organization, the Local Enterprise Assistance Fund (LEAF) Revolving Loan Fund (previously the ICA Revolving Fund), provided a key $80,000 loan for the buyout.[7] A similar organization in Ohio—the Northeast Ohio Employee Ownership Center—with funding from the Cleveland Foundation, the Gund Foundation, and the Ohio State Department of Development, assists unions and workers interested in employee ownership. The center runs workshops, provides legal/technical advice for unions and workers in a buyout, and assesses feasibility.

In a major rust-belt region embracing Cleveland and Pittsburgh, foundations have underwritten comprehensive approaches to economic revitalization. In the late 1980s, the Cleveland and Gund foundations teamed up with the United Labor Agency, the human-services arm of area unions, to create the Regional Industry Center (RIC). Collaborating in the center are Cuyahoga Community College, Cleveland State University, and a grassroots coalition of labor (combining efforts by the local AFL-CIO, the Teamsters, and the UAW), religious organizations, and neighborhood groups. The RIC operates an early warning system that trains workers to recognize signals that their plant is in trouble. It has helped retain many jobs, especially in small- and medium-sized businesses, though it did not succeed in persuading the *Cleveland Plain Dealer* to remain in the city. Gund helped the agency raise an additional $1.2 million in 1991 to offset government cutbacks and layoff-related declines in union contributions.

In Pittsburgh an intensive program of job retention measures was organized in 1994 by labor unions collaborating with foundations (including

Alcoa, Benedum, two Heinz foundations, Hillman, and R. K. Mellon) in a Regional Economic Revitalization Initiative, aimed at creating 80,000 to 100,000 new jobs by the year 2000. (The percentage of manufacturing jobs lost around Pittsburgh between 1970 and 1990 was the largest of any region in the country: 157,000 jobs).[8] Business, civic, government, education, religious, and cultural figures have also been involved in analyzing the competitiveness of the Greater Pittsburgh Region and devising plans to revive its economy. In a survey conducted for the group by Carnegie Mellon University's Center for Economic Development, Duquesne University, and Price Waterhouse, one-third of the firms interviewed said a general perception of poor labor/management relations had a negative effect on the region. Many believed, as one of the Initiative's reports stated, that "a lack of understanding and commitment by both management and labor have hindered the adoption of more empowering, flexible work practices."[9] The Initiative's efforts to improve labor/management relations resulted in the Pittsburgh Pledge, an agreement signed by business and labor leaders committing them to use all means possible to resolve disputes without a strike.[10]

Strategies that use union pension funds and other workers' savings for community investment are being developed by the Steel Valley Authority in western Pennsylvania. The SVA will build on its creation, together with the United Steelworkers, of a regional investment fund for jobs in manufacturing, which is regarded as a national model of industrial retention. Funders include the MacArthur, Ford, Rockefeller, and Pittsburgh foundations, the Veatch Program, and the Jewish Fund for Justice.

Job dislocation is another focus of foundation-union economic development programs. With support from the Greater Cincinnati Foundation, for example, the National Association of Working Americans provided some four hundred families affected by six plant closings with short-term financial assistance, counseling, and placement in new jobs. The Northwest Area Foundation funded a major workplace effort to raise wage and skill levels for low-income adult workers; organized labor was involved in Oregon, Minnesota, and Seattle. With a foundation grant the University of Oregon Labor Education and Research Center established an Ecosystem Workforce Project, in which the United Brotherhood of Carpenters was a participant and advocate. The project used the federal "Jobs in the Woods" program to train dislocated timber workers in watershed restoration and to promote quality jobs. Started with Northwest Area funds, the project attracted six federal demonstration projects in watershed restoration.[11] Under a $570,000 Kellogg Foundation grant, the Minnesota AFL-CIO cooperated with seventeen colleges and universities in an Adult Learner Services network to provide workers wishing to return to school with counseling and flexible course offerings.

In Flint, Michigan, a community hard hit by layoffs from General Motors, the Charles Stewart Mott Foundation financed an autoworker retraining project at local colleges. The foundation also funded an allied project by the National Center for Research in Vocational Education, which was supported by the UAW-GM Human Resource Center as well.

Sophisticated legal representation for the casualties of plant closings has been provided by the Maurice and Jane Sugar Law Center, founded in 1991 and based in Detroit (Maurice Sugar, long-time general counsel of the United Auto Workers, was fired by Walter Reuther for left-wing activities). The center's first priority is to ensure enforcement of the Workers Adjustment Retraining Notification Act (WARN), which requires that workers be notified in advance of mass layoffs or plant closings. The center brings suits on behalf of individual workers or unions against companies allegedly violating the act (the Oil, Chemical and Atomic Workers, for example, retained the Sugar Law Center for all its WARN cases). In May 1996 the center won a major victory when the U.S. Supreme Court ruled unanimously that unions may sue for money damages on behalf of their members when an employer violates the WARN Act (*United Food & Commercial Workers Union v. Brown Shoe Co.*).[12] A handful of foundations supplement the support the Sugar Law Center receives from unions. Kary L. Moss, executive director, says it is extremely difficult to obtain foundation grants: "Many foundations are not interested in funding litigation-driven work, and few seem to understand the importance of plant closing work to the issue of economic justice and the labor union movement."[13]

A subcategory of plant closings and cutbacks, particularly painful in some parts of the country, has resulted from changes in the defense industry. Post-Cold War defense reductions have cost more than one million jobs. The Center for Economic Conversion, based in Mountain View, California, and funded mainly by foundations, reports that many efforts to convert military industrial facilities to peacetime production ones now are led by organized labor. "Unions have emerged as some of the major forces working for changes at the local, regional, and national levels," according to a center official.[14] The center is a clearinghouse for information, research on conversion issues, and technical assistance to unions, managers, and public officials confronting military cutbacks. For example, in South Bend, Indiana, the UAW ratified a contract with AM General Corp. that provides job security through redirection of the company's program to produce civilian versions of the four-wheel-drive Humvee transports it makes for the army. In Philadelphia, the Samuel S. Fels Fund and local unions planned industrial reconversion of portions of the Philadelphia Naval Yard.[15]

The principal labor-led effort is the Workplace Economic Conversion

Action Network (WE-CAN), founded in 1993 under the leadership of Peter diCicco, a high-ranking AFL-CIO official. It identifies conversion opportunities and tries to spur community economic development around new manufacturing jobs. The "Better Business" part of its agenda encourages firms to improve their competitiveness and support community and state strategies for retention of industry and job creation. WE-CAN helped obtain authorization for $15 million in the defense budget for market feasibility studies for proposed new businesses and a $50 million loan guarantee. But the group had no success in getting foundation funds, diCicco recalled:

> I don't blame them for it. We just haven't been able to put it together. In the meantime, the AFL-CIO carries most of the costs, though I don't know whether they consider it worthwhile. I haven't had much success in bringing them on board on this. One argument was, "Why should we do something for military workers now when they've been on the take for so long with high wages sponsored by the federal government? Now it may be somebody else's turn." I was stunned with disbelief at this view, but there it is.
> I don't think that we know how to work with foundations, though I think there could be natural alliances. Some of them have told us to use our own money, but my resources are limited. Seed money from foundations would help us staff up with people who could penetrate various barriers, get more people within labor on board.[16]

The Living Wage Movement

With the passage of national welfare reform legislation in 1996, state and local governments are tackling the urgent issue of work-based alternatives to welfare. Guideposts may be available in an economic development effort in Milwaukee, the New Hope Project. With grants totaling $650,000 from the Rockefeller Foundation, $5 million from the Annie E. Casey Foundation, and funds from federal, state, and business sources, it combines the development of private-sector jobs with wages above the poverty line, health and child care, and publicly subsidized community-service jobs when private employment is not feasible.[17] A union-supported organization, the Campaign for a Sustainable Milwaukee, acts as a watchdog over plant closings and flawed tax breaks and city contracts, and promotes training, community job banks, and credit and capital vehicles for small business. An official of the New Hope Project helped plan the Campaign, and in turn the director of Sustainable Milwaukee, Bruce Colburn, secretary-treasurer of the Milwaukee County Labor Council, serves on the board of New Hope.[18]

In several cities unions are part of campaigns to require companies that receive municipal contracts or subsidies to provide liveable wages and job security to their employees. Even after the 1996 increase in the minimum wage, the movement continues because what a full-time worker paid at that rate earns is still far enough below the poverty line to require welfare and food stamps, perpetuating the "working poor" class.[19]

The Los Angeles Living Wage Coalition was instrumental in having the city council pass a job-protection ordinance that requires companies receiving city subsidies or contracts to retain workers for at least ninety days and then offer them permanent employment if their work is satisfactory. A later ordinance provided some five-thousand such workers $7.25 an hour plus benefits or $8.50 an hour without benefits. The coalition emerged in response to a UCLA study that followed the 1992 riots, and receives funds from several foundations, including Veatch, Liberty Hill, the Jewish Fund for Justice, and the Campaign for Human Development. The New World Foundation arranged a briefing on the coalition project for twenty foundations at the 1995 AFL-CIO convention in New York.[20]

Similar drives are under way in Boston, New York, Dallas, Milwaukee, Minneapolis, New Orleans, Little Rock, and Baltimore. Baltimoreans United in Leadership Development (BUILD), a citywide church-based organization that receives major funding from AFSCME, teamed up with unions to win legislation guaranteeing that employees of companies with city contracts receive wages of $6.60 an hour. The issue arose when downtown developers assigned high-paying jobs to workers from outside Baltimore, leaving the remaining low-wage, dead-end jobs to local workers.[21]

Long-Range Economic Planning

The most far-ranging economic development effort supported by unions and foundations was the Los Angeles Manufacturing Action Project (LAMAP). Begun in 1994 with a Rosenberg Foundation grant, it also received funds from the New World, Veatch, McKay, and Liberty Hill foundations. LAMAP aimed at industry-wide organizing rather than organizing piecemeal, firm by firm. It hoped to reinforce this strategy with community support and potential mass mobilization of workers (boycotts and strikes, for example) to win union recognition. Recognition was the alternative to the election process, which involved recourse to the National Labor Relations Board, which could take years in some cases. David Sickler, the regional AFL-CIO director, lamented the "many years when we walked in lockstep with the N.L.R.B., organizing one shop at a time. It was a failed approach."[22]

This strategy proved successful in a truck driver organizing campaign, but it also accounted for the demise of the overall project in 1997. The participating unions were reluctant to continue the heavy front-end contributions required, according to Sickler, and the bottom fell out when the Teamsters, a major source of funding, withdrew as a result of the financial scandal growing out of the fiercely contested election for the union presidency. The project is worth describing nonetheless because of the scale and innovative approach, which Sickler predicts will one day be revived in another effort.[23]

LAMAP was a major project aimed at economic upgrading and multiunion organizing in the Alameda Corridor, a twenty-one-mile stretch running from the edge of downtown Los Angeles to the Port of Los Angeles/Long Beach. With 717,000 workers, it is the largest manufacturing complex in the country, depending mainly on immigrant workers—Latinos in particular—who live in East, Southeast, and South-Central Los Angeles, "communities largely disorganized and left out of the political and social discourse of the Southland," according to LAMAP's mission statement.[24] Besides the Teamsters, the cooperating unions were the Carpenters, the Garment Workers, the Machinists, the Oil, Chemical, and Atomic Workers, the Steelworkers, and the Food and Commercial Workers. Faculty and students at the University of California, Los Angeles, provided research for the project.

LAMAP targeted industries that employ mainly immigrant workers (apparel, food processing, printing, plastics, and warehousing) who are overwhelmingly low-wage and nonunion. An estimated 120,000 people work in Los Angeles's garment sweatshops. LAMAP's project coordinator, Peter Olney, believes that economic and social stability can be attained in the city's immigrant communities by increasing manufacturing wages and offering a selection of comprehensive employer-financed benefits. To achieve these goals, as an article in *The Nation* noted, LAMAP became "the largest-scale, most meticulously planned organizing effort mounted by the labor movement and its allies in many years. It draws on the immigrant experience, following the immigrant work force through the plants and barrios of the nation's most concentrated manufacturing district."[25]

Some economists warned that LAMAP's plan could backfire, forcing industry out of Los Angeles, the *Los Angeles Times* reported. "Organizing would contribute to the departure of at least some companies," said Ed Lawler, professor of management and organization at the University of Southern California. "The win-win argument is that if you uplift your work force with good wages and good jobs, you create a positive economic cycle. But there are some kinds of [low-skilled] work that don't lend themselves to that sort of scenario and can be done cheaply in mainland China or somewhere else." Olney pointed out, however, that most job losses in the previous decade and a half were in the steel and other durable goods industries; jobs in nondurable goods, LAMAP's target, stayed almost level.[26]

LAMAP was building on a record of labor militancy in Los Angeles in the 1990s. Immigrant workers walked out of the huge industrial sweatshops of American Racing Equipment and Cal Spas. They won union recognition from the developer of Century City office towers. Drywallers successfully shut down construction sites across Southern California's three most populous counties. In the Justice for Janitors campaign of the SEIU, immigrant janitors, taking to the streets, won contracts for 6,500 workers from building owners. Joel Ochoa, a LAMAP staff member and former organizer for the California Immigrant Workers Association, observed, "The immigrant community is targeting labor and not necessarily the other way around. The United Farm Workers pioneered many of the organizing ideas that LAMAP is adapting, such as heavy reliance on rank-and-file participation."[27]

In the radically different Silicon Valley, in California's Santa Clara County, a coalition of unions, community organizations, and academics called Working Partnerships USA began in 1995 to reshape regional economic policy. Despite the soaring success of the area's electronic industries, the growth in jobs has consisted mainly of increased contingent work, with resulting low wages, lack of benefits, and economic insecurity for employees. As in other high-tech boom areas (Austin, Eugene, Seattle, Boston), affordable housing is scarce, and child poverty and high school dropout rates have been increasing. Working Partnerships was founded by Amy Dean, head of the South Bay AFL-CIO, in an effort to broaden discussion of economic policy beyond domination by high-tech industry. Staff research, augmented by focus groups, deals with the region's economy, education, housing, and the environment. It sponsors popular economics education, develops worker representation models to help temporary and contingent employees obtain living wages, health care, pensions, and career advancement, and works with labor-management committees to design high-performance work systems in the private and public sectors.[28] Funders include foundations ranging from Ford to New World, McKay, and Solidago, and the County of Santa Clara and the Federal Mediation and Conciliation Service.

So swiftly are economic changes affecting American workers that issues like plant closings (although they continue) have a ring of the past. Since the late 1970s foundations have proven to be adept at community development projects that include jobs and infrastructure elements as well as social services.[29] Increasingly, as noted here, they are joining with unions to deal with economic challenges that affect localities and regions. As foundations pay more attention to national and international as well as local and regional facets of these issues, such ties seem likely to strengthen.

12

Public Policy

Despite self-imposed and external constraints, organized labor and philanthropic foundations have been players in the formation of public policy. Two instances were cited earlier—the deep involvement of the Twentieth Century Fund in the drafting and passage of the National Labor Relations Act (1935) and the stimulus provided by foundations to state legislation for Chicago public school reform, despite a reluctant teacher union. One of the most fiercely argued public policy issues in recent years—the North American Free Trade Agreement (NAFTA)—also engaged foundations and unions.

Nonalignment vs. Activism

The political history of the American labor movement has been marked by clashes between the concept of collective concerns vs. individual interests. The "pure and simple" business unionism of the early AFL was aimed at the advancement of the individual worker; Gompers cautioned against all but the narrowest involvement in politics, but many lower-rank union leaders rushed to expand their influence in local and state politics. Even Gompers was forced to venture into politics in an attempt to influence Congress to curtail the widespread, destructive use of court injunctions by employers to bar union organizing, and as Republicans grew increasingly antiunion, the AFL not only campaigned vigorously for Woodrow Wilson's reelection in 1916, it then launched its own National Non-Partisan Campaign Committee, which helped elect several progressive senators and representatives.[1] With the Democratic Party's conservative shift in the 1920s, the federation supported the Progressive Robert La Follette in 1924. When the Depression struck, as David Greenstone observed, "the New Deal helped create a far larger American labor movement, with a constituency that resembled the still larger constituency of the Democratic party in spirit, class composition, and ethnic heterogeneity."[2]

A notable contribution of unions to American politics was organized labor's invention of the Political Action Committee (PAC), which allows individuals who would be affected by legislation to pool their resources to try to influence the outcome of an election; all the players—business, political, labor, and other "special interests"—have employed this device.

For their part, foundations have been criticized for too much or too little engagement in public policy. At the outset, they viewed themselves as opening paths to legislative and policy changes in the states and, as the federal role expanded, at the national level as well. Along with experiments and demonstration programs, research was one of their principal instruments. Thus a 1910 study of industrial accidents by the Russell Sage Foundation and the U.S. Bureau of Labor was instrumental in fostering a more favorable attitude toward workingmen's insurance.[3] By 1920 all but six states and the District of Columbia had enacted workmen's compensation laws.

Without much support from organized labor, a body of protective legislation (on safety and health, child labor, maximum hours, and minimum wages) was built in the industrial states through agitation by humanitarian reformers working in small but remarkably effective organizations. Foremost were the National Child Labor Committee (NCLC) and the American Association for Labor Legislation (AALL), both important beneficiaries of foundations, and state and national consumers' leagues.[4]

Critics of foundations say that as gatekeepers of social research, foundations resent criticism and are reluctant to be examined. In a submission to the Commission on Private Philanthropy and Public Needs (the Filer Commission), Reynold Levy and Waldemar Nielsen called for giving "at least modest funding to the work of thoughtful critics of the performance of nonprofit organizations, including foundations." They asserted, "The power of the nonprofit sector's establishment has been so great and intimidating upon scholarly and intellectual critics, and its response to criticism in some cases has been so hostile and vengeful, that an attitude of hospitality to research and writing by independent and in some cases dissident voices will not be easy to create."[5] In fact, the decades since the Filer Commission have seen a flowering of critiques of foundations, ranging from the work of independent scholars to a newspaper with an investigative bent, *The Chronicle of Philan-*

thropy, to scholarly journals (e.g., the *Nonprofit and Voluntary Sector Quarterly*). Along the way, a dozen or so academic centers for research on the voluntary sector have been established, as well as a fund for research, the Aspen Nonprofit Sector Research Fund.

The attacks on foundations in the McCarthy era, coupled with restrictions in the Tax Reform Act of 1969 (discussed in Chapter 3) chilled their inclination to grapple directly with public policy, but indirect involvement continued. One prominent area was the encouragement of wider participation in the political process. Beginning in the 1960s, as foundations became deeply involved in the civil rights movement, they provided major support for voter registration and education programs, notably the Voter Education Project. Voter education and registration of union members had long been a staple of organized labor's political activity.[6] In the early 1980s AFSCME, the UAW, the Machinists, and the Food Workers established Project Vote, a nonpartisan, tax-exempt organization that sought to bring politically inactive persons onto the voting rolls, using tactics such as enlisting people waiting on lines for unemployment checks or food stamps. Project Vote also obtained grants from several foundations and many other unions, as well as individual contributions. The organization claims to have registered more than two million persons.[7]

The extent and propriety of foundation participation in public policy have been argued from various ideological viewpoints. More than a half-century ago, a pacesetter of foundation philanthropy, Julius Rosenwald, forcefully advocated public responsibility for many activities established by private philanthropy: "My personal hope is that more and more the greater government units, like the county, city, state, and nation, will take over and operate tried and true social agencies for the betterment of mankind that have been originated by private initiative and funds."[8] But in our own time, G. William Domhoff, Mary Anna Colwell, Robert Arnove, and other radical critics deplore what they construe as the use of foundations by social and economic elites as a means of influencing the formation of public policy. They point to overlapping board membership of corporate executives in foundations and policy organizations, such as Brookings, the Committee for Economic Development, the Hoover Institution, the American Enterprise Institute, and the Council on Foreign Relations.[9] Conservative foundations have used the courts to influence policy regarding organized labor. The F. M. Kirby Foundation funded the important court case brought by the National Right to Work Legal Defense and Education Foundation which limited unions' use of members' dues to support political candidates. The ruling, in *Communications Workers v. Beck*, (1988) said than union members may request refunds on the portion of their dues used for political candidates. President George

Bush backed up the Supreme Court decision with an executive order requiring that notices of the limitation be posted in workplaces.

On the other hand—given the charged atmosphere following the capture of Congress in 1994 by conservative Republicans and their threats to curtail social programs—liberal foundations have been faulted for avoiding a debate on national policy, leaving the field to conservative foundations that fund think tanks and publications tilted to the right. David Callahan, a resident scholar at the Twentieth Century Fund, attacks liberal foundations that "poured money into activist groups and community programs . . . unconnected to a national ideological vision." He calls on foundations to support liberal think tanks because "the left is suffering from a massive strategic planning void." Liberals have not invested in intellectual elites to frame the debate, as conservative foundations have done, he complains, "and in contrast to the well-funded and politically influential polemic of conservative foundations, most liberal books and magazines do not receive funding."[10] The fierce debate on the federal budget in 1995 prompted a paper from the National Committee for Responsive Philanthropy that criticized foundations for supporting research to the exclusion of participating in the political debate: "We have found [foundations] to be sitting on the sidelines as some of the most dramatic events of the last 30 years have been taking place."[11]

The Case of NAFTA

The NAFTA dispute embroiled two presidents (and a maverick presidential candidate), Congress, the corporate community, organized labor, and a wide array of other interests and organizations—environmentalists, farmers, church and grassroots groups, think tanks, and foundations. (The agreement was approved in October 1993 and took effect January 1, 1994, with implementation spread over a decade.) Despite the controversial nature of the issue, some foundations openly supported anti-NAFTA organizations, and others funded research clearly intended to advance pro-NAFTA positions. Some grants supported projects dealing with the consequences of NAFTA or conditions along the U.S.-Mexico border and in Mexico. The Charles Stewart Mott Foundation, one of the country's largest, held back its funds until the agreement was approved, then weighed in with a dozen grants related to its environmental aspects.

The AFL-CIO, working with the Bush and Clinton administrations to fashion side agreements that provided fines and sanctions for violations of environmental and labor protections, aimed to make the package palatable, but when the Clinton administration announced them, they fell far short of labor's hopes. Unions then mobilized more money, troops, and lobbying muscle than they had deployed on any issue since Taft-Hartley to defeat the legislation. Organized labor would not buy such moderate opinions as "Jobs and profits would undoubtedly be lost in labor-intensive, low-wage American industries, but threats of massive job and investment loss are likely to be muffled because the Mexican economy is tiny compared to the U.S. one."[12]

A trustee of the Boehm Foundation, Reynaldo R. Guerrero of the Center for Immigrants Rights, challenged the general prediction that the Mexican government's commitment to free markets would assure a long-term boost to American industries. "The relocation of multinationals has resulted in the reduction of real wages, deindustrialization and an eradication of job security in the U.S," he wrote. Relocated firms are facing cross-border "grassroots movements comprised of workers, religious and community organizations, unions in Mexico, Canada, and the U.S. that seek better health, safety, environmental, and labor standards and counter growing and inadequately monitored economic power."[13]

Arrayed against the agreement's opponents was USA* Nafta, a coalition of over 2,700 companies. The major academic underpinnings of the pro-NAFTA forces were provided by the Washington-based Institute for International Economics (IIE), which is heavily funded by foundations. On the critical issue of NAFTA's effects on jobs, a major IIE study estimated that NAFTA would create 600,000 jobs in Mexico and 130,000 jobs in the United States and lead to an improvement of about $10 billion annually in the American trade balance.[14] This research was supported by the Charles R. Bronfman, John D. and Catherine T. MacArthur, Tinker, and Dayton Hudson foundations.

The single largest foundation source for NAFTA-related work was the Ford Foundation, which made grants to organizations, including IIE, whose research supported the agreement. In 1990 Ford commissioned a trade economist, Thomas O. Bayard, to survey the U.S.-Canada Free Trade Agreement (FTA) and draw lessons for a possible NAFTA. He reported that while very little research had been done on the FTA in the United States, the Canadians had produced "an enormous body of public and private research and extensive public debate."[15] A Ford grant had enabled a Canadian center to bring U.S. congressional representatives and their staffs to meet with high-level Canadian policy and business people, which "helped to turn potential into actual supporters." Predicting that the U.S.-Mexican negotiations would be far more difficult, Bayard suggested that the foundation act quickly—"in time to influence the negotiations and the ratification process." In recommending empirical research on potential gains, Bayard argued: "It is important to identify the sectoral winners and losers to help mobilize support from the winners and provide an independent assessment of the often highly exaggerated cries of pain from the potential losers that are usually far more vociferous than the gainers and can block the agreement."[16] The foundation also made grants to environmental groups and to the Southwest Voters Research Institute to convene forums on NAFTA. These resulted in an alliance of one hundred Latino organizations and elected officials—the Latino Consensus on NAFTA—which provided conditional support for the agreement.[17]

At the opposite pole from IIE was the Economic Policy Institute (EPI), a research center unique in that it is funded by labor unions and foundations. William Spriggs, a former EPI economist, claims it was instrumental in discovering major flaws in computer-generated models used by the International Trade Commission to back NAFTA. The EPI's testimony shocked senators, he says.[18]

The Institute for Policy Studies (IPS), another Washington think tank, the recipient of grants from several liberal and generally smaller foundations, concentrated on the environmental and labor rights aspects of NAFTA. Focusing on actual conditions in Mexico, IPS specialists argued that many parts of the agreement would hamper the Mexican government if it chose to spread development more evenly among the population.[19]

A focus on the agricultural consequences of NAFTA was provided by the Institute for Agriculture and Trade Policy (IATP) in Minneapolis, which generated information needed to help grassroots organizations spread a message about "creating sustainable economies through sound agriculture and trade practices." For its research and analysis of NAFTA, the institute organized a team of agricultural and environmental leaders from the United States, Mexico, and Canada, published a daily news bulletin covering trade and environmental developments, and staged events in several states to alert citizens about NAFTA's potential impact on their state's agriculture. The IATP received support from two dozen foundations.[20]

The most extensive grassroots effort to defeat NAFTA was the Fair Trade Campaign (FTC), a coalition of thirty-one organizations formed in 1990 to introduce a "citizens agenda" of environmental, labor, consumer, and human rights into the NAFTA and GATT treaties. Funded by many foundations, it publicized potential environmental hazards and U.S. job losses due to NAFTA and appealed to union members and religious leaders "concerned about the dreadful working and living conditions of many Mexican workers in the new factories opened by multinational corporations."[21]

Public Citizen, Ralph Nader's consumer advocacy organization (which received grants from twenty foundations in 1993), formed a Citizens Trade Program embracing sixty national organizations—unions, environmental organizations, and consumer and farm groups. The campaign maintained a database of documents and published a newsletter exposing corporations'

alleged domination of government-sponsored trade negotiating committees. "We tried to bring home this arcane, esoteric topic to the average citizen, who doesn't know how trade impacts our daily life," says Gabriella
Boyer, a staff member.[22] Along with the Sierra Club and Friends of the
Earth, the Nader group scored a temporary victory in a suit asking that the
administration submit an Environmental Impact Statement before sending
NAFTA to Congress, but the case was overturned on appeal. The NAFTA issue
divided major environmental groups (all of which have foundation support)
on the issue of whether any side agreement was better than none. The Sierra
Club called attention to what it called "four key flaws" in the environmental
side agreements, but the Environmental Defense Fund and the National
Audubon Society believed that the agreements would improve enforcement
of environmental laws and promote joint efforts to solve environmental
problems.[23]

NAFTA opponents hold conflicting views on the role of foundations. Most
of the Fair Trade Campaign's proposals to foundations were rejected. According to the co-director, Don Wiener, "If we got on a foundation's docket
we usually succeeded because we were pretty good face-to-face. Most often
we were rejected because we were too political." Were legal restrictions a
constraint? The FTC used the Tides Foundation as fiscal agent for its grants
because the FTC itself engaged in some direct lobbying, and care had to be
taken, says Wiener, not to exceed the legal lobbying limit. He places emphasis on contributions to organizing as well as to research: "Without foundation money you couldn't get together a thing like the Fair Trade Campaign. It couldn't be done on labor money alone, and there could not have
been a NAFTA campaign without Veatch [a church-related foundation]. By
giving money early in this important policy area, foundations enabled us to
come close even though outnumbered. Unions were late in marshaling opposition because they thought they could cut a deal with the Administration."[24] Four years later, the union movement scored a major victory by
helping to defeat President Clinton's "fast track" trade bill.[25]

In contrast to foundations that were involved in the NAFTA debate, the
Charles Stewart Mott Foundation intentionally made no grants that dealt directly with the issue until after the vote. "We did not want to be perceived as
having taken sides," said Edward Miller, a Mott program officer. "We do not
have a policy that is pro- or anti-trade liberalization. These agreements
could be a threat or an opportunity. We believe it's important for a vibrant
nonprofit sector to be monitoring what is happening in trade agreements
that may have significant environmental impacts."[26]

13

Union Democracy

Among the few direct engagements of foundations in union affairs has been their support of union democracy movements—efforts by dissident union members to overturn apparently corrupt or ineffective labor leaders. This connection bears out the observation in a Filer Commission report that "a range of philanthropically supported institutions, particularly 'advocacy' projects, have made remarkable gains in reversing repressive, corrupt, and discriminatory practices on the part of major institutions."[1]

Dissension has long been a feature of the labor movement—differences over jurisdiction, struggles within local and national unions for leadership, and contention between the AFL and CIO before their merger in 1955. The national furor over Communists and Communist sympathizers in the 1940s led to several unions being purged from the CIO.

In recent decades, a generation of unionists reared during the civil rights and anti-Vietnam movements broke with the tradition whereby unions agree not to speak ill of one another, and mounted efforts for more democratic participation in union affairs. The targets, as analyzed by Victor Reuther, are twofold:

> The same sinister forces that often prey upon business enterprises [infiltrated] the labor movement, attracted by union treasuries, welfare and pension funds, and the opportunities of selling, or selling out, services in collective bargaining. Racketeers and corruptionists can succeed in debasing unions only because they are frequently encouraged by employers and

tolerated by government officials. . . . A different kind of malady sometimes arises from within. As unions become larger, more diverse in membership, and more complicated in structure, there is a possibility that control may slip out of the hands of the membership. When internal union
democracy is completely eroded, as in the United Mine Workers under
Tony Boyle, the union begins to serve its officials first and its members
last.[2]

Despite prominent congressional investigations of corruption and racketeering and turmoil within the Teamsters, hotel workers, and other unions,
many labor leaders have been apathetic, if not wholly indifferent, to the development of self-serving oligarchies within unions.

Observations about union corruption go back a century.[3] Granted that a
combination of malfeasance and "adroit publicity" by the NAM reinforced a
widespread attitude that "unions are a racket," labor scholars expressed concerns about union democracy long before foundations became involved in
the issue.[4] In 1938 the noted economists Summer Slichter and William H.
Davis posed questions before the Twentieth Century Fund regarding union
responsibility—in particular, responsibility to account for the disposition of
funds and preserve democratic control.[5] Slichter's concern persisted; in 1943
he wrote:

> In view of the position which collective bargaining now occupies in our so-
> ciety, what is the position of the trade union? Should it be regarded as a
> private club? May any union which sees fit refuse to admit women, or Ne-
> groes? Should unions be free to charge any initiation fee they see fit?
> Should they be free to confer upon their presidents any authority which
> they see fit, including authority to set aside the constitution of the union?
> Should unions be free to expel members, suspend them, or fine them with-
> out appeal to outside agencies so long as the constitution of the union it-
> self is not violated? In short, what moral and legal responsibility must
> unions now be prepared to assume in view of the fact that the government
> encourages membership in them?[6]

Union reform has given rise to such organizations as Miners for Democracy, Teamsters for a Democratic Union, and Steelworkers Fight Back. Miners for Democracy (MFD) was organized in 1970, when Joseph "Jock"
Yablonski and members of his family were murdered after his unsuccessful
campaign against W. A. "Tony" Boyle for the presidency of the United Mine
Workers. (Boyle was later convicted of the murders.) Two years later, the 1969
election was overturned and an MFD slate won. MFD received support from

the Field Foundation, the Stern Family Fund, the Public Welfare Foundation, and the J. M. Kaplan Fund, but appeals to a dozen other foundations, including several that styled themselves as "progressive," were rejected.[7]

Serving this movement by providing research, technical assistance, and public information is the Association for Union Democracy (AUD), established in 1970 by Herman Benson, a labor activist and journalist. Its earliest foundation support came from the Hopkins Funds of California, a small civil liberties fund established by a friend of Norman Thomas.[8] The AUD has provided guidance and at times intervened in court cases with amicus briefs involving several important unions. Half its budget comes from foundations and the rest from three thousand individual contributors.

By the 1970s workplace disputes and membership revolts stimulated organized reform movements and individual dissident candidates. Among the most prominent was Steelworkers Fight Back, led by Edward Sadlowski, a young crane operator. One of Sadlowski's supporters described the Steelworkers union as "torpid, old, bureaucratic," and the object of rank-and-file anger over its "quiet decision to castrate itself in the early seventies by giving up the right to strike, even when the contract had expired."[9] Assisted by the AUD, Sadlowski won election as head of the Steelworkers of America's largest district, in Chicago, but failed in his bid for the international presidency at the head of an insurgent ticket in 1973.

Several foundations supported the Sadlowski group's second bid in 1977 by funding extensive monitoring supervised by the AUD. Grants were also made to insurgent groups in other unions, including the Teamsters for a Democratic Union (TDU). Not surprisingly, such funding provoked hostility to foundations from established unions. The newsletter of a Detroit local of the International Brotherhood of Electrical Workers, also the target of an insurgent movement backed by the AUD, commented, "[The AUD] . . . receives a major portion of its finances from large tax exempt foundations that were established by corporate interests. For example, the Rockefeller Family Fund. . . . Makes you wonder why the Rockefellers are so interested in 'union democracy,' doesn't it?" Replying, the AUD noted that two official sections of the AFL-CIO (the Coalition of Labor Union Women and the A. Philip Randolph Institute) received funds from the Rockefeller Family Fund, that AFL-CIO president Lane Kirkland and UAW Public Review Board member Eleanor Holmes Norton had been Rockefeller Foundation board members, and that the New York AFL-CIO had backed Nelson Rockefeller in his gubernatorial campaign against labor lawyer Arthur Goldberg. "So," concluded Benson in the AUD newsletter, "our labor officials . . . support Rockefellers for high public office. They welcome Rockefeller support. But their eyebrows lift with affected horror only when checks are made out for union democracy. What bothers them is not who gives the money but for what."[10]

Still, even liberal labor leaders frown on such intervention, however well meant. Unions that are targets of insurgents are particularly hostile. The grounds on which the Steelworkers union sued eight foundations and the AUD in 1978 for supporting a project to ensure fairness in the Sadlowski election were that the foundations' investment portfolios made them "employers," who are prohibited by the Landrum Griffin Act from supporting candidates in union elections. The suit was dismissed because the funds were not earmarked for candidates, but the AUD's Benson reported, "Half our foundations got cold feet and pulled away."[11]

Ten years later, in 1989, the International Brotherhood of Teamsters sought another way of curbing foundation involvement in union democracy movements. Into a consent decree with the federal government to settle RICO (Racketeer-Influenced Corrupt Organizations) charges of corruption and ties to organized crime, Teamster lawyers slipped language to prohibit candidates for union office from accepting funds from outsiders—redundant because existing law carried such a prohibition.[12] Nevertheless, the AUD was able to get foundation funding for its Teamster Fair Election Project. The consent decree opened the way to the first secret rank-and-file vote for officers of the International Brotherhood of Teamsters, which Ronald Carey won on a reform platform in 1991. Carey's narrow victory in 1996 for reelection against the challenge of James Hoffa Jr. was invalidated the following year by a federal monitor because of financial irregularities in the campaign. Carey was also barred from running in a new election.

The rationale for foundations supporting insurgents in the internal affairs of unions was expressed by Phil Sparks, a former mine union official: "It is similar to foundation intervention where human or civil rights are being violated. In autocratic situations where entrenched union leadership commands great financial and legal resources, funding of union members seeking a democratic organization is an attempt to level the playing field."[13]

More than thirty-five years ago George Meany urged members of the AFL-CIO to read Solomon Barkin's book on the decline of the labor movement, which included warnings of the effects of corruption on union effectiveness and public perception.[14] That message took a long time to sink in, but reform elements have prevailed in several major unions. In at least one— UAW dissidents' New Directions Fund (supported for several years by the New World Foundation)—the union democracy movement has taken on new dimensions. The group's leader, Jerry Tucker, inspired by Brookwood Labor College and the Highlander Folk Center, has created schools for union activists "not only to receive tactical and strategic training, but also to help them think about the larger relationship between labor and capital."[15] Tucker's "Solidarity Schools" are thus reminiscent of past union efforts to promote class consciousness and solidarity alongside struggles for bread-and-butter victories. New Directions' goal of creating "a new vision for the labor movement" and encouraging closer ties between workers and intellectuals (the Solidarity Schools are attended by writers, college teachers, and labor educators along with rank-and-file workers and local union officers and staff) resonate with the platform of John Sweeney's new administration at the AFL-CIO. Further expansion of union democracy would serve the labor movement's major new emphasis on stronger organizing efforts.

14

Organizing

The industrial model of unionism that emerged in the 1930s in response to the needs of blue-collar males toiling in large industrial plants is increasingly outmoded for today's transformed work environment, where technological innovations and services are overturning traditional work structures, roles, and functions. The growing use of part-time and contingent workers and "consultants" poses complex questions about the application and enforcement of the Fair Labor Standards Act and labor-management regulations. Contingent workers receive lower hourly wages and fewer—if any—employer-paid benefits than their full-time counterparts, and part-timers may be excluded from federal minimum wage and overtime provisions. So unions are beginning to turn their energies toward organizing and representing the interests of such workers.[1]

One of the least visible but most substantive connections between organized philanthropy and labor unions was forged over two decades by the Youth Project, a public foundation established in 1970. With roots in the civil rights, women's, student, and anti-Vietnam movements, the Project sought to respond to a broadly felt sense of hopelessness. It assisted hundreds of community-based organizations throughout the country with funds and technical assistance on fund-raising, legal matters, and other management affairs. Financing, which averaged $1 million a year, came from established foundations, corporations, churches, and individual donors, some of whom used the project as a vehicle to insure anonymity.[2]

The Youth Project also sought to raise the level of consciousness among mainstream foundations and other funders about the importance of grass-

172

roots organizing. It often served as an intermediary, opening doors to New York foundations for struggling organizations that lacked access. Labor-related organizations and projects were the most difficult to interest other funders in, recalls Karen Paget, executive director from 1981 to 1985, among them the Teamsters Rank and File Educational and Legal Defense Fund (TRF), arm of Teamsters for a Democratic Union.[3] The Project assisted the TRF's expansion to Appalachia and the efforts of the Women's Employment Information Service to give women their fair share of jobs in the coal industry. Miners for Democracy was stimulated by a Project organizer, Ed James, who joined with Don Stillman, then a journalism teacher at West Virginia State University. Stillman had started *Miner's Voice*, a crucial alternative to the Boyle-controlled union newsletter. After the MFD won, both went into service with the union.

Labor-related grants funded organizations concerned with issues ranging from the environment and occupational health and safety to tax policy. In San Diego and other cities, the Project assisted in organizing domestic workers around work-related and social issues.[4] Occasionally unions were assisted directly, as in the case of Local 925 of the Service Employees International Union (SEIU) in its effort to organize clerical workers in the Boston area. In addition to grants for the Association for Union Democracy, the Project gave funds in Seattle to a Rank and File Committee for its efforts to overcome racial and sexual discrimination within unions. In Greenville, South Carolina, aid was given to enable a Workers' Rights Project to address issues of unjust firings, polygraph testing, blacklisting, and lack of job security.

"Although the Project's direct contact with organized labor was limited," says Paget, "we were keenly aware that there was a war on for the soul of labor within labor. We were alert to which unions were at the grassroots and which were not." Present and future union officials served on the Project board, including Stillman (United Auto Workers) and James Andrews, secretary-treasurer of the North Carolina AFL-CIO. "Our basic mission was organization of voiceless and powerless people," says Paget. Many Youth Project staff had roots in the Saul Alinsky organizational approach, and Alinsky's critique of organized labor was that it no longer cared about organizing the unorganized. "We, along with organizations like Citizen Action, sought to build alliances, such as those between working-class whites—union or non-union—and racial minorities. We saw that antagonism between them, coming in part out of the Vietnam conflict and the candidacy of George Wallace, was shattering the entire base for social reform."[5]

Paget's successor, Margery Tabankin, recalls that the Youth Project's funders viewed union democracy efforts and union/community coalitions (whether on health, environmental, or other issues) from a civil liberties perspective. "Labor was bigger than we were," she says, "and after Reuther few unions pursued a social agenda, so we were not interested in helping unions organize just to serve their own members. But when unions could unite with grassroots people on White Lung, Brown Lung, nuclear, and energy issues, or when we could help level the playing field in a union plagued by corrupt and abusive power, our funders were attracted."[6]

The Project's most dramatic engagement with a labor struggle centered on the Brookside coal mine strike of 1973–74. As a Project evaluator described the situation, the mine's owner, Duke Power Company, "launched a vicious union busting campaign, importing scabs by the busload, invoking the contempt of court and injunctive power of local judges to prevent miners from picketing, directing local law enforcement authorities to arrest miners' wives when they came to uphold the picket lines . . . and refusing to bargain."[7] The Project helped assemble a citizens' public inquiry, composed of distinguished academic and public figures. Leslie Dunbar, president of the Field Foundation, which helped finance the panel, speaking of exploitation of coal miners, noted, "Only now and then has resistance arisen and been effective. One of those times was 1974 at Brookside, when the Youth Project helped focus workers' desperation and win some relief from injustice."[8] Supported by Project grants, the Duke Power Project was organized by the Institute for Southern Studies and the North Carolina Public Interest Research Group. Analyzing the Duke Power Company's corporate structure and rate increase requests, the research group "led a public outcry that combined themes of consumer rip-off and mineworkers repression," Dunbar said. In the aftermath of the killing of a striker by a company foreman, the company settled the strike. The real outcome, a Youth Project evaluation noted, "was that young activists had innovated a whole new model of organizing going far beyond the particular workplace or grievance. They helped build strong local support for the strikers and the union . . . [and] reached out into other communities, . . . made the struggle regional and even national."[9] The Project also assisted Barbara Kopple with her Academy Award–winning film about the strike, *Harlan County USA*.

Under the pressure of financial and organizational difficulties, the Youth Project closed its doors in 1992.

The stepped-up drive to build union membership since John Sweeney became president is based at the AFL-CIO's Organizing Institute, set up in 1989 to concentrate on recruiting and training young organizers, especially from minority and working-class backgrounds. Half the trainees are staff members sent by their unions. Richard Bensinger, its director, notes, "We try to tap the idealism of college students, some of whom may be skeptical or ignorant of the labor movement. Those who complete the program and take union jobs learn that labor organizing is a tough career, in which ideal-ism carries you only to a point. Many of the new recruits are the sons and daughters of people who have been downsized."[10]

Although the Organizing Institute receives no foundation funds, two re-lated organizations do—the National Organizers Alliance and Jobs with Jus-tice. Since it was founded in 1993, the NOA has attracted three thousand dues-paying members among labor and community organizers. It sponsors a pension plan for organizers who work for groups too small to have pen-sions. The NOA's founder, Kim Fellner, a veteran of twenty years in union organizing, broke the ice at the left-wing National Network of Grantmak-ers by holding a labor roundtable at its 1994 annual convention. She recalls:

> NNG, many of whose members support liberal movements in Central America, was at arm's length from unions in part because of the AFL-CIO's hostility toward such movements. There is a cultural strain on the left, including progressive foundations, that is a lot more "touchy-feely" than the real lives of low-wage workers. But I have been talking to foun-dations about the importance of having a strong labor movement if they want to maintain a healthy progressive presence in this country at all. It is in their interests to look at the whole union organizing sector differently from the way they have been.[11]

Fourteen national unions participate in Jobs with Justice, established in 1987 as an outgrowth of a machinists' strike against Eastern Airlines. A na-tional community/labor coalition is supported by Veatch, the Funding Ex-change, and other "alternative-type" foundations. "Although this support is helpful, we have not tried the big foundations because we do not want to be beholden to them," says Fred Azcarati, director of JWJ. "Also, organizing is a long-term process, and foundations do not stay with most projects long enough."[12]

Worker Centers

At the same time, immigrant and minority workers ignored by traditional unions are creating worker centers throughout the country to improve their working conditions, again with funding from alternative-type foundations. The centers, for which Asian and Latina women are mainly responsible, fill a vacuum left by the failure of existing unions to address low-wage and other conditions in sweatshops (employers who regularly violate wage-and-hour, child-labor, and safety and health regulations). "That regular unions have not done so is a combination of lack of will and the weak condition of the labor movement before the election of John Sweeney," says Jeanine Appelman, a former program officer at the Jewish Fund for Justice and onetime community organizer in the Midwest. She doubts that such groups will seek union affiliation:

> There is a lot of bad feeling about unions. Moreover, these worker centers embrace a much broader role, serving such needs as child care and teaching English as a second language (ESL). They also do what the most profound organizing efforts have always sought to accomplish—they transform the people involved. For example, a number of women workers who were battered wives and mothers have learned to turn around the rest of their lives. Also, the children of members tend to do better in school.[13]

Worker centers are suspicious of contractual relationships, observes Seth Borgos of the Veatch Program (Unitarian Universalist Church), a major funder. "They take on specific grievances, but see disputes as a way of educating worker communities, building indigenous leadership. Some of them are educating unions about immigrant workplaces, and in fact some large union locals are arising that are very different from traditional unions, in their concern for economic justice and readiness to fight for it."[14]

The national Consortium of Independent Workers' Centers, established in 1994, has eleven members, from Hempstead, New York, to Oakland, California. The group draws a sharp distinction between worker centers and unions. One of its brochure states: "Even the best unions are institutions centered on the collective bargaining process. Workers' centers aren't alternative unions or pre-union formations, but places for workers to address all their needs using every tactic necessary. Centers may support particular bargaining struggles, but as tactics in the broader fight for liberation."[15] And they are effective with employers. The groups are small and local, but often the local victories they achieve have ripple effects. The actions of the Asian Immigrant Women's Advocates (AIWA) in Oakland, for example, shook up the garment industry throughout the state, prompting state agencies to improve enforcement of workplace regulations.

Foundations—by providing seed money for organizing before income from dues sustains their budgets—are critical to worker centers. This relationship has met opposition from some unions. For example, Rosenberg and several other foundations have assisted the AIWA, a civil rights–style organization that exerts pressure and builds national awareness. "While AIWA supports the International Ladies Garment Workers Union [now UNITE]," according to Kirke Wilson of Rosenberg, "it is unlikely to accept traditional collective bargaining. Its objective is the restructuring of labor relations—making the manufacturer responsible for the sins of the contractor rather than site-by-site organizing, recognition, and bargaining."[16]

Home care is a rapidly expanding occupation for low-income workers, and with foundation assistance, they can turn to organizations such as the long-established Women for Economic Justice in Boston, which obtained a grant from the Haymarket People's Fund for a Home Care Workers' Campaign to raise wages and job status. The campaign affiliated with a program in the Bronx (supported by the New York Community Trust) that trained home health care aides to develop a workers' cooperative. Household Worker Rights, in San Francisco, received a grant from the San Francisco Foundation to press for enforcement of legislation covering household employment.

The AFL-CIO, showing greater awareness of immigrant workers than in the past, has created the California Immigrant Workers Association, a Latino group. "Latinos have faced a long history of rejection . . . by a number of institutions—labor included—which has forced this community to develop a strong sense of self reliance," says Joel Ochoa, a CIWA official. Although waves of anti-immigrant/antiworker attacks over the years weakened Latino mutual aid societies and union locals, Ochoa says that in the face of California's Proposition 187, "labor . . . rose to the occasion and openly defended immigrants by taking a public position and organizing against the initiative. Despite a high level of acceptance among Latinos, labor is still perceived as 'outside' the community. Bureaucratic mistakes and other external factors allowed labor to alienate itself from a changing non-farm workforce. This course can be shifted if labor cultivates roots in the Latino community, by understanding and building upon the tradition of self-reliance."[17]

In South Carolina, the 1,000-member Carolina Alliance for Fair Employment (CAFE) worked with established unions to improve conditions of hotel workers at resorts in Hilton Head and later focused on the conditions of contingent and temporary workers. Serving both nonunion and unionized immigrants workers in Boston (e.g., in SEIU locals of building maintenance workers), the Immigrant Workers Resource Center operates as a broker between immigrants and unions. "Such centers support unions and have some union people on their boards of directors, but their concern is directed to immigrant workers who have connected to their center," observes Henry Allen of the Hyams Foundation, which has a long-standing interest in immigrants and refugees. "They are not interested in developing into union locals. They serve their clients by working through unions, supporting union drives, being advocates for their members in the workplace. For more progressive unions, who see that their future is rooted in the immigrant force, [they] are a real ally and resource."[18]

Union advocates maintain that the tendency of such organizations to distance themselves from the mainstream weakens them. Says one: "An organization interested in empowering low-income workers on the job will languish if it fails to use the weapon of unionization . . . to link itself with the philosophy and institutional support of the national labor movement."[19] Peter Olney, a longtime labor organizer in Los Angeles, welcomes the movement to establish worker centers, especially in immigrant communities, but "confining yourself to providing services and building worker consciousness without collective bargaining and ultimately confronting corporate power doesn't get you far."[20]

Organizing in the South

Nowhere was opposition to unionism more bitter than in the South, and where labor organizing involved black workers, resistance has been particularly intense. Several Southern agencies assisted by foundations have been struggling against such intransigence. One of the earliest, the Georgia Workers Education Service, received the bulk of its financing from 1946 to 1950 from the Rosenwald Fund. Its programs were desegregated, its director remembers, "which restricted its activities with a number of unions and earned it the enmity of others."[21] When Rosenwald funds ran out, the Ella Lyman Cabot Trust supported an Atlanta Labor Education Association.

The Atlanta-based Southern Regional Council, the most ambitious agency for reconciling organized labor with racial justice, was founded in 1944 out of dissatisfaction among liberal blacks and whites with the equivocal approach of the Commission on Interracial Cooperation to desegregation. The SRC attracted foundation support initially from the North, later from the South as well, and for a ten-year period was headed by George M. Mitchell, a former staff member of the CIO's Political Action Committee. The council was assisted during that time by the Whitney, Field, and Ford foundations.[22]

The SRC cooperated with the Jewish Labor Committee on a survey of racial patterns and attitudes in southern unions (with grants from the Fund for the Republic) and then employed, as a full-time labor consultant, Emory Via of the University of Wisconsin Workers School, who had worked on the survey. "The rationale for picking me was straightforward," Via recalls. "It was rare to find a Southern white, of moderately good education, sympathetic and familiar with unions, who was 'right on race' and who had labor education skills." Before joining the council, Via had conducted union staff training institutes in the South with support from the New World Foundation. "The programs brought together twenty or so union staff persons across union and racial lines," he recalls. Living and studying together, they sharpened basic union skills and got a substantial dose of the issues facing a changing South—politically, economically, in race relations in the labor movement, and civil rights.[23] An SRC proposal to the Ford Foundation observed, "Lower-middle-class and lower-income Southern whites are insulated from intellectual and moral leadership toward new patterns of human relations. For example, they typically do not belong to the church denominations actively and unambiguously advocating new outlooks. One of the few institutional settings where a significant number may be reached is within unions."[24] The national staff of the AFL-CIO cooperated with the SRC's efforts, according to Via. "They welcomed having a Southern voice to reach out constructively to unions in the South, and those that were approachable were not always, by a long shot, those with the largest civil rights reputations."[25]

The low-profile but highly effective Institute for Southern Studies in Durham, N.C., founded in 1970, conducts strategic research for labor organizing, and its magazine, *Southern Exposure*, covers labor issues extensively. The Field Foundation and the Stern Family Fund were early supporters of the institute's union work, notably the long struggle of textile unions to organize the J. P. Stevens Company, but union contributions account for less than 1 percent of its funds, and it mutes its connections to organizing. Two-thirds of its $600,000 budget comes from foundations, says Robert Hall, the institute's director. "In our proposals to them we never use the word union. It's OK to talk about grassroots efforts, health, and human suffering, but if something even suggests union-style organizing they will tell us to put it differently." Support from two major North Carolina foundations, the Mary Reynolds Babcock and Z. Smith Reynolds foundations, for the Brown Lung Association (cotton mill dust) and the Women's Center for Economic Alternatives (services for workers in the huge southern poultry industry) has been particularly valuable.[26]

Southerners for Economic Justice (SEJ), also based in Durham, began with funding from the Amalgamated Clothing and Textile Workers to build community support—or at least neutralize antagonism—for labor organizing drives. It is now funded by foundations, church groups, and individuals. Although the SEJ's board includes union officials, Leah Wise, its former director, is somewhat disenchanted with unions, remarking that the North Carolina AFL-CIO, for example, "feels threatened by organizing efforts by non-union, community self-help organizations. Unions have been known to leave just before a certification election, subjecting workers to reprisals. In other cases, unions have started multi-plant organizing drives and then narrowed down from, say, ten [plants] to two and then just one."[27] The SEJ acts as a sounding board for worker grievances, conducts research on plant closings, racial discrimination, and health and environmental hazards, and lobbies for legislative reforms, as in the aftermath of fire in a Hamlet, North Carolina, poultry plant that took twenty-five lives, injured sixty, and left twenty orphaned children and two hundred unemployed workers.

The Z. Smith Reynolds and Mary Reynolds Babcock foundations have funded several agencies in North Carolina that help working women deal with workplace problems: Working Women's Organizing Project, Southeast Regional Economic Justice Network, Center on Women's Economic Alternatives, Women in the Work Force, and N.C. Association of Working Women 9 to 5. Reynolds also funds an A. Philip Randolph Institute program in the state enabling students from black colleges to serve internships with black union members.

The continuing plight of workers in the region has been described by SEJ officials: "We are witnessing plant closings; the demise of black-owned farms and farmers; a rising incidence of workplace injuries and deaths; forced overtime and violations of wage, hour, and child labor laws; workers' compensation under siege; severe environmental contamination, particularly in communities of color; increasing racist violence; and the emergence of contingent work as the fastest growing job sector."[28]

Not only do blacks now make up an estimated 21 percent of total union membership, a higher percentage than that of blacks in the total population, but organized labor has begun to recognize that its greatest potential for growth lies among service and government employees where blacks and other minorities are a growing proportion, and in sectors largely unorganized and populated by low-wage minority workers, including immigrants.[29] More than ever, then, organized labor's embrace of blacks and other minorities will become a necessity, not only an act of racial justice.

15

Prospects

A major shift of strategy by the labor movement, and of attitudes toward it by various parts of the public, began with the changing of the guard at the AFL-CIO in 1995 when John Sweeney was elected president in the first contested election in the organization's history. Enhancing the new look was the elevation of Richard Trumka (head of the United Mine Workers and veteran of the foundation-supported Miners for Democracy movement) to secretary-treasurer, and election of the first woman to a top office (executive vice president), Linda Chavez-Thompson of AFSCME.

Sweeney's accession energized labor's outreach to old and new constituencies, including the intellectual-academic community, with which foundations have always had an affinity. The strong bonds liberals and intellectuals forged with organized labor in the 1930s and 1940s had loosened after World War II. Disenchantment arose from disclosures of corruption and racketeering, jurisdictional disputes, featherbedding, denial of the democratic rights of members, and, as one historian put it, "the failure of spirit and imagination to stage forceful drives for new adherents in territories untouched by unions."[1] Union purges of Communist elements and continued discrimination against minorities also cooled the ardor of many intellectuals. Unflagging AFL-CIO loyalty to White House policies throughout the cold war, and during the Vietnam War in particular, further distanced labor from potential allies among intellectuals. But one month after Sweeney's election, forty-three men and women representing the top rank of American sociologists, economists, historians, editors, and philosophers issued a statement celebrating "the rebirth of a strong and progressive labor movement." The statement declared:

181

We believe the revitalization of the American labor movement can fashion a new politics of social solidarity and economic justice, and reverse the country's descent into the kind of mean-spirited selfishness that so discolors the contemporary political scene. . . . As intellectuals, educators, and professionals we . . . extend our support and cooperation to this new leadership and pledge our solidarity with those in the AFL-CIO dedicated to the cause of union democracy and the remobilization of a dynamic new labor movement.[2]

In October 1996, some of the signatories organized a labor teach-in at Columbia University. It drew an overflow crowd of 1,700 and was followed by two dozen teach-ins around the country.

Another group moving closer to organized labor consisted of religious leaders, echoing the tenets of the nineteenth century's social gospel movement. Drawing support from foundations and unions, the National Interfaith Committee for Worker Justice was organized in 1996 to encourage dialogues with employers and workers and among the clergy and congregants on labor issues. In several cities the clergy's support for unions is expressed in sermons, petitions, pastoral letters, protest marches, sit-ins, and meetings with corporate management. The rationale for action was voiced by Paul Sherry, president of the 1.5 million-member United Church of Christ: "By being more supportive of trade unions, we do not intend to be anti-business. As religious leaders, we're trying to find ways to assist a society to become more balanced in terms of the way it allocates its benefits. We believe the balance is now against working people, and has to be righted."[3]

The years following the Sweeney election brought an unprecedented wave of direct and conscious foundation action. For example:

- A Task Force on the Future of the American Labor Movement (made up of labor and business leaders, government officials, and academics) was established by the Twentieth Century Fund in 1995. In the belief that profound changes in the economy create "a need for fundamental institutional and behavioral transformations that would strengthen the ability of unions to help workers regain [their] sense of security," the task force set out to examine how labor should apportion its time and resources among organizing efforts, labor-management cooperation, services to members, political activities, and observance of international labor standards.[4] Consistent with this agenda, John Sweeney advocated an alliance between business and labor to increase corporate competitiveness and promote social equity in a rapidly changing workplace by treating workers as assets, through training and cooperation, instead of cutting wages and laying workers off.[5]

- The New World and other foundations in 1996 established the Phoenix Fund for Workers and Communities, which makes grants and administers contributions from foundations and individuals who do not want to be identified with supporting unions or economic justice. The Phoenix Fund focuses on empowering the working poor (union and nonunion) to challenge such practices as denial of benefits to contingent workers, the exploitation of immigrants in sweatshops, and health hazards in unregulated industries.

- Also in 1996, the Ford Foundation began a major program titled "Business, Labor, and Community: Redefining Accountability," directed toward new social and economic challenges faced by American society. Under it, for example, a $500,000 grant was made to the Center on Wisconsin Strategy at the University of Wisconsin to link labor and community groups in promoting sustainable economic development and to rebuild local and regional central labor councils. Through a newly funded Institute for Work and Employment Research at the Massachusetts Institute of Technology, a multidisciplinary task force is analyzing possible changes in the governance of the labor market—laws and regulations, training and education systems, unions and professional associations, and the structure of corporate decision making.

- Smaller foundations with no previous interest in the labor movement are taking on union-related work. The Discount Foundation, for instance, announced that it would assist projects that defend the rights of workers to join a union and bargain collectively.

- Responding to troublesome new workforce patterns, foundations funded a new organization, Working Today, which targets problems of that growing "nonstandard" part of the workforce (representing 29.4 percent, or more than 36 million workers) that is contingent, part-time, self-employed, temporary, or under independent contract. These workers typically lack job security, health, pension, and other benefits, and labor-law protection. They also earn significantly less than full-time workers in traditional employment.

A salient feature of most of these programs is the inclusion of labor unions as players or as partners with others—business, policy makers, academics. Having for several years (with foundation assistance) joined community coalitions addressing problems ranging from environmental pollution to the living wage, unions in many places have provided models for implementing a central objective of the new AFL-CIO administration—a wider public agenda in partnership with a variety of groups.[6] Reflecting this trend, a new foundation-supported Labor Leadership Forum, developed by the Harvard Trade Union Program, brings together emerging labor leaders with their counterparts in other fields. New conditions also require wider participation by workers within their unions on policies and strategic priorities; a Labor Renewal Project run by the San Francisco–based Organize Training Center and assisted by several foundations trains staff and members of a diverse range of union locals in assessing and renewing their structure, culture, and practices.

Since most foundations operate at local and regional, rather than national, levels (including, of course, community foundations, a major part of the foundation universe), they could help meet the challenges presented by the devolution from federal to local responsibility in social welfare. Given their support of welfare reform experiments and evaluations, for example, foundations can shed some light on the nettlesome issue of job competition between welfare clients and the working poor, including unionized employees. In 1995, state employee unions bitterly criticized proposals by major nonprofit organizations for revisions in the welfare system that could eliminate union jobs.[7] In New York, James Butler, president of the Municipal Hospital Workers Union, argued, "Because these workers are filling these jobs under the threat of loss of their welfare benefits, they are, in effect, indentured servants."[8] Moving beyond such overheated rhetoric, community organizations funded by foundations (for instance, the New York Association of Community Organizations for Reform Now [ACORN] and Baltimoreans United in Leadership Development [BUILD]) began organizing drives to win recognition and bargaining rights for thousands of welfare clients employed in duties ordinarily done by unionized city workers, and unions themselves have signed up workfare clients.

Foundations were well positioned to play expanded roles in other areas of concern to organized labor as the twenty-first century approached. Wage stagnation, massive layoffs at both blue-collar and managerial levels, and the export of jobs to low-wage countries in the 1990s, along with the growth of outsourcing and part-time work (which was the crux of the massive United Parcel Service strike in 1997), have heightened the issue of corporate accountability, a concern of many foundations. Foundation assets were $226.7 billion in 1995, and labor's capital was even greater—an estimated $5 trillion in deferred worker wages in pension funds and retirement plans, including $1.5 trillion in collectively bargained plans—altogether nearly one-third of all U.S. financial assets. As substantial stockholders, unions and foundations had begun to challenge questionable corporate practices (as they had done with respect to investments in South Africa during apartheid, for example). Unions were also in the lead among proxy activists (52 percent of the dollar total of stock held by such activists in 1996). In environmental affairs, several foundations that owned stock in the giant computer-chip manufacturer Intel Corporation prodded it to respond to concerns over toxic chemicals released during its production process.[9] The Teamsters Pension Fund, with $46 billion heavily invested in major corporations, issued a list of the "least valuable" board members of poorly performing companies with highly paid CEOs, in an "attempt to put a face on inefficient board oversight."[10]

Since the 1960s, several foundations have added "social benefit" to their criteria for investing assets, without sacrificing returns that traditional investment would yield. The Foundation Partnership on Corporate Responsibility was formed in 1996, in cooperation with the Interfaith Center on Corporate Responsibility, to provide information to foundations that planned to become more active shareholders. This step paralleled the creation of an AFL-CIO Department of Corporate Affairs, to promote new strategies for the use of labor's capital through "shared capitalism." For example, "One could increase the amount of capital available for 'high road' [quality, innovation, and service competition] rather than 'low-road' [wage competition] economic development which has adversely affected American labor markets and led to depressed family incomes," observes Lance Lindblom of the Ford Foundation. "Different labor capital strategies could limit some of the potential deleterious effects of economic globalization, curb domestic investments' sensitivity to speculative international capital flows, reducing capital market volatility. Such changes could be of great interest to the business community by increasing the amount of capital for investment while reducing pressures for short-term profits."[11] In this spirit, the AFL-CIO Housing Investment Trust targets investments in affordable housing in poor neighborhoods, and a Union-Labor Life Insurance Company was investing in construction projects using union labor to ensure good wages.[12]

At the same time, the concept of corporate social responsibility—embracing sympathetic policies on issues ranging from the environment to affirmative action—has come under strong attack by conservatives as being inimical to stockholder rights. Such an assault runs counter to a long history of efforts by corporations to act as public-minded citizens. Even the 1920s brand of welfare capitalism, calculated in large part to squelch union organizing, acknowledged the need for sensitivity to employee needs and support of government social services. In a larger sense, the drumbeat of criticism is a throwback to the division in corporate America on the New Deal—which on the one hand was viewed as a prelude to socialism, on the other as a means of rescuing capitalism.

Structural change wrought by advancing technology is hardly new in American industry. In the 1920s, technology that revolutionized factories resulted in the first decline of workers in manufacturing while output increased 60 percent. Despite plant closings and downsizing, productivity in American manufacturing rose since the 1980s and in the service sector since the early 1990s. The income gap between the rich and the middle class and poor grew. Between 1968 and 1994 it widened by 22.4 percent; the income of the richest fifth of the population expanded to 49.1 percent from 42.8 percent, while that of the lowest fifth inched up only 8 percent.[13] At the same time, work has become more cerebral and abstract. The earnings differential between the well educated and the less educated was steadily widening. In 1995 the MacArthur Foundation's Working Poor Project estimated that while by 2005 half the new jobs would require only a high school education, none of those was projected to pay enough to cover even a minimal budget for a family with two children—a living wage defined as about $23,000 a year.

The connection between education and economic status has long been recognized. In 1960 John Gardner, president of Carnegie Corporation, noted that young people who dropped out of high school had an even harder time than those who did not go on to college. Criticizing employers and unions, he said, "Neither . . . welcome [youth's] appearance on the labor market, and juvenile unemployment is a serious problem today, particularly in the big cities. It may become considerably more serious in the years ahead."[14]

Foundations have been the most consistent source of nongovernmental support for improved education, and it seems obvious that they and unions should collaborate in this enterprise—foundations learning more about workplace needs from unions, and unions supporting policies that encourage more government, philanthropic, and corporate investment in public education and reform, along the lines followed by the National Research Council. John Sweeney, recognizing these new opportunities, wrote several years ago:

> Historically there has been a certain amount of mutual suspicion on the part of labor unions and philanthropic organizations. However, at present there seems to be a major convergence in the goals of both entities, especially in the inseparable matters of education and economic development. I think it would be very advantageous for foundations and unions to collaborate on activities. . . . Foundations want to educate minorities and the disenfranchised; unions, to a great extent, represent them. Unions make natural conduits to a foundation's targeted population. To use SEIU's one million members as an example, over 30 per cent are minorities, 50 per cent women.[15]

Unions and foundations have also been challenged by onrushing economic globalization. With the vast sum of $1 trillion traded daily on foreign exchange markets, national economic sovereignty has been greatly reduced. Capital is organized across national lines; labor is not, and progressives are deeply concerned that workers are being played off against one another worldwide, as capital seeks the lowest-wage, least-organized labor force. For a long time unions were complicit, argued Professor Orlando Patterson at the Columbia University labor teach-in, because the lost jobs affected "second tier" largely nonunion workers—minorities, women, Appalachian whites. Patterson urged unions to recognize that cheap, illegal labor introduced to control the supply of labor worsens joblessness among the urban poor and drives down domestic wages.[16]

Foundations have established a precedent for fostering organized labor abroad, strengthening unions in South Africa and Eastern Europe. American unions, too, are involved; the United Electrical Workers and the Teamsters, for example, help the Authentic Labor Front, Mexico's independent labor federation, maintain a Workers' Center in Ciudad Juárez, across the border from El Paso, which deals with conditions in the area's U.S.-owned maquiladoras.[17] The ARCA Foundation supports three organizations that monitor international codes of behavior toward workers—the Labor Institute, the International Labor Rights Fund, and the U.S.-Guatemala Labor Education Project. Four foundation-assisted organizations (Cornell University's School of Industrial and Labor Relations, the Economic Policy Institute, the Institute for Policy Studies, and the International Labor Rights Fund) and the AFL-CIO began working together in 1997 (along with representatives from developing countries) to craft policies to deal with economic globalization. Specifically, their aims were to prevent abuse of workers' rights in countries to which American and other corporations have shifted production to take advantage of cheap and compliant labor; to promote competition on the basis of factors other than lower wages, and to devise trade and investment policies that benefit workers and strengthen their communities. The targets include overseas subcontracting, through which corporations obtain products without owning or operating factories abroad; it is estimated that there are more than 10 million children under the age of fourteen in bonded labor in South Asia alone.[18]

Is there something in the makeup and outlook of foundations that has inhibited closer ties to organized labor? Most foundation trustees and many staff members belong at least to the middle class, if not an "overclass."[19] Does that preclude their dealing with unions? Or is the problem that the *unions* are too middle class and foundations are fixated on the downtrodden, as asserted by Peter Frumkin, a former foundation official who has studied foundation staffs?[20] That is hardly borne out by the variety of items on foundation agendas—not only poverty, social welfare, employment training, and related issues, but also the arts, higher education, environmental quality, and other middle-class interests. And in fact unions are less terra incognita than Frumkin supposes. In addition to the initiatives of the 1990s noted above, a consortium of more than one hundred private and community foundations and corporate givers, called the Neighborhood Funders Group (NFG), added unions to their interests. The NFG in 1997 set up a Working Group on Organized Labor and Communities, declaring, "Organized labor . . . represents a potential ally of enormous significance for low-income and working class communities. . . . Many unions have established a credible record of working with community-based organizations on issues such as affordable housing, job training, health care, day care, voter registration, and living wage campaigns. A number of funders have supported these efforts."[21]

Moreover, foundations are likely to become more sensitive to organized labor as more white-collar and professional workers become unionized. Fifty years ago, Edward Wieck of the Russell Sage Foundation wrote: "The manual workers need the white collar and professional workers in the labor movement, and the latter need the labor movement just as badly. . . . Any worker, whatever may be his trade or profession, who fails to join with his fellow workers in the labor movement neglects not only his own interests but the interests of the country as well."[22] Enough professionals had joined the labor movement by the late 1990s—schoolteachers, college faculty, nurses, resident physicians—to be a factor in the hospitals, universities, and other nonprofit organizations with which foundations deal.[23] An increase in the number of unionized nonprofit institutions has been forecast. In large part this prediction is based on the fact that government is a major source of income for most types of nonprofit organizations, and the number of employees belonging to public sector unions has been on the rise.[24] In addition, foundations were increasing direct contact with labor leaders at the national and local levels since the new AFL-CIO administration. The labor movement began recruiting staff from foundation ranks. More significant, the AFL-CIO hired a full-time staff person in 1998 to serve as liaison with the foundation community—the former executive director of the Arca Foundation, Janet Shenk.[25]

In "Dear Brother Sweeney," an open letter to the new president of the AFL-CIO, the labor lawyer and author Thomas Geoghegan proffered a basketful of advice, including "Ask to get on every foundation board you can."[26] In fact, at the time of Sweeney's election fewer labor leaders were on foundation boards than there had been twenty years earlier, and even then they had constituted no more than a handful. In 1949 Edwin Embree, president of the Rosenwald Fund, deplored the absence of labor representation on the boards of large foundations, coupling that with criticism of foundations for not following Rosenwald's lead in placing blacks on their boards. But Embree disputed the claims of some critics that trustees used the power of foundations to bolster the status quo and oppose change. "The real criticism is not that foundations are vicious but that they are inert," he said.[27]

By the mid-1950s, C. Wright Mills pointed out, members of a "labor elite" were sharing the stage with business and other leaders (receiving honorary degrees, seats on college boards, and appointments to prestigious commissions), but seats on foundation boards were not among the accoutrements of status and prestige.[28] Beginning in the 1970s, many foundation boards became more diverse in race and gender, but seldom added men and women from the labor movement. Carnegie Corporation provided an early exception by creating a "labor seat" on its board when Alan Pifer became president in 1966. It was first held by Howard Samuel, head of the Industrial Union Department of the AFL-CIO, then by Thomas R. Donahue, secretary-treasurer of the AFL-CIO.[29] Glenn Watts, president of the Communications Workers of America, served on the board of the Ford Foundation, but when he left in 1988 no other union member was appointed; in fact the proportion of business executives grew. Other exceptions were Lane Kirkland, former president of the AFL-CIO, on the Rockefeller Foundation board, and Albert Shanker of the American Federation of Teachers, on the boards of the Spencer Foundation and the Twentieth Century Fund.[30]

As unions build coalitions with environmental, civil rights, senior citizen, and other advocacy groups, many of which receive foundation support, labor's political influence may be expected to grow. The boundaries of foundation political engagement have been stretched over the last two decades by the growing size and number of grants from conservative foundations like Olin and Bradley to right-wing organizations and publications—for example, the Heritage Foundation, the Hudson Institute, and similar think tanks, and the *American Spectator* and *New Criterion* magazines. The output of conservative centers feeds into the right-wing agendas of politicians as well as activist right-wing groups. Of course what's good for the goose should be good for the gander, and union-friendly think tanks such as the Economic Policy Institute do enjoy foundation support. But liberal foundations have not developed the comprehensive funding strategies, political goals, and media acumen of conservative foundations. Also, the latter vastly outspend their progressive counterparts, four-to-one, according to a study by the Center for Policy Alternatives.[31]

Conclusion

Unlike their engagement with traditional fields such as education and health, foundations' relations with organized labor have been neither tidy, continuous, nor always perceived as such. But as this book makes clear, the arena for these relations has been wide and varied. Research is the most continuous thread, but conflict is also part of the story, and sometimes, as with the Rockefeller Foundation's foray into industrial relations experiments after the Ludlow Massacre, or the Ford Foundation's role in New York City's school decentralization reform, interventions have had unintended consequences.

Although foundations have generally flinched from controversy (in different places at different times the very word *union* was controversial), some grasped the nettle, combating racial discrimination, intransigence toward labor organizing, and offenses against worker health and safety. Foundations generally claim to stand above the battle, but many have tackled heated union-related public policy issues, ranging from the Wagner Act of the 1930s to NAFTA in the 1990s.

The foundation players have included giants—Ford, Rockefeller, and Carnegie—and such little-known ones as the Garland and Shalan funds. Historic steps were taken by some of the oldest foundations, such as Russell Sage, and others that no longer exist, such as the Rosenwald and Stern funds. Newcomers such as the Annie E. Casey Foundation have undertaken important initiatives. Also involved have been self-styled "progressive" foundations such as the North Star Fund, despite their ambivalence toward labor's social and political stance. And avowedly conservative foundations of the 1980s and 1990s have financed groups espousing an antiunion ideology.

Union attitudes toward institutional philanthropy have ranged from downright hostility, as in calls for Congress to limit the lifetime of foundations, to collaboration, as in voter registration and community development projects. Foundation executives' attitudes have ranged from the disdain of John D. Rockefeller Sr.'s confidant Frederick Gates, to the empathy of John D. Rockefeller Jr.'s foundation steward Raymond Fosdick, to the ardor of Russell Sage's Mary Van Kleeck. In between is the indifference of most of the upper-class men and women who populated foundation boards almost exclusively until the last quarter of the twentieth century, and of middle-class professionals who staff the foundations. Some philanthropoids take a cautiously sympathetic interest in organized labor, but there are few out-and-out partisans.

Foundations have never been immune to general public perceptions, so the decline of unions and a widespread, longstanding impression of them as obsolescent—if not corrupt—inhibited foundations from any strong embrace of the labor movement. Despite unions' 16.2 million members (45 million when dependents are included) and their status as the country's largest organized social force apart from religion, the labor movement has not consistently inspired confidence. And for a community that prides itself on knowledge and broad perspectives, foundations often seemed to suffer from amnesia regarding organized labor's part in public policy innovations in the general interest—social security, unemployment insurance, and the minimum wage—and in fueling economic growth by increasing consumer demand. Nor did they credit unions for being the most consistent mechanism for closing the race and gender wage gaps, and for disproportionately representing African American and Hispanic workers.

Still, foundations and unions share certain ideals. Foundations express them in broad statements of mission (the Rockefeller Foundation's "Toward the Well-Being of Mankind," the Ford Foundation's "To Advance Human Welfare"). Organized labor's desires were expressed a century ago by Samuel Gompers in terms that resonate: "What does labor want? It wants the earth and the fullness thereof . . . . We want more schoolhouses and less jails; more books and less arsenals; more learning and less vice; more constant work and less crime; more leisure and less greed; more justice and less revenge."[1]

At mid-century, although Walter Reuther had concluded that socialism per se was unattainable in the American environment, he aimed, as his biographer put it, "to lead organized labor beyond the specifics of economic gains to a broad, progressive role in society at large." Labor's struggles, Reuther believed, "were linked intimately with the plight of the poor and the powerless everywhere."[2] This vision faded in the next decades as labor concentrated on wage and benefit gains and bargaining for union members alone.[3] Union workers who arrived in the middle class increasingly distanced themselves from the working poor. Nevertheless, Reuther's ideal of lifting the entire working class appeared to be renewed in an AFL-CIO Executive Council mission statement in 1996: "to bring economic justice to the workplace and social justice to our nation." If the union movement follows up by organizing the unorganized and forcefully advocating progressive social and economic policies—restoring the social mission of labor—it can profit from the rich store of experience among foundations that address such issues. Mark Elliott of the Ford Foundation expressed it well in 1996:

> The challenges facing us as grantmakers and practitioners are not small. If the globalization of markets is reducing national sovereignty, what does that imply for communities? If firms are able to shift their functions within a worldwide network of people and facilities, what does this turbulence imply for workers? For the already unemployed? Who better than we to enter these debates about the common good? For we are blessed with the rare ability to invest resources that can make a difference in how problems are understood and solved; how the debate is framed and undertaken; and how communities respond.[4]

Yet despite their contributions to American society, foundations and unions also share an uncertain claim to the confidence of the public—even a stigma, one might say. Unions, assailed as threats to the social order in their early history, are now tarred as a "special interest," even as their strength has faded. Foundations have been criticized as unaccountable, privileged-class instigators of ultraliberal (if not subversive) activities, at odds with the wishes of their founders. Lester M. Solomon director of the Johns Hopkins Institute for Policy Studies and a foremost analyst of the philanthropic community, remarked that the nonprofit sector, of which foundations are a prominent part, "has been implicated in the general assault on . . . the American version of the welfare state and is being painted with the same broad brush of criticism."[5]

Intellectual dialogue began swirling in the mid-1990s around calls for renewal of civil society—the middle ground between government and the business sector. The political scientist Benjamin R. Barber cautioned against traditional civic institutions such as foundations, schools, and voluntary associations being regarded as "special interests," as unions were "when they tried to break the stranglehold of corporations over labor, [and] were labeled as . . . another special interest group no better than those against whom they struck."[6] Applied by conservative forces that became increasingly adept in swaying public opinion, the "special interest" and "welfare state" labels place unions and foundations on the defensive. The most potent response in gaining public regard might be a common effort by organized labor and philanthropic foundations to see that more people enjoy "the earth and the fullness thereof"—a combined effort more productive than either could make alone. In the historical record disclosed in this book, in developments of the 1990s, and in extraordinary new conditions in the American workplace may lie the seeds of such a new relationship.

Notes

Preface

1. See, for example, Elizabeth A. Fones-Wolf, *Selling Free Enterprise: The Business Assault on Labor and Liberalism, 1945–60* (Urbana: University of Illinois Press, 1994); Sarah Lyons Watts, *Order against Chaos: Business Culture and Labor Ideology in America, 1880–1915* (Westport, Conn.: Greenwood, 1991), pp. 1–31; and Gary Gerstle, *Working Class Americanism: The Politics of Labor in a Textile City, 1914–1960* (New York: Cambridge University Press, 1989).

2. Howard M. Gitelman, *Legacy of the Ludlow Massacre: A Chapter in American Industrial Relations* (Philadelphia: University of Pennsylvania Press, 1988), p. 5.

3. The American Newspaper Guild, which I joined in Dayton, Ohio, withdrew its attempt to represent the newspaper I worked for before a vote could be taken. Later, in New York, I was fired from Paramount News (with the union's acquiescence and a token settlement) for joining the International Association of Theatrical Stage Employees.

4. Gloria Garrett Samson, *The American Fund for Public Service: Charles Garland and Radical Philanthropy, 1922–1941* (Westport, Conn.: Greenwood, 1996).

5. See Daniel J. Leab and Philip P. Mason, eds., *Labor History Archives in the United States: A Guide for Researching and Teaching* (Detroit: Wayne State University Press, 1992).

Introduction: An Untold Tale

1. Maurice F. Neufeld, Daniel J. Leab, and Dorothy Swanson, *American Working Class History: A Representative Bibliography* (New York: Bowker, 1983); John Schacht, "Labor History in the Academy," *Labor's Heritage* 5 (Winter 1994): 4-21; David W. Noble, *The Paradox of Progressive Thought* (Minneapolis: University of Minnesota Press, 1988), pp. 138–41, 150–51, 158–61, 164–65, 172–73.

2. John R. Commons et al., *A Documentary History of American Industrial Society,* 11 vols. (Cleveland: A. H. Clark, 1910–11).

3. Michael H. Frisch and Daniel J. Walkowitz, eds., *Working-Class America: Essays on Labor, Community, and American Society* (Urbana: University of Illinois Press, 1983), p. xi. See also Herbert G. Gutman, *Work, Culture, and Society in Industrializing America* (New York: Vintage Books,

1977); David Brody, ed., *Workers in Industrial America: Essays on Twentieth-Century Struggles*, 2d ed. (New York: Oxford University Press, 1993); David Montgomery, *Workers' Control in America: Studies in the History of Work, Technology, and Labor Struggles* (New York: Cambridge University Press, 1979).

4. Daniel J. Leab, ed., *The Labor History Reader* (Urbana: University of Illinois Press, 1985), p. xiv.

5. Richard Magat, Introduction to Eduard C. Lindeman, *Wealth and Culture: A Study of One Hundred Foundations and Community Trusts and Their Operations during the Decade 1921–1930* (1936; New Brunswick, N.J.: Transaction Books, 1988), p. xxi. See also Richard Magat, "Wilmer Shields Rich: The First Lady of Organized Foundations," *Foundation News*, March/April 1983; "Out of the Shadows: Communications in Foundations," *Foundation News*, September/October 1984.

6. Quoted in Horace Coon, *Money to Burn: Great American Foundations and Their Money* (1938; New Brunswick, N.J.: Transaction Books, 1990), pp. 334–35.

7. U.S. Department of the Treasury, Commission on Private Philanthropy and Public Needs, *Giving in America: Toward a Stronger Voluntary Sector*, 5 vols. (Washington, D.C., 1977).

8. James Douglas, *Why Charity? The Case for a Third Sector* (Beverly Hills, Calif.: Sage, 1983), pp. 29–31.

9. *Report of the Princeton Conference on the History of Philanthropy in the United States* (New York: Russell Sage Foundation, 1956), p. 34. Yet in 1989 I found, in a wide-ranging survey of future research needs in philanthropy and the voluntary sector, that none of some sixty scholars and practitioners interviewed raised the subject. See *Prospective Views of Research on Philanthropy and the Voluntary Sector* (New York: Foundation Center, 1989). A more recent compendium listed only one labor-related project among 372 reported by 407 scholars. See *Research in Progress, 1989–92* (Indianapolis: Indiana University Center on Philanthropy, 1993).

10. It is also commemorated in the title of one of the most informative—and wry—books I encountered during my research, Thomas Geoghegan's *Which Side Are You On? Trying to Be for Labor When It's Flat on Its Back* (New York: Farrar, Straus & Giroux, 1991).

Chapter 1. Social Order, Social Progress

1. Philip S. Foner, *History of the Labor Movement in the United States*, vol. 2, *From the Founding of the American Federation of Labor to the Emergence of American Imperialism* (New York: International Publishers, 1975), p. 384.

2. Toni Gilpin, "New Feet under the Table," *Labor's Heritage* 4 (Spring 1992): 7.

3. Kathleen D. McCarthy, *Noblesse Oblige: Charity and Cultural Philanthropy in Chicago, 1849–1925* (Chicago: University of Chicago Press, 1982), pp. 120–21, 153.

4. New World Foundation, *Annual Report, 1954–61*, p. 5.

5. Union membership declined 30 percent between 1975 and 1991, from 23.7 million to 16.5 million (U.S. Department of Labor). During the same period the number of foundations grew 52.5 percent, from 21,877 to 33,356, and assets increased 113.3 percent, from $1.2 billion to $2.26 billion (in constant 1967 dollars) (Foundation Center).

6. Quoted in Robert H. Wiebe, *Businessmen and Reform: A Study of the Progressive Movement* (Cambridge: Harvard University Press, 1962), pp. 2, 125.

7. David W. Noble, *The Paradox of Progressive Thought* (Minneapolis: University of Minnesota Press, 1958), pp. 139–40.

8. Herbert G. Gutman, *Work, Culture, and Society in Industrializing America* (New York: Vintage Books, 1977), pp. 82–105.

9. Robert H. Wiebe, *The Search for Order, 1977–1920* (New York: Hill & Wang, 1967), p. 138.

10. G. William Domhoff, *The Higher Circles: The Governing Class in America* (New York: Random House, 1970), p. 159.

11. Noble, *Paradox of Progressive Thought*, p. 172.

12. E. Digby Baltzell, *Philadelphia Gentlemen: The Making of a National Upper Class* (Glencoe,

Ill.: Free Press, 1958), pp. 234–36. The social gospel was not entirely a Protestant construct. The encyclical *Rerum novarum* (On the condition of the workers), issued on May 15, 1891, by Pope Leo XIII, was a liberal statement of the view that the "possessing classes," including employers, have important moral duties to fulfill, and one of the first duties of society is to improve the position of workers.

13. Frederick Gates, "Essay on Capital and Labor," in Gates Papers, box 1, folder 9, Rockefeller Archive Center, Pocantico Hills, N.Y.; hereafter RAC.

14. Elizabeth Anne Payne, *Reform, Labor, and Feminism: Margaret Dreier Robins and the Women's Trade Union League* (Urbana: University of Illinois Press, 1988), p. 161.

15. Wiebe, *Search for Order*, p. 157.

16. James Weinstein, *The Corporate Ideal in the Liberal State, 1900–1918* (Boston: Beacon, 1968), p. xiv.

17. Barry D. Karl and Stanley N. Katz, "The American Private Philanthropic Foundation and the Public Sphere, 1890–1930," *Minerva*, Summer 1981, p. 253.

18. Gerald Jonas, *The Circuit Riders: Rockefeller Money and the Rise of Modern Science* (New York: Norton, 1989), p. 35.

19. Andrew Carnegie, *The Gospel of Wealth* (1884; Garden City, N.Y.: Doubleday, Doran, 1933), p. 279. The staying power of Carnegie's exhortation is evident—a century after his remarks—in a statement by Walter Annenberg, a major philanthropist of the present era: "If you have been fortunate economically in life, I think you have a very important obligation to share and support others less fortunate than you. And if you don't understand that you're a rather shabby citizen": "Walter Annenberg's Aim: Give It All Away," *Chronicle of Philanthropy*, January 11, 1994, p. 11.

20. "Wealth—A Decree of Justice," *Independent*, May 1, 1902, p. 1028.

21. Sheila Slaughter and Edward T. Silva, "Looking Backwards: How Foundations Formulated Ideology in the Progressive Period," in *Philanthropy and Cultural Imperialism: The Foundations at Home and Abroad*, ed. Robert F. Arnove (Bloomington: Indiana University Press, 1980), p. 59.

22. Robert H. Bremner, *From the Depths: The Discovery of Poverty in the United States* (1956; New Brunswick, N.J.: Transaction Books, 1992), p. 155.

23. Lawrence Orton, "The Russell Sage Foundation and Industrial Studies" (1927), in Collections of the Russell Sage Foundation, box 1, folder 15-4, RAC.

24. Guy Alchon, "Philanthropy and the Woman Intellectual: Mary Van Kleeck's Passage to the Russell Sage Foundation," paper presented at the annual meeting of the Association for Research on Nonprofit Organizations and Voluntary Action (ARNOVA), Toronto, October 1993.

25. Bremner, *From the Depths*, p. 235.

26. Mary Van Kleeck, *Women in the Bookbinding Trade* (New York: Survey Associates, 1913). See John M. Glenn, Lillian Brandt, and F. Emerson Andrews, *Russell Sage Foundation, 1907–1946*, 2 vols. (New York: Russell Sage Foundation, 1947), 1:155–56.

27. RSF made grants to the National Child Labor Committee for an office in Cincinnati to investigate industrial conditions in the Ohio Valley and parts of the South. "Shocking facts about the employment of children in cotton mills, in glass and cigar factories, in canneries, the coal mines, mercantile establishments, and street trade, were discovered and put on record, and important legislation was added [in] ten or twelve states" (Glenn et al., *Russell Sage Foundation*, p. 229).

28. Mary Van Kleeck to John Glenn, memorandum, October 25, 1919, in Mary Van Kleeck Papers, Sophia Smith Collection, Smith College, Northampton, Mass.

29. Quoted in Glenn et al., *Russell Sage Foundation*, p. 169.

30. Guy Alchon, "Mary Van Kleeck and Social-Economic Planning," *Journal of Policy History* 3 (1991): 2.

31. Mary Van Kleeck and Ben M. Selekman, *Employees' Representation in Coal Mines: A Study of the Colorado Fuel and Iron Company. Summary* (New York: Russell Sage Foundation, 1925). This study was singled out in William Leiserson's article "Company Unions" in *Encyclopaedia of*

the Social Sciences (New York: Macmillan, 1930–35), 4:125. Regarding Rockefeller's attempt to suppress publication, see Howard M. Gitelman, *Legacy of the Ludlow Massacre: A Chapter in American Industrial Relations* (Philadelphia: University of Pennsylvania Press, 1988), p. 336. Ten years later, when Van Kleeck reviewed advances in labor relations in the western mines of another Colorado coal company, she found that its general manager, Josephine Roche, "is not an absentee owner [and] has separated herself from the policies of the owner class . . . by inviting the United Mine Workers to join with the company in the collective agreement in which she has declared that the organized miners . . . have the right to share with the management in all decisions regarding conditions of employment": Mary Van Kleeck, *Miners and Management* (New York: Russell Sage Foundation, 1934), pp. 25–37, 228–33. See also John R. Commons, *Industrial Goodwill* (1919; New York: Arno, 1969), p. 112: "The Rockefeller plan was adopted . . . with recognition of organized labor. In this respect it is paternalistic rather than democratic. It is handed down rather than forced up."

32. Philip Taft, *Organized Labor in American History* (New York: Harper & Row, 1964), p. 431.

33. Van Kleeck memorandum, June 20, 1948, RSF Collections, box 14, folder 123, RAC.

34. RSF press release, May 4, 1942. Wieck was a former coal miner and union officer. His history of the first American miners' union, *The American Miners Association* (New York: Russell Sage Foundation, 1941), was acclaimed in both scholarly reviews and the labor and general press. Edward Wieck's personal papers are archived at the Reuther Library, Wayne State University (see Series II); RSF press releases and book reviews are in RSF Collections, RAC.

35. Van Kleeck, memorandum, May 13, 1943, RSF Collections, box 14, folder 123, RAC.

36. Slaughter and Silva, "Looking Backwards," p. 62.

37. Ibid., pp. 56, 62.

38. Peter diCicco, secretary-treasurer of the Industrial Union Department of the AFL-CIO, recalls various successful joint ventures with foundations in human service programs when he was an official of the electrical workers' union in Massachusetts. The union was engaged in a workfare program, and secured foundation funds to form a nonprofit agency to move welfare recipients to private employment. "Our professional staff was very successful in helping clients bridge some of the barriers to employment," he recalls. Another program, initially funded by three foundations (Elvirita Lewis, Edna McConnell Clark, and Burden), concentrated on first-time juvenile offenders, offering alternatives to incarceration. The union provided mentors (mostly retired union members). The program was later funded by the Commonwealth of Massachusetts, but dissolved in the face of an economic turndown and budget cuts: Peter diCicco, interview with author, March 21, 1995.

39. Wiebe, *Search for Order*, pp. 2, 78, 79.

40. Barry D. Karl and Stanley N. Katz, "Foundations and Ruling Class Elites," *Daedalus* 116 (Winter 1987): 22.

41. Gloria Garrett Samson, *The American Fund for Public Service: Charles Garland and Radical Philanthropy, 1921–1941* (Westport, Conn.: Greenwood, 1996), p. 61. Most of the material on the Garland Fund comes from this book.

42. Ibid., p. 17.

43. Ibid., p. 93.

44. Eduard C. Lindeman, *Wealth and Culture: A Study of One Hundred Foundations and Community Trusts and Their Operations during the Decade 1921–1930* (1936; New Brunswick, N.J.: Transaction Books, 1988), pp. 59–62.

45. Charles Forcey, *The Crossroads of Liberalism: Croly, Weyl, and Lippmann and the Progressive Era, 1900–1925* (New York: Oxford University Press, 1961), p. 158.

46. Samson, *American Fund*, p. 221.

47. Karl and Katz, "American Private Philanthropic Foundation," p. 263.

48. Quoted in Peter D. Hall, *Inventing the Nonprofit Sector and Other Essays on Philanthropy, Voluntarism, and Nonprofit Organizations* (Baltimore: Johns Hopkins University Press, 1992), p. 160. Hanna's company was the first to recognize the Miners National Association and to adopt the principle of arbitration in the settlement of wage disputes.

49. Weinstein, *Corporate Ideal*, p. 6.

50. Paul Starr, *The Social Transformation of American Medicine* (New York: Basic Books, 1982), p. 251.

51. John R. Commons, *Myself* (New York: Macmillan, 1934), p. 84.

52. Karl and Katz, "American Private Philanthropic Foundation," p. 263.

53. Weinstein, *Corporate Ideal*, p. 121.

54. G. William Domhoff, *The Powers That Be* (New York: Random House, 1978), p. 225.

55. Harold L. Miller, "The American Bureau of Industrial Research and the Origins of the 'Wisconsin School' of Labor History," *Labor History* 25 (Spring 1984): 165–88.

56. Theda Skocpol, *Protecting Soldiers and Mothers: The Political Origins of Social Policy in the United States* (Cambridge: Belknap Press of Harvard University Press, 1992), p. 183.

57. Ibid., pp. 205–7. For an analysis of the views of two AALL officers (John R. Commons and John B. Andrews) favorable to worker rights, see John Dennis Chasse, "The American Association for Labor Legislation: An Episode in Institutionalist Policy Analysis," *Journal of Economic Issues* 225 (September 1991): 799–828.

58. Samuel Gompers, quoted in Skocpol, *Protecting Soldiers and Mothers*, p. 207. Starr, *Social Transformation*, p. 251.

59. Elizabeth A. Fones-Wolf, *Selling Free Enterprise: The Business Assault on Labor and Liberalism, 1945–60* (Urbana: University of Illinois Press, 1994), pp. 1, 2.

60. Robert Bremner, "Private Philanthropy and Public Needs: Historical Perspectives," in *Giving in America: Toward a Stronger Voluntary Sector*, report of the Commission on Private Philanthropy and Public Needs, U.S. Department of the Treasury (Washington, D.C.: Government Printing Office, 1975).

61. Charles E. Harvey, "John D. Rockefeller, Jr. and the Social Sciences: An Introduction," *Journal of the History of Sociology* 4 (Fall 1982): 1–31.

62. Loren Renz et al., *Foundation Giving: Yearbook of Facts and Figures on Private, Corporate, and Community Foundations* (New York: Foundation Center, 1995), p. 3.

63. Rady A. Johnson, Preface to Marvin Olasky, Daniel T. Oliver, and Robert V. Pambianca, *Patterns of Corporate Philanthropy: Funding False Compassion*, ed. William T. Poole (Washington, D.C.: Capital Research Center, 1991), pp. iv–v.

64. Quoted in Stuart R. Brandes, *American Welfare Capitalism, 1880–1940* (Chicago: University of Chicago Press, 1976), p. 124.

65. Milton Derber, *The American Idea of Industrial Democracy, 1865–1965* (Urbana: University of Illinois Press, 1970), p. 212.

66. Harry Millis and Royal Montgomery, *The Economics of Labor*, vol. 3 (New York: McGraw-Hill, 1945), p. 837.

67. Raymond B. Fosdick, *John D. Rockefeller, Jr.: A Portrait* (New York Harper & Row, 1956), pp. 177–78.

68. Quoted in Harvey, "John D. Rockefeller, Jr.," p. 7.

69. Despite the growth of employee participation arrangements, in which some unions acquiesce, suspicion continues. Anger and resentment can run deep at disparities between compensation at the top and conditions in the ranks. In Canton, Ohio, for example, the annual compensation of the chief executive of a unionized company grew nearly five-fold, to $2.37 million over five years in the 1990s, while workers' pay dropped and the workforce was slashed from 800 to 58 when the company shifted work to outside contractors and to nonunion plants in the South. See Michael Winerip, "Canton's Economic Seesaw: Managers' Fortunes Rise as Workers Get Bumpy Ride," *New York Times*, July 7, 1996, p. 10. The issue later spread to the Internet. See Robert L. Rose, "Call to Action: Labor Has Discovered the Perfect Issue for Galvanizing Workers: CEO Pay," *Wall Street Journal*, April 9, 1998.

70. Richard B. Freeman and Joel Rogers, "Who Speaks for Us? Employee Representation in a Nonunion Labor Market," in *Employee Representation: Alternatives and Future Directions*, ed. Bruce E. Kaufman and Morris M. Kleiner (Madison, Wis.: Industrial Relations Research Association, 1993), pp. 13–80; "Worker Representation and Participation Survey: Second Report of

Findings," Princeton Survey Research Associates, June 1, 1995. The gospel of labor-management cooperation has been preached by the Work in America Institute since it was founded in 1975 by Jerome M. Rosow, former assistant secretary of labor. Heavily supported by foundations, the institute develops case studies of successful efforts to improve quality, productivity, and competitiveness.

71. Thomas R. Brooks, in *The Federationist*, October 1972, quoted in *The Worker and the Job: Coping with Change*, ed. Jerome Rosow (Englewood Cliffs, N.J.: Prentice-Hall, 1974), p. 101.

72. Richard B. Freeman and Joel Rogers, "A New New Deal for Labor," *New York Times*, March 10, 1993.

73. Commission on the Future of Worker-Management Relations, "Fact-Finding Report: Executive Summary" (Washington, D.C.: U.S. Department of Labor, Department of Commerce, May 1994); Jane Slaughter and Ellis Boal, "Unions Slam Dunlop Commission Proposals," *Labor Notes*, February 1995, pp. 1, 14.

74. Public employee unions grew rapidly in the 1960s, and by 1971 AFSCME had signed 1,200 contracts with state and local governments. See Sterling D. Spero and John M. Capozzola, *The Urban Community and Its Unionized Bureaucracies* (New York: Dunellen, 1973), p. 6. New unions of postal, transit, hospital, and other public employees staged 254 work stoppages in 1968, compared to 15 in 1958.

75. But in an independent evaluation in 1977, the LMRS's relations with other major public employee unions were said to be good. See "Helping City Hall Get Organized for Organized Labor," report no. 4870, Ford Foundation Archive, New York City (August 1977), pp. 24, 25, 31.

76. Marcia Calicchia and Laura Ginsburg, "Caring for Our Children: Labor's Role in Human Services Reform," report on a project funded by the Annie E. Casey Foundation, Baltimore, 1996.

77. Raymond D. Fosdick, *The Story of the Rockefeller Foundation* (New York: Harper, 1952), p. 204.

Chapter 2. Dimensions of Connection and Mistrust

1. Burton A. Weisbrod, *The Nonprofit Economy* (Cambridge: Harvard University Press, 1988), pp. 9, 10.

2. James Douglas, *Why Charity? The Case for a Third Sector* (Beverly Hills, Calif.: Sage, 1983), p. 67; see also pp. 29–31.

3. David Hammack, "Putting the First Amendment into Practice: A Historical Perspective on the Nonprofit Sector in the United States," paper presented at the Independent Sector Research Forum, Alexandria, Va., March 23–24, 1995, p. 11.

4. President's Research Committee on Social Trends, *Recent Social Trends*, 2 vols. (New York: McGraw-Hill, 1933).

5. *Foundation Giving* (New York: Foundation Center, 1996).

6. *Labor Union–Related Grants by Foundations, 1984–1992* (New York: Foundation Center), Dialog (database): file 27.

7. Craig Jenkins, "Channeling Social Protest: Foundation Patronage of Contemporary Social Movements," in *Private Action and the Public Good*, ed. Walter Powell and Elisabeth Clemens (New Haven: Yale University Press, 1998), p. 407.

8. Marilyn Fischer, "Philanthropy and Injustice in Mills and Addams," paper presented at the annual meeting of the Association for Research on Nonprofit Organizations and Voluntary Action (ARNOVA), Berkeley, Calif., October 21, 1994, p. 270.

9. F. Emerson Andrews, ed., *Foundations: Twenty Viewpoints* (New York: Russell Sage Foundation, 1965), p. 47.

10. Cited in Alan Rabinowitz, *Social Change Philanthropy in America* (Westport, Conn.: Quorum Books, 1990), pp. 40–41.

11. David Montgomery, *Workers' Control in America: Studies in the History of Work, Technology, and Labor Struggles* (New York: Cambridge University Press, 1979), p. 158.

12. *Mechanics Free Press* (Philadelphia), June 28, 1828, quoted in David Montgomery, *Citizen Worker: The Experience of Workers in the United States with Democracy and the Free Market during the Nineteenth Century* (New York: Cambridge University Press, 1994), p. 82.

13. Theodore Roosevelt, quoted in Gerald Jonas, *The Circuit Riders: Rockefeller Money and the Rise of Modern Science* (New York: Norton, 1989), p. 33; Barry D. Karl and Stanley N. Katz, "The American Private Philanthropic Foundation and the Public Sphere, 1890–1930," *Minerva*, Summer 1981, p. 253.

14. Quoted in Howard M. Gitelman, *Legacy of the Ludlow Massacre: A Chapter in American Industrial Relations* (Philadelphia: University of Pennsylvania Press, 1988), p. 5.

15. Quoted in Thomas R. Brooks, *Toil and Trouble: A History of American Labor* (New York: Dell, 1965), p. 87.

16. Quoted in William Serrin, *Homestead: The Glory and Tragedy of an American Steel Town* (New York: Times Books, 1992), p. 71.

17. Quoted in Herbert G. Gutman, *Work, Culture, and Society in Industrializing America* (New York: Vintage Books, 1977), pp. 104–5.

18. Barry D. Karl and Stanley N. Katz, "Foundations and Ruling Class Elites," *Daedalus* 116 (Winter 1987): 22.

19. Raymond D. Fosdick, *The Story of the Rockefeller Foundation* (New York: Harper, 1952), p. 303.

20. Quoted in Arthur Kornhauser, Robert Dunn, and Arthur M. Ross, eds., *Industrial Conflict* (New York: McGraw-Hill, 1954), p. 245.

21. American Federation of Labor, Executive Committee Minutes of 1907, in *American Federation of Labor—History Encyclopedia, Reference Book*, 3 vols. (Washington, D.C.: AFL, 1919), 1:209.

22. Samuel Gompers, *Seventy Years of Life and Labor: An Autobiography*, ed. Nick Salvatore (Ithaca: ILR Press, 1984), pp. 34–35.

23. John D. Rockefeller to Starr Murphy, November 21, 1919, quoted in Charles E. Harvey, "John. D. Rockefeller Jr. and the Social Sciences: An Introduction," *Journal of the History of Sociology* 4 (Fall 1982): 8.

24. Cited in Leon Fink, *In Search of the Working Class: Essays in American Labor History and Political Culture* (Urbana: University of Illinois Press, 1994), p. 215.

25. AFL, *American Federation of Labor—History*, 1:262.

26. Ibid. p. 315.

27. Quoted in Fink, *In Search of the Working Class*, p. 214.

28. Robert Kanigel, *The One Best Way: Frederick Winslow Taylor and the Enigma of Efficiency*, (New York: Viking, 1997), p. 1. See also Charles D. Wrege and Ronald G. Greenwood, *Frederick W. Taylor, the Father of Scientific Management: Myth and Reality* (Homewood, Ill.: Business One Irwin, 1991), p. 207: "My contention . . . remains that the union is absolutely unnecessary and only a hindrance to the quick and successful organization of any manufacturing establishment"; and John R. Commons, *Industrial Goodwill* (1919; New York: Arno, 1969), p. 15: "Scientific management carries to the final limit that disintegration of the workman's skill and its transfer to the employer, which began a hundred and fifty years ago with the inventions of power machinery, the steam engine, and division of labor."

29. Charles J. McCollester, "Turtle Creek Fights Taylorism: The Westinghouse Strike of 1914," *Labor's Heritage* 4 (Summer 1991): 4–27.

30. Wrege and Greenwood, *Frederick W. Taylor*, p. 209; John M. Jordan, *Machine-Age Ideology: Social Engineering and American Liberalism, 1911–1939* (Chapel Hill: University of North Carolina Press, 1994), p. 64.

31. Quoted in Robert F. Arnove, ed., *Philanthropy and Cultural Imperialism: The Foundations at Home and Abroad* (Bloomington: Indiana University Press, 1980), pp. 88–89.

32. The project was directed by Paul Jacobs, labor writer on the staff of the Institute of Industrial Relations at the University of California. In books, pamphlets, and position papers, intellectuals who had served the labor movement and some labor officials themselves grappled with issues confronting the labor movement, acknowledging its achievements and strengths but also dealing with troubling aspects—ranging from excessive bureaucracy to corruption and shortsightedness.

33. Brendan Sexton, "The Intellectuals and Trade Unions," in *Proceedings of the Sixteenth Annual Meeting of the Industrial Relations Research Association, Boston, December 27–28, 1963,* (Madison, Wis.: Industrial Relations Research Association, 1964), pp. 249–52.

34. Karen J. Winkler, "Precipitous Decline of American Unions Fuels Growing Interest among Scholars," *Chronicle of Higher Education,* November 12, 1986, p. 5.

35. Michael H. Frisch and Daniel J. Walkowitz, *Working-Class America: Essays on Labor, Community, and American Society* (Urbana: University of Illinois Press, 1983), p. xiii. See also Seymour Martin Lipset, *Unions in Transition: Entering the Second Century* (San Francisco: ICS Press, 1986).

36. Mitchell Sviridoff, oral history interview, February 12, 1975, in Ford Foundation Archive, New York.

37. Robert Emerson, interview with author, April 29, 1995.

38. Robert S. Keener, personal communication, July 28, 1993.

39. Ron Myslowka, personal communication, July 16, 1993.

40. Charles E. Bradford, personal communication, February 28, 1994.

41. Gordon H. Bream, personal communication, February 16, 1994.

42. Anne C. Green, personal communication, December 22, 1993.

43. Moe Biller, personal communication, September 1, 1993.

44. Susan Bianchi-Sand, interview with author, March 22, 1995.

45. Terry N. Saario, personal communication, October 29, 1992.

46. Larry Kirkman, interview with author, September 15, 1992. Before joining the Benton Foundation, Kirkman was founding executive director of the Labor Institute of Public Affairs, AFL-CIO.

47. Kirke Wilson, personal communication, August 31, 1992.

48. Willard J. Hertz, personal communication, September 29, 1992.

49. Thomas W. Lambeth, personal communication, November 11, 1992.

50. Joel D. Getzendanner, personal communication, October 16, 1992.

51. Peter Bell, personal communication, September 29, 1992.

52. Larry Kressley, personal communication, February 28, 1993.

Chapter 3. Congressional Intervention

1. U.S. Congress, House of Representatives, Select Committee to Investigate Tax-Exempt Foundations and Comparable Organizations (hereafter Cox Committee), *Hearings,* 81st Congress, 1st sess., 1952, p. 789.

2. U.S. Congress, Senate, Commission on Industrial Relations (hereafter Walsh Commission), Final Report and Testimony, 64th Cong., 1st sess., Senate Document no. 415, 9 vols. (Washington: G.P.O., 1916). Allen F. Davis, "The Campaign for the Industrial Relations Commission, 1911–1913," *Mid-America, An Historical Review* 45 (October 1963): 211–28. The commission's members included Walsh, John R. Commons, and Florence (Mrs. J. Borden) Harriman (public representatives); Frederick Delano, Harris Weinstock, and S. Thurston Bullard (representing capital); and Austin Garretson, James B. Lennon, and James O'Connell (labor representatives). For the first time a study commission had a research director, in this case Selig Perlman, who became a noted labor historian. The commission issued its final report in 1916.

3. John Lankford, *Congress and the Foundations in the Twentieth Century* (River Falls: Wisconsin State University, 1964), p. 8.

4. Robert H. Bremner, *American Philanthropy,* 2d ed. (Chicago: University of Chicago Press, 1988), p. 113.

5. Howard M. Gitelman, *Legacy of the Ludlow Massacre: A Chapter in American Industrial Relations* (Philadelphia: University of Pennsylvania Press, 1988), p. 29 and passim.

6. Quoted in W. T. Davis, "The Strike War in Colorado," *Outlook,* May 9, 1914, p. 73.

7. John E. Harr and Peter J. Johnson, *The Rockefeller Century* (New York: Scribner's, 1988),

p. 123. By 1914 the Rockefeller Foundation board was seriously considering the establishment of a network of research institutes to apply scientific methods to the study of—and solutions to—human problems, as it had already done in medicine and public health. Gerald Jonas, *The Circuit Riders: Rockefeller Money and the Rise of Modern Science* (New York: Norton, 1989), pp. 92, 94.

8. Rockefeller Foundation, *Annual Report*, 1913–14, p. 18.

9. Joseph C. Goulden, *The Money Givers: An Examination of the Myths and Realities of Foundation Philanthropy in America* (New York: Random House, 1971), p. 39.

10. Irving Bernstein, *The Turbulent Years: A History of the American Worker, 1933–1941* (Boston: Houghton-Mifflin, 1970). See also Mary Van Kleeck and Ben Selekman, *Employee Representation in Coal Mines: A Study of the Colorado Fuel and Iron Company*—Summary (New York: Russell Sage Foundation, 1925).

11. Quoted in Lankford, *Congress and the Foundations*, pp. 27–28. The commission also charged the Rockefeller's General Education Board with bribery for having given unrestricted grants of $100,000 to Colorado College and to the University of Denver, whose president and dean of liberal arts, respectively, had organized a public appeal asking the miners to return to work (Goulden, *Money Givers*, p. 39).

12. Quoted in Robert F. Arnove, ed., *Philanthropy and Cultural Imperialism: The Foundations at Home and Abroad* (Bloomington: Indiana University Press, 1980), p. 35.

13. Dwight Macdonald, *The Ford Foundation: The Men and the Millions—an Unauthorized Biography* (New York: Reynal, 1956), p. 23.

14. Walsh Commission, *Final Report*, 9:8006, 8119.

15. Quoted in Lankford, *Congress and the Foundations*, p. 30.

16. Quoted in Gustavus Myers, *History of the Great American Fortunes* (New York: Modern Library, 1936), p. 703. The commission embraced an array of issues beyond foundations, such as the secondary boycott and public representation in labor disputes. Commons, the great labor historian and a commission member, regretted differing with the three labor members of the commission. This division reflected his view that labor should focus on collective bargaining rather than politics: "I thought . . . that [they] were being misled by the general labor unrest into throwing their movement into politics. I wanted them . . . to direct their energies toward what I knew was the policy of Samuel Gompers in building up strong organizations of self-governing unions able to meet the employers' associations on an equality." John R. Commons, *Myself* (New York: Macmillan, 1934), p. 167.

17. Lankford, *Congress and the Foundations*, p. 31.

18. Quoted in Jonas, *Circuit Riders*, p. 94. King shifted from the foundation to Rockefeller's personal staff until he returned to Canadian politics, becoming prime minister in 1921 and serving for twenty-one years.

19. U.S. Congress, Senate, Subcommittee on Interstate and Foreign Commerce, *Investigating Closing of Nashua, N.H., Mills and Operation of Textron, Inc.*, Hearings and Summary of Report, 80th Cong., 2d sess., February 17, 1949, p. 58.

20. Ibid., p. 59.

21. Ibid., p. 1032.

22. John A. Edie, *Congress and Private Foundations: An Historical Analysis* (Washington, D.C.: Council on Foundations, 1987), p. 5.

23. Cox Committee, *Hearings*, Executive Session, July 4, 1952, p. 4.

24. Edwin R. Embree, "Timid Billions—Are the Foundations Doing Their Job?" *Harper's*, March 1949, p. 302.

25. Cox Committee, *Hearings*, p. 359.

26. Ibid., pp. 431, 433.

27. Ibid., p. 650.

28. Ibid., p. 694.

29. Ibid., p. 703.

30. Lankford, *Congress and the Foundations*, p. 46.

31. U.S. Congress, House of Representatives, Special Committee to Investigate Tax-Exempt

Foundations and Comparable Organizations (Reece Committee), *Hearings, Parts I and II*, 83d Cong., 2d sess. 1954, pp. 162, 1158–69.

32. Ibid., p. 1159. Even the conservative Alfred P. Sloan Foundation was criticized, because Public Affairs Committee pamphlets it financed were recommended by the Affiliated Schools for Workers.

33. U.S. Congress, House of Representatives, Report of the Special Committee to Investigate Tax-Exempt Foundations and Comparable Organizations, 83d Cong., 2d sess., Report no. 2681, p. 34.

34. F. Emerson Andrews, *Foundation Watcher* (Lancaster, Pa.: Franklin and Marshall College, 1973), p. 146.

35. U.S. Department of the Treasury, *Report on Private Foundations*, for the Senate Committee on Finance, February 2, 1965.

36. Waldemar Nielsen, *The Big Foundations* (New York: Columbia University Press, 1972), p. 5.

37. Quoted in Mitchell Sviridoff, "Organized Labor and Organized Philanthropy: A Discussion Paper" (New York: Ford Foundation, n.d.), p. 2.

38. The source for Sanders's and Degnan's comments is a memorandum issued by the Council on Foundations for its members on March 6, 1969, summarizing statements before the House Ways and Means Committee through February 27, 1969. UFT president Albert Shanker himself, still smarting over his union's encounter with the Ford Foundation, declared in 1971, "The foundations are today responsible neither to elected public officials nor to stockholders interested in the efficiency of the enterprise. Legally they are responsible only to their self-perpetuating boards of trustees . . . it is indeed strange that the matter of their accountability has until now virtually been ignored." Quoted in Sviridoff, "Organized Labor," p. 3.

Chapter 4. Research

1. John R. Commons et al. *A Documentary History of American Industrial Society*, sponsored by the Carnegie Institution of Washington, 11 vols. (Cleveland: A. H. Clark, 1910–11); Commons et al., *History of Labour in the United States*, 4 vols. (New York: Macmillan, 1918, 1935).

2. Among the financial contributors was Stanley McCormick, the youngest son of Cyrus Hall McCormick. Commons also worked on the Russell Sage Foundation's Pittsburgh Survey, 1905–6.

3. Quoted in Robert F. Arnove, ed., *Philanthropy and Cultural Imperialism: The Foundations at Home and Abroad* (Bloomington: Indiana University Press, 1980), p. 65.

4. Peter D. Hall, personal communication, April 25, 1993.

5. James L. Cochrane, *Industrialism and Industrial Man in Retrospect: A Critical Review of the Ford Foundation's Support for the Inter-University Study of Labor* (New York: Ford Foundation, 1979), p. 10. Roger L. Geiger, *To Advance Knowledge: The Growth of American Research Universities, 1900–1940* (New York: Oxford University Press, 1986), p. 145.

6. Frederick T. Gates to John D. Rockefeller Jr., March 19, 1914, quoted in Geiger, *To Advance Knowledge*, p. 144.

7. Arnove, *Philanthropy*, p. 74.

8. Geiger, *To Advance Knowledge*, pp. 145, 148; Commonwealth Fund, *Annual Report*, 1919, p. 14.

9. Kenneth Prewitt, *Social Sciences and Private Philanthropy: The Quest for Social Relevance*, Essays on Philanthropy No. 15 (Indianapolis: Indiana University Center on Philanthropy, 1995), pp. 1–2.

10. Geiger, *To Advance Knowledge*, pp. 146–51.

11. In 1927, Brookings received additional donations from Robert Brookings and the Carnegie, Rockefeller, and George Eastman foundations. See G. William Domhoff, *The Higher Circles: The Governing Class in America* (New York: Random House, 1970), pp. 182–83.

12. Charles E. Harvey, "John D. Rockefeller, Jr. and the Social Sciences: An Introduction," *Journal of the History of Sociology* 4 (Fall 1982): 19.

13. Among Wolman's publications for the NBER were *The Growth of American Trade Unions 1880–1923* (1924) and *Ebb and Flow in Trade Unionism* (1936). He had also worked for the U.S. Commission on Industrial Relations and served on the board of the Garland Fund.

14. "The First Three Years of the National Bureau of Economic Research: An Informal Account of How the Bureau Works," LSRM Collection, series 3, box 51, folder 538, Rockefeller Archive Center, Pocantico Hills, N.Y.; hereafter RAC.

15. National Bureau of Economic Research, *Annual Report of the Director of Research*, 1924, pp. 12–13.

16. Norma MacKenzie, NBER staff member, personal communication, November 24, 1992.

17. Ronald W. Schatz, "From Commons to Dunlop: Rethinking the Field and Theory of Industrial Relations," in *Industrial Democracy in America: The Ambiguous Promise*, ed. Nelson Lichtenstein and H. J. Harris (New York: Cambridge University Press, 1993), pp. 87–88.

18. John R. Commons, *Myself* (New York: Macmillan, 1934), p. 73.

19. Geiger, *To Advance Knowledge*, pp. 140–42; also cited in Prewitt, *Social Sciences and Private Philanthropy*, p. 19.

20. Geiger, *To Advance Knowledge*, p. 145; Harvey, "John D. Rockefeller, Jr.," p. 12.

21. Geiger, *To Advance Knowledge*, p. 145.

22. Harold Laski, "Foundations, Universities, and Research," in *The Dangers of Obedience and Other Essays* (New York: Harper, 1930), pp. 154–77.

23. Local Community Research Committee, Report to the President of the University of Chicago, February 1, 1927, in LSRM Collection, series 3, box 71, folder 752, RAC.

24. Ibid., folder 749.

25. Raymond B. Fosdick, *The Story of the Rockefeller Foundation* (New York: Harper, 1952), p. 204.

26. David L. Featherman, "SSRC: Then and Now: A Commentary on a Recent Historical Analysis"; *Items* [newsletter], March 1994, pp. 13–22; Martin Bulmer, review of Donald Fisher, *Fundamental Development of the Social Sciences: Rockefeller Philanthropy and the United States Social Sciences Research Council*, in *Science*, October 8, 1993, pp. 259–60; and Howard Brick's review of Fisher's book in *Journal of American History* 81 (September 1994): 770.

27. Quoted in Guy Alchon, *The Invisible Hand of Planning: Capitalism, Social Science, and the State in the 1920s* (Princeton: Princeton University Press, 1985), pp. 144–45.

28. Robert S. Lynd and Helen M. Lynd, *Middletown: A Study in American Culture* (New York: Harcourt, Brace, 1929), and *Middletown in Transition: A Study in Cultural Conflicts* (New York: Harcourt, Brace, 1937). For Robert Lynd's philosophy of sociological research, see his *Knowledge for What? The Place of Social Science in American Culture* (Princeton: Princeton University Press, 1939).

29. Charles E. Harvey, "Robert S. Lynd, John D. Rockefeller, Jr., and *Middletown*," *Indiana Magazine of History*, 1982, pp. 330–47.

30. Ibid., p. 331. "Raymond D. Fosdick was Rockefeller's key advisor . . . who held the purse-strings of the sponsoring agency."

31. Lynd and Lynd, *Middletown*, pp. 76–77.

32. Lee W. Minton, *Flame and Heart: A History of the Glass Bottle Blowers Association of the United States and Canada* (GBBA, n.d.). Under various names, the union—proud of its craft—went back to the early nineteenth century.

33. Lynd and Lynd, *Middletown in Transition*, pp. 70, 89.

34. Ibid., pp. 77–81; Elizabeth Fones-Wolf, *Selling Free Enterprise: The Business Assault on Labor and Liberalism, 1945–60* (Urbana: University of Illinois Press, 1994), p. 16.

35. Joseph Galvin Jr., research director, Glass, Molders, Pottery, Plastics & Allied Workers International Union, interview with author, February 20, 1996.

36. Douglas A. Bakken, executive director, Ball Brothers Foundation, personal communication, February 9, 1996.

37. *Annual Reports*, 1985–94; *The Social Change Report*, vols. 1–4 (through 1996), Center for Middletown Studies, Ball State University, Muncie, Indiana 47306, Dwight W. Hoover, Director.

38. Alchon, *Invisible Hand of Planning*, cited in Joseph C. Kiger, *Historiographic Review of Foundation Literature: Motivations and Perceptions* (New York: Foundation Center, 1987), p. 28.

39. Guy Alchon, "Mary Van Kleeck and Scientific Management," in *A Mental Revolution: Scientific Management since Taylor*, ed. Daniel Nelson (Columbus: Ohio State University Press 1992), p. 103.

40. Guy Alchon, "Mary Van Kleeck and Social-Economic Planning," *Journal of Policy History* 3 (1991): 6.

41. John M. Jordan, *Machine-Age Ideology: Social Engineering and American Liberalism, 1911–1939* (Chapel Hill: University of North Carolina Press, 1994), pp. 202–3.

42. *International Encyclopedia of the Social Sciences* (New York: Macmillan/Free Press, 1968), s.v. "Elton Mayo," by William F. Whyte.

43. Harvey, "John D. Rockefeller, Jr.," pp. 20, 21.

44. Whyte, "Elton Mayo."

45. Cochrane, *Industrialism*, p. 10. The IRC's staff was among the few expert enough to advise policy makers on the early administration of the National Labor Relations Board (Harvey, "John D. Rockefeller, Jr.," p. 14).

46. Alchon, *Invisible Hand of Planning*, p. 66.

47. Alchon, "Mary Van Kleeck and Scientific Management," p. 112.

48. Ellis W. Hawley, "Herbert Hoover, the Commerce Secretariat, and the Vision of the 'Associative State,' 1921–1928," *Journal of American History* 60 (June 1974): 116–17.

49. Some of Franklin Roosevelt's major programs in social reform had their origins in the efforts of one or more private foundations. The creation of the Executive Office of the President, which gave him funds to carry out research, was based on a Brookings study financed in part by the Rockefeller Foundation through the Social Science Research Council.

50. President's Research Committee on Social Trends, *Recent Social Trends*, 2 vols. (New York: McGraw-Hill, 1933).

51. Jordan, *Machine-Age Ideology*, p. 180.

52. President's Research Committee, *Recent Social Trends*, 2:830.

53. Ibid., p. 804.

54. The fund evolved from the Cooperative League, established by Edward and his brother Lincoln with the strong encouragement of their lawyer, Louis D. Brandeis. I am indebted to Professors Andrew Workman (Mills College) and Meg Jacobs (Claremont McKenna College) for information on the Twentieth Century Fund's relations with policy makers of the 1930s on economic matters such as mass consumption, collective bargaining, and labor legislation.

55. Adolf A. Berle, *Leaning against the Dawn* (New York: Twentieth Century Fund, 1969), p. 11.

56. Meg Jacobs, "The Promise of Purchasing Power: Edward A. Filene and the Creation of an American Consumer Society," draft of a paper presented to the Social Science History Association, Chicago, November 1995. Filene was no hypocrite. Within his own business, he had established the Filene Cooperative Association (FCA), a means of giving his employees a voice in the operation of the company and a vehicle by which they would eventually own it. The employees did not take advantage of the ownership opportunity, but used the FCA to secure better working conditions. An exhaustive (480 pp.) Russell Sage Foundation study pointed to employee satisfaction in many areas, concluding that the FCA prevented labor trouble: Mary LaDame, *The Filene Store: A Study of Employee Relations in a Retail Store* (New York: Russell Sage Foundation Industrial Series, 1930).

57. Quoted in Berle, *Leaning against the Dawn*, p. 13.

58. Ibid., p. 95.

59. Jacobs, "Promise of Purchasing Power," pp. 1–3 and passim.

60. Steven Fraser, *Labor Will Rule: Sidney Hillman and the Rise of American Labor* (Ithaca: Cornell University Press, 1991), p. 262.

61. J. Joseph Huthmacher, *Senator Robert F. Wagner and the Rise of Urban Liberalism* (New York: Athenaeum, 1968), pp. 192–93; see also Fraser, *Labor Will Rule*, pp. 330–33; and Jacobs, "Promise of Purchasing Power," p. 23.

62. Alfred L. Bernheim and Dorothy Van Doren, eds., *Labor and the Government: An Investigation* (New York: Twentieth Century Fund, 1935); Louis Stark, "New Labor Agency Proposed in Book," *New York Times*, May 24, 1935, p. 2.

63. *Summary of Minutes of the Labor Committee*, Twentieth Century Fund, December 2, 1938.

64. Sterling Spero memorandum, ibid., February 14, 1938.

65. Louis Stark to Evans Clark, February 22, 1938, Twentieth Century Fund, New York City.

66. *Summary of Minutes of the Labor Committee*, July 2, 1940; Harry Millis, *How Collective Bargaining Works: A Survey of Experience in Leading American Industries* (New York: Twentieth Century Fund, 1942). Milton Derber and Philip Taft, who worked under Millis, became noted labor scholars.

67. Andrew Workman, personal communication, May 11, 1995.

68. Davis's recommendation is noted in the *Summary of the Minutes of the Labor Committee*, December 14, 1946; Garrison to Clark, August 14, 1946, in *Minutes of the Labor Committee*. The committee was completing a special report in advance of final work on the Taft-Hartley Act.

69. Charles C. Heckscher, *The New Unionism: Employee Involvement in the Changing Corporation*. A Twentieth Century Fund Book (1988; Ithaca: Cornell University Press, 1997); Richard C. Edwards, *Rights at Work: Employment Relations in the Post-Union Age* (Washington, D.C.: Brookings Institution Press, 1993).

70. RG 1.1, series 200, U.S.-S.S., box 39, folder 3797-99, RAC.

71. RG 1.1, series 200, box 413, folder 4908-10, RAC. Also, the University of Chicago's Industrial Relations Center received Rockefeller grants for studies of white-collar workers and unionization and the ingredients of "constructive" relations between labor and management. See 1.1, RG series 216 (IL), box 21, folder 287, RAC.

72. Brookings began publishing a series of pamphlets and labor books in the early 1930s, generally recognized as the last word on a subject.

73. Lichtenstein and Harris, *Industrial Democracy in America*, p. 115.

74. Quoted in Thomas A. Kochan, Harry C. Katz, and Robert B. McKersie, *The Transformation of American Industrial Relations* (1986; Ithaca: ILR Press, 1994), p. 255.

75. Gary Burtless, interview with author, September 18, 1992. Labor-management research is also commissioned from outside scholars by the W. E. Upjohn Institute for Employment Research, an offshoot of a trust established by the founder of the Upjohn Company to deal with unemployment during the Depression. An influential Upjohn study in 1984 dealt with worker participation in industry, and others have focused on the role of collective bargaining in plant closings.

76. This summary of the background of "industrial relations" is drawn largely from Bruce E. Kaufman, *The Origins and Evolution of the Field of Industrial Relations in the United States* (Ithaca: ILR Press, 1993).

77. Cochrane, *Industrialism*, p. 9.

78. Harry Millis and Royal Montgomery, *The Economics of Labor*, vol. 1: *Labor's Progress and Some Basic Labor Problems*, vol. 2: *Labor's Risks and Social Insurance*; vol. 3: *Organized Labor* (New York: McGraw-Hill, 1938, 1938, 1945).

79. Walter Galenson and Seymour Martin Lipset, eds., *Labor and Trade Unionism: An Interdisciplinary Reader* (New York: Wiley, 1960).

80. Kaufman, *Origins*, pp. 191, 193; Thomas Kochan, interview with author, October 15, 1993.

81. John Dunlop, "Discussion: Collective Bargaining, Wages, and the Price Level," in Industrial Relations Research Association, *Proceedings of the First Annual Meeting*, San Francisco, December 29–30, 1948, ed. Milton Derber (1949), pp. 53–54.

82. Solomon Barkin, *The Decline of the Labor Movement and What Can Be Done about It* (Madison, Wis.: Industrial Relations Research Association, 1961), p. 8; Clark Kerr, *Unions and Union Leaders of Their Own Choosing* (New York: Fund for the Republic, 1957); Paul Jacobs, *Dead Horse and the Featherbird*, (Santa Barbara: Center for the Study of Democratic Institutions 1962).

83. John B. Judis, "The Pressure Elite: Inside the Narrow World of Advocacy Group Politics," *American Prospect*, 2 (Spring 1992): 24.

84. Request for Grant Action, Grant no. 870-0604, August 31, 1989, p. 3, Ford Foundation Archive, New York City; hereafter FFA.

85. Roger Hickey, interview with author, November 10, 1993. In 1989, the EPI issued a statement signed by over three hundred economists, including six Nobel Laureates, calling for increased public investment in human capital and economic infrastructure. It attracted media notice and led to hearings by the Joint Economic Committee of Congress.

86. Request no. USIAP-227, Grant no. 900-1344, June 17, 1993, FFA. A think tank more directly linked to union interests is Citizens for Tax Justice. Some foundations have provided support to its sister organization, the Institute on Taxation and Economic Policy, but the bulk of its funds come from unions, and its officers and board consist mainly of presidents of major unions.

87. "The Economic Policy Institute: New Rhetoric, Old Message," *Organization Trends* (Washington, D.C.: Capital Research Center, February 1993), pp. 6, 8; Doug Bandow, "New Democrats Lose Think-Tank War," *Wall Street Journal*, March 18, 1993.

88. Heritage Foundation, Washington, D.C., executive memorandum, March 12, 1991.

89. Reed Larson, "Labor Unions and Political Reform," Heritage Lecture no. 242, 1990. The Fisher Institute in Dallas, also supported by conservative foundations, publishes antiunion works, such as *Deregulating Labor Relations* (1981), the authors of which charge, for example, that the Occupational Safety and Health Act has failed to reduce work-related accidents and illness significantly, and propose to eliminate it and substitute higher wages for higher risks. One of the authors, James T. Bennett, is also funded by the John M. Olin Foundation, which provided major support to the National Right to Work Legal Defense Foundation, another of whose important funders, from 1972 to 1991, was the Pew Charitable Trusts.

90. Derek C. Bok and John T. Dunlop, *Labor and the American Community* (New York: Simon & Schuster, 1970), pp. 484–85.

91. Laura Ginsburg, interview with author, March 25, 1996. See also Sally Covington, *Moving a Public Agenda: The Strategic Philanthropy of Conservative Foundations* (Washington, D.C.: National Committee for Responsive Philanthropy, 1996).

92. Alfred P. Sloan Foundation, *Annual Report*, 1994, pp. 6–10; 1995, pp. 45–53; Hirsh Cohen, interview with author, February 13, 1996.

93. This array of Sloan Foundation programs is ironic in view of the strong antiunion view of its founder, General Motors' chairman Alfred P. Sloan. Livid over the New Deal, industrial magnate/philanthropists including Sloan, the Du Ponts, and J. Howard Pew of Sun Oil wanted recognition that it was their efforts—not government's or labor unions'—that guaranteed a good life for the American people. Thus Sloan supported ultraconservative organizations such as the Liberty League and the National Industrial Information Council, an extremist spin-off of the National Association of Manufacturers. On the heels of Sloan's failure to persuade state or federal officials to remove sit-in strikers from GM plants, and his accession to most of the union demands, he greatly enlarged his small family foundation in 1937 with a gift of $10 million and dedicated it exclusively to economic education and research from a conservative viewpoint. See David Farber, "Cars Are Us: Alfred P. Sloan of GM and the Body Politic," unpublished paper, Barnard College, n.d.

94. Eric Wanner, personal communication, May 4, 1994; Russell Sage Foundation Board meeting dockets, November 1995, June 1996; "The Future of Work," in *Biannual Report*, 1994–95.

95. Richard Freeman, "How Much Has Unionization Contributed to the Rise in Male Earnings Inequality?" in *Uneven Tides: Rising Inequality in America*, ed. Sheldon Danziger and Peter Gottschalk (New York: Russell Sage Foundation, 1994), p. 134.

Chapter 5. Black Workers

1. James Weldon Johnson, *Negro Americans, What Now?* (New York: Viking, 1934), p. 66.

2. The earliest were the Anna T. Jeanes Fund and the Peabody Education Fund, followed by Rockefeller's General Education Board, the Carnegie Endowment for the Advancement of Education, the Julius Rosenwald Fund, and the Phelps-Stokes Fund.

3. Sterling Spero and Abram Harris, *The Black Worker: The Negro and the Labor Movement* (New York: Columbia University Press, 1931), p. 15. Spero reiterated this point in his essay "The Negro Problem" for the 1933 edition of the *Encyclopaedia of the Social Sciences*, 11:340.

4. Spero and Harris, *Black Worker*, p. 34.

5. Quoted in Thomas R. Brooks, *Toil and Trouble: A History of American Labor* (New York: Dell, 1965), p. 46.

6. Charles H. Wesley, *Negro Labor in the United States* (New York: Vanguard, 1927), p. 276.

7. Laura Spelman Rockefeller Memorial Papers, series 3, box 99, folder 1005, Rockefeller Archive Center, Pocantico Hills, N.Y.; hereafter RAC.

8. Nancy J. Weiss, *The National Urban League 1910–1940* (New York: Oxford University Press, 1974), p. 157. The league persuaded the Carnegie Corporation to give $10,000 to the New York Public Library to purchase the invaluable Schomburg Collection—books, prints, and other material on black history and culture—in 1926. The collection contains the league's publications and, notably, the papers of the Myrdal study, *An American Dilemma* (see n. 14).

9. LSRM Papers, series 3, box 98, folder 1001, RAC.

10. Ira DeReid, ed., *Negro Membership in American Labor Unions* (New York: Alexander Press, 1930). It was reprinted in 1969 by the Negro University Press.

11. Weiss, *National Urban League*, pp. 67 (quotation), 242–44.

12. LSRM papers, series 3, box 99, folder 1005, RAC. The Rockefeller Foundation, which absorbed the LSRM in 1929, continued to fund the league through 1937.

13. Spero and Harris, *Black Worker*, pp. 464–65.

14. Gunnar Myrdal [with the assistance of Richard Sterner and Arnold Rose], *An American Dilemma: The Negro Problem and Modern Democracy* (1944; New York: Harper & Row, 1962), p. 840.

15. Speech delivered at conference, December 19–21, 1927, LSRM Papers, series 3, box 98, folder 1001, RAC, p. 98. In a rare activist mode for a foundation, J. H. Dillard (president of the Jeanes and Slater funds) asked the LSRM in 1927 if it could intervene with the Railroad Brotherhoods, which were ruthlessly eliminating blacks from railroad jobs in the South. See memorandum from Leonard Outhwaite in LSRM Papers, Series 3, box 101, folder 1021.

16. Gloria Garrett Samson, *The American Fund for Public Service: Charles Garland and Radical Philanthropy, 1922–1941* (Westport, Conn.: Greenwood, 1996), pp. 27–28, 49–52, 83–84, 87–88, 111–12, 159.

17. Alfred L. Bernheim and Dorothy Van Doren, eds., *Labor and the Government: An Investigation* (New York: Twentieth Century Fund, 1935), pp. 300–301.

18. The books, all published by the University of North Carolina Press in Chapel Hill, are: Charles S. Johnson, Edwin R. Embree, and Will W. Alexander, *The Collapse of Cotton Tenancy* (1935); Arthur F. Raper, *A Preface to Peasantry* (1936); and Horace C. Cayton and George S. Mitchell, *Black Workers and the New Unions* (1939).

19. Lester Granger, "The National Negro Congress: An Interpretation," Document no. 116 in *Black Workers: A Documentary History from Colonial Times to the Present*, ed. Philip S. Foner and Ronald L. Lewis (Philadelphia: Temple University Press, 1989), pp. 484–88.

20. Michael K. Honey, *Southern Labor and Black Civil Rights: Organizing Memphis Workers* (Urbana: University of Illinois Press, 1993), pp. 200–207.

21. Myrdal, *American Dilemma*, p. 402.

22. Anson Phelps Stokes, *Negro Status and Race Relations in the United States, 1911–1946: The Thirty-Five-Year Report on the Phelps-Stokes Fund* (New York: Phelps-Stokes Fund, 1948), pp. 103–5.

23. Robert E. Skinner, "The Black Man in the Literature of Labor: The Early Novels of Chester Himes," *Labor's Heritage* 1 (July 1989): 60. Rosenwald Fund fellowships, Skinner notes (p. 54), were awarded to black and white southerners "for academic study, music, literature, the arts, labor, business, the ministry, or any other field in which the individual gives promise of some special contribution to American life."

24. Myrdal, *American Dilemma*, p. 789.

25. Ralph Bunche, "Conceptions and Ideologies of the Negro Problem" (March 1940), in Carnegie-Myrdal Papers, Schomburg Center for Research in Black Culture, New York, microfilm no. 323, 173C, reels 1 and 2.

26. Quoted in John H. Stanfield, *Philanthropy and Jim Crow in American Social Science* (Westport, Conn.: Greenwood, 1985), pp. 108–9. In a memorandum Charles S. Johnson wrote, "The characteristic movements among Negroes are now for the first time becoming proletarian, as contrasted to the upper class in intellectual influence that was typical of previous movements." He and others influential in racial affairs believed that "there is likelihood (and danger) that the movement may be seized upon by some much more picturesque figure who may be less responsible and less interested in actual improvement of conditions." Quoted in Richard M. Dalfiume, "The 'Forgotten Years' of the Negro Revolution," *Journal of American History* 55 (June 1968): 100.

27. Creel quoted in Kenneth W. Rose, "The Rockefellers in Harlem: Rockefeller and the African-American Community in New York City, 1920–1950," paper presented at the Rockefeller Archive Center Conference, Tarrytown, N.Y., September 25, 1992.

28. I am indebted to Walter A. Jackson, *Gunnar Myrdal and America's Conscience: Social Engineering and Racial Liberalism, 1938–1987* (Chapel Hill: University of North Carolina Press, 1990), for much of this discussion of *An American Dilemma*. Other interesting accounts are Stanfield, *Philanthropy and Jim Crow*, pp. 139–84, and Ellen Condliffe Lagemann, *The Politics of Knowledge: The Carnegie Corporation, Philanthropy, and Public Policy* (Middletown, Conn.: Wesleyan University Press, 1989), pp. 136–42, passim. How Myrdal came to direct the study exemplifies the way the philanthropic network operated in the social science community: by the mid-1930s, Newton Baker (a distinguished public servant and Carnegie Corporation board member), and Frederick Keppel, Carnegie's president, were seriously doubting the efficacy of twenty years and $1.7 million in grants for black education in the South and believed that a fresh look and new perspective were needed on the entire issue of the African American condition. For help in selecting a study director, Keppel turned to Donald Young of the foundation-supported Social Science Research Council and Melville Herskovits, an outstanding anthropologist specializing in African American culture. They argued that an objective outlook demanded a non-American from a nonimperialist country. Beardsley Ruml recommended Myrdal, whom he had met when Myrdal and his wife, Alva (also an economist), were Rockefeller Foundation Social Science Fellows in the United States in 1929–30, and Ruml headed the Laura Spelman Rockefeller Memorial. Myrdal had become a well-respected economist and member of the Swedish parliament who shared the ideals of the Progressive movement—its rational, optimistic views and commitment to social engineering, exemplified by the work of Commons and Dewey.

29. Paul Norgren, "Negro Labor and Its Problems," Carnegie-Myrdal Papers, Schomburg Center, New York, microfilm no. 323, 173C, reel 10, pp. 4, 7, 386, 387. Although Norgren's was the only one of thirty specialized memoranda to deal with Negro labor, several others also examined economic status: "The Negro's Share: In Consumption, Housing and Public Assistance" (Richard Sterner), "The Negro in Agriculture" (T. C. McCormick), and "The Negro in the American Economic System" (Ira DeReid). In 1959 Norgren authored *Employing the Negro in American Industry* (New York: Industrial Relations Counselors), and in 1964, with assistance from the Taconic Foundation, he authored *Toward Fair Employment* (New York: Columbia University Press).

30. Myrdal, *American Dilemma*, pp. 401, 402, 713, 849.

31. Bunche, quoted ibid., p. 793.

32. Myrdal, quoted in Jackson, *Gunnar Myrdal and America's Conscience*, p. 130.

33. Ibid., pp. 209, 211.

34. Quoted in Bayard Rustin, "The Blacks and the Unions," *Harper's*, May, 1971, p. 75.

35. AFL-CIO press release, Washington, D.C., September 5, 1966.

36. Miners for Democracy Collection, boxes 15, 20, 24, 25, Walter Reuther Library, Wayne State University.

37. For example, funds were earmarked by the New York Foundation in 1972 and 1974, and later by other foundations, for a project to enable black-owned construction companies to over-

come discriminatory practices by bonding companies in the construction industry, a bastion of discriminatory unions.

38. Gilbert Jonas, interview with author, October 21, 1996. In 1974, Jonas recalls, leaders of the National Urban League and the A. Philip Randolph Institute and William Pollard of the AFL-CIO demanded a meeting with Roy Wilkins, president of the NAACP, to protest Herbert Hill's criticism of their worker training programs and to demand that he be fired. "Wilkins said that they had failed to prove a single false statement by Hill and that he worked for the NAACP, not for them," Jonas said. Hill remained with the NAACP until Wilkins retired. Hill's criticism appeared in Herbert Hill, "Labor Union Control of Job Training: A Critical Analysis of Apprenticeship Outreach Programs and the Hometown Plans" (Washington, D.C.: Howard University/Institute for Urban Affairs and Research, 1974).

39. Herbert Hill, personal communication, September 10, 1996. See also Herbert Hill, "Black Workers, Organized Labor, and Title VII of the 1964 Civil Rights Act: Legislative History and Litigation Record," in *Race in America: The Struggle for Equality*, ed. Herbert Hill and James E. Jones Jr. (Madison: University of Wisconsin Press, 1993), pp. 269–70; and Herbert Hill, "The Problem of Race in American Labor History," *Reviews in American History* 24 (June 1996): 109–208.

40. Robert H. Zieger, *The CIO, 1935–1955* (Chapel Hill: University of North Carolina Press, 1995), p. 418. See also Bruce Nelson et al., "Robert Zieger's History of the CIO," *Labor History* 37 (Spring 1996): 157–88.

41. Request for Grant Action, National Urban League, PA 650-0374, September 30, 1965, p. 1, in Ford Foundation Archive, New York City (hereafter FFA).

42. Mitchell Sviridoff, oral history interview, February 12, 1975, p. 26, FFA.

43. Hill, personal communication, September 10, 1996.

44. *Final Report*, FFA Grant no. 6822, February 15, 1971.

45. William B. Gould, *Black Workers in White Unions: Job Discrimination in the United States* (Ithaca: Cornell University Press, 1977), p. 15.

46. A. Philip Randolph Institute, "Objectives, Principles, Organizational Structure and Operating Policies" (New York, December 1992), p. 2.

47. John N. Sturdivant, personal communication, July 27, 1993.

Chapter 6. Working Women

1. Quoted in William L. O'Neill, *Everyone Was Brave: The Rise and Fall of Feminism in America* (Chicago: Quadrangle, 1969), p. 134.

2. Ibid., p. 151.

3. John M. Glenn, Lilian Brandt, and F. Emerson Andrews, *Russell Sage Foundation, 1907–1946*, 2 vols. (New York: Russell Sage Foundation, 1947), 1:152. See also Robert Bremner, *From the Depths: The Discovery of Poverty in the United States* (1956; New Brunswick, N.J.: Transaction Books, 1992), chap. 13, especially pp. 230–40.

4. Nancy S. Dye, *As Equals and as Sisters: Feminism, the Labor Movement, and the Women's Trade Union League of New York* (Columbia: University of Missouri Press, 1980), p. 8; Philip Foner, *Women and the American Labor Movement*, vol. 2: *From World War I to the Present* (New York: Free Press, 1980), p. 222.

5. Elizabeth B. Butler, *Women and the Trades: Pittsburgh, 1907–08*, vol. 1 of *The Pittsburgh Survey*, 6 vols. (New York: Russell Sage Foundation, 1909). The survey was expected to be not merely research but "an object lesson not only to the city . . . itself but to American industrial cities." Glenn et al., *Russell Sage Foundation*, 1:34; see also David Hammack, *The Russell Sage Foundation: Social Research and Social Action in America, 1902–1947*, guide to the microfiche edition (Frederick, Md.: UPA Academic Editions, 1988), pp. 14–17.

6. Susan Lehrer, "A Living Wage Is for Men Only: Minimum Wage Legislation for Women, 1910–1925," in Christine Bose, Rosyln Feldberg, and Natalie Sokoloff, eds., with the Women and Work Research Group, *Hidden Aspects of Women's Work* (New York: Praeger, 1987), pp. 157, 211.

7. O'Neill, *Everyone Was Brave*, p. 95–97.

8. On protective legislation for women see Bremner, *From the Depths*, pp. 233–35.

9. Alice Kessler-Harris, *A Woman's Wage: Historical Meanings and Social Consequences* (Lexington: University Press of Kentucky, 1990), p. 156; Philip S. Foner, *History of the Labor Movement in the United States*, vol. 3: *The Policies and Practices of the American Federation of Labor, 1900–1909* (New York: International, 1981), p. 223; Bremner, *From the Depths*, pp. 235–36.

10. Van Kleeck took a leave to work in Washington when the War Industries Board asked the Russell Sage Foundation to look into the possibilities of replacing men with women in the government's warehouses. She served on the War Labor Policies Board, wrote a memorandum on labor standards that was adopted by the Chief of Ordnance, and organized and directed a women's branch in the War Department's Industrial Service Section (the Woman in Industry Service) which after the war was established as the Women's Bureau of the Department of Labor (as per Van Kleeck's recommendation). Glenn et al., *Russell Sage Foundation*, 1:256–58.

11. O'Neill, *Everyone Was Brave*, pp. 116, 117, 138.

12. Foner, *Women and the American Labor Movement*, p. 230; Dye, *As Equals*, p. 38; Alice Kessler-Harris, *Out to Work: A History of Wage-Earning Women in the United States* (New York: Oxford University Press, 1982), pp. 22, 205, 208. In 1950, much of its work having been taken over by the labor movement, the WTUL dissolved. See Mary Elizabeth Pidgeon, *Towards Better Working Conditions for Women: Methods and Policies of the National Women's Trade Union League of America*, U.S. Department of Labor, Women's Bureau Bulletin 252 (Washington D.C.: GPO, 1953). See also Theda Skocpol, *Protecting Soldiers and Mothers: The Political Origins of Social Policy in the United States* (Cambridge: Belknap Press of Harvard University Press, 1992), p. 319.

13. Louise C. Odencrantz, *Italian Women in Industry: A Study of Conditions in New York City* (New York: Russell Sage Foundation, 1919), p. 292; Dye, *As Equals*, p. 3.

14. Sophonisba P. Breckinridge, "Women in the Twentieth Century: A Study of Their Political, Social and Economic Activities," in President's Research Committee on Social Trends, *Recent Social Trends*, 2 vols. (New York: McGraw-Hill, 1933).

15. Joyce L. Kornbluh and Mary Frederickson, eds., *Sisterhood and Solidarity: Workers' Education for Women, 1914–1984* (Philadelphia: Temple University Press, 1984), pp. xvi–xvii.

16. Barbara M. Wertheimer, "To Rekindle the Spirit: Current Education Programs for Women," in Kornbluh and Frederickson, *Sisterhood and Solidarity*, p. 306.

17. Gloria Garrett Samson, *The American Fund for Public Service: Charles Garland and Radical Philanthropy, 1922–1941* (Westport, Conn.: Greenwood, 1996), p. 88; Robin Miller Jacoby, "The Women's Trade Union League: Training School for Women Organizers," in Kornbluh and Frederickson, *Sisterhood and Solidarity*, pp. 18–20.

18. Rita Heller, "Blue Collars and Bluestocking: The Bryn Mawr Summer School for Women Workers," in Kornbluh and Frederickson, *Sisterhood and Solidarity*, p. 113.

19. Ibid., pp. 120, 122, 129. The Bryn Mawr School trained one hundred women during eight-week summer sessions annually, with rich extracurricular activities. It set the pattern for later college-based education programs.

20. Mary Frederickson, "Citizens for Democracy: The Industrial Programs of the YWCA," in Kornbluh and Frederickson, *Sisterhood and Solidarity*, pp. 149–68. Samson refers to the $12,000 in her doctoral dissertation, "Toward a New Social Order—The American Fund for Public Service: Clearinghouse for Radicalism in the 1920s" (University of Rochester, 1987), p. 369, but not in her book.

21. Theresa Wolfson, *The Woman Worker and the Trade Unions* (New York: International, 1926), p. 199. A fuller description of Brookwood Labor College can be found in Chapter 9.

22. Marion W. Roydhouse, "Partners in Progress: The Affiliated Schools for Women Workers, 1928–39," in Kornbluh and Frederickson, *Sisterhood and Solidarity*, p. 204.

23. Joyce Kornbluh, interview with author, April 18, 1995. Kornbluh herself received funds from the Rockefeller Foundation for an oral history project, "Twentieth Century Trade Union

Women: Vehicle for Social Change." It appears that foundations that funded adult education shied away from unionism. See O'Neill, *Everyone Was Brave*, p. 151.

24. National Manpower Council, *Womanpower* (New York: Columbia University Press, 1957).

25. These models offered a combination of traditional undergraduate course (economics, political science) and union leadership curricula (role-playing, organizing).

26. Sandy Morales Pope reported in "What Do Unions Do for Women," *Women and Foundations/Corporate Philanthropy News*, Economic Justice supplement, Fall 1993–94, p. S1, that unionized women, from clerical workers and bank tellers to professors and salespersons, earn 30 percent more than nonunionized women workers, though the pay gap between men and women is 20 percent even in union jobs. Also, union women have better benefits across the board than nonunion women.

27. Stephen L. Fisher, ed., *Fighting Back in Appalachia: Traditions of Resistance and Change* (Philadelphia: Temple University Press, 1993), p. 151.

28. But the number of women in the mines fell to 1 percent in 1995, in part because they lack seniority and are first to be laid off. See *Wall Street Journal*, February 6, 1995.

29. Chris Weiss, "Appalachian Women Fight Back: Organizational Approaches to Nontraditional Job Advocacy," in Fisher, *Fighting Back*, chap. 8.

30. Lauren Sugarman, interview with author, January 12, 1993. Sugarman also founded the National Tradeswoman Network, representing 25,000 women. Also training women for the trades in Chicago is the Midwest Women's Center, which targets minority women.

31. Roberta Trace, executive director, enTrade Women's Training and Support Center, Berkeley, Calif., personal communication, November 6, 1993; "Breaking Out of the Pink-Collar Ghetto," *Ford Foundation Report*, Spring, 1993, p. 24.

32. Statement of Purpose, Coalition of Labor Union Women, adopted at the Founding Conference, New York, March 23–24, 1974; Diane Balser, *Sisterhood and Solidarity: Feminism and Labor in Modern Times*, (Boston: South End Press, 1987), chap. 7, esp. pp. 156, 160, 163, 205.

33. Balser, *Sisterhood and Solidarity*, p. 192.

34. Bose, Feldberg, and Sokoloff, *Hidden Aspects of Women's Work*, p. 316. In 1981 the Service Employees International Union (SEIU) gave a charter to a union spin-off of 9 to 5, called District 925, which was started in Boston as Local 925 and has organized over 10,000 women office workers. 9 to 5 continues to operate independently as a nonunion advocacy organization. In Cincinnati, the 9 to 5 chapter responded strongly to a plan by Lazarus Department Stores to eliminate seven hundred nonunion jobs of office and middle-management staff. It devised a program of reemployment, retraining, job search workshops, and a package to give hourly employees the same severance as managers—also under an umbrella of community support. See *9 to 5 Newsline*, March/April 1995, no. 2, 3.

35. *Wall Street Journal*, May 14, 1995.

36. Balser, *Sisterhood and Solidarity*, p. 189; no. 790-0161A, April 17, 1979, Ford Foundation Archives, New York City. Additional Ford Foundation grants in the 1970s sponsored Louise Kapp Howe for *Pink Collar Workers* (New York: Putnam, 1977), and Barbara Wertheimer for *We Were There: The Story of Working Women in America* (New York: Pantheon, 1977). Ford also financed Patricia Cayo Sexton's book *The New Nightingales* (New York: Enquiry, 1982), about hospital workers, commissioned by CLUW and SEIU—the fifth-largest union in the country, with more than one million workers. Sexton is a sociologist and former officer of a UAW local. The Rockefeller Foundation's Gender Roles Program supported Alice Kessler-Harris's *A Woman's Wage: Historical Meanings and Social Consequences* (Lexington: University Press of Kentucky, 1990). Rockefeller also funded a conference at the Brookings Institution, which published *Gender in the Workplace* (1987), edited by Clair Brown and Joseph A. Pechman. The Andrew W. Mellon Foundation backed Bose, Feldberg, and Sokoloff, *Hidden Aspects of Women's Work*, and Elizabeth Payne's book *Margaret Dreier and the Women's Trade Union League* (Urbana: University of Illinois Press, 1988). The film *The Life and Times of Rosie the Riveter*, produced and directed by Connie Field, was distributed in 1980 with funds from the Ford Foundation.

37. *Wall Street Journal*, August 10, 1993.

38. The program's Trade Union Advisory Committee included female officials of some dozen unions. New York State and Cornell's SILR agreed to assume nearly all costs of the program by 1979. Susan Berresford, Request for Grant Action, grant no. 740-0024, September 30, 1975, p. 1.

39. NOW Legal Defense Fund, *Annual Report*, 1993, pp. 8, 9.

40. Miriam Louie, "Organizing Immigrant Women," *Women and Foundations/Corporate Philanthropy News*, Economic Justice Supplement, Fall 1993–94, p. S7.

Chapter 7. Farm and Southern Labor

1. *New York Times*, December 12, 1914; U.S. Commission on Industrial Relations, "The Seasonal Labor Problem in Agriculture." *Final Report 5* (Washington, D.C.: GPO, 1916), pp. 4911–5027.

2. Edwin R. Embree, "Southern Farm Tenancy: The Way Out of Its Evils," *Survey Graphic* 25 (March 1936): 149; Donald H. Grubbs, *Cry from the Cotton: The Southern Tenant Farmers Union and the New Deal* (Chapel Hill: University of North Carolina Press, 1971), p. 5; Louis Cantor, *A Prologue to the Protest Movement: The Missouri Sharecropper Roadside Demonstrations of 1939* (Durham: Duke University Press, 1969), pp. 18–23; Dick Meister and Anne Loftus, *A Long Time Coming: The Struggle to Unionize America's Farm Workers* (New York: Macmillan, 1970), pp. 49–57; David E. Conrad, *The Forgotten Farmer: The Story of Sharecroppers in the New Deal* (Urbana: University of Illinois Press, 1965), pp. 6–9, 14–17, 90–94, 112–13, 157–58.

3. Jerold S. Auerbach, "Southern Tenant Farmers: Socialist Critics of the New Deal," *Labor History* 7 (Winter, 1966): 3–5.

4. Howard Kester, *Revolt among the Sharecroppers* (1936; New York: Arno Press, 1969), p. 73. In addition, Mitchell had to contend with "the Communist Party [which] tried to get control of the STFU but never had much success. After 1939 the Party tried to prevent any recognition of our work in the South." Mitchell to Auerbach, April 26, 1993, Wilson Library Collection, no. 3472, box 40, University of North Carolina Libraries at Chapel Hill. See also Vivian Gornick, *The Romance of American Communism* (New York: Basic Books, 1977), p. 98.

5. H. L. Mitchell, *Mean Things Happening in This Land: The Life and Times of H. L. Mitchell* (Montclair, N.J.: Allanheld Osmun, 1979), p. 137; Grubbs, *Cry from the Cotton*, pp. 78–80.

6. Cantor, *Prologue to the Protest Movement*, pp. 77–78. For Mitchell's quote on philanthropists, see Grubbs, *Cry from the Cotton*, p. 80.

7. Merle Curti, "Subsidizing Radicalism: The American Fund for Public Service: 1921–1941," *Social Science Review* 33 (September 1959): 285–86. The Garland Fund had unexpectedly received repayment of a loan made in the 1920s to the Reconstruction Farms of Russia, which led to a false story that the Russians were subsidizing radicalism in America by funneling Russian gold through the Garland Fund (Mitchell, *Mean Things*, p. 138).

8. Cantor, *Prologue to the Protest Movement*, p. 163.

9. "South's Land Evils Assailed in Report," *New York Times*, March 31, 1935; Alfred Gilbert Belles, "The Julius Rosenwald Fund: Efforts in Race Relations, 1928–1948," diss., Vanderbilt University, 1972, p. 107; Conrad, *Forgotten Farmer*, pp. 122–23. Charles S. Johnson, Edwin R. Embree, and Will W. Alexander, *The Collapse of Cotton Tenancy* (Chapel Hill: University of North Carolina Press, 1935), includes the report of the Committee on Minority Groups in the Economic Recovery.

10. Sidney Baldwin, *Poverty and Politics: The Rise and Fall of the Farm Security Administration.* (Chapel Hill: University of North Carolina Press, 1968), p. 170; Auerbach, "Southern Tenant Farmers," p. 16.

11. Baldwin, *Poverty and Politics*, p. 149; Grubbs, *Cry from the Cotton*, p. 139.

12. Cantor, *Prologue to the Protest Movement*, pp. 142–46; Mitchell, *Mean Things*, pp. 132–33, 136.

13. Kirke Wilson, personal communication, August 22, 1996.

14. Joan London and Henry Anderson, *So Shall Ye Reap: The Story of Cesar Chavez and the Farmworkers' Movement* (New York: Crowell, 1970), p. 40; quote is from Anthony P. Dunbar, *Against the Grain: Southern Radicals and Prophets* (Charlottesville: University Press of Virginia, 1981), p. 256.

15. Baldwin, *Poverty and Politics*, pp. 411, 414. Rural poverty is still acute in the South, where one third of the nation's population but 40 percent of its poor live: "Of the 242 persistently poor nonmetropolitan counties identified by the U.S. Department of Agriculture, 223 are in the South:" "Rural Development: New Southern Initiative," *Responsive Philanthropy*, Spring 1993, p. 10. The Southern Rural Development Initiative, a project of Funders who Fund in the South (an affinity group of foundations and individual grantmakers) wants to find "creative solutions" to the area's substandard resources, noted in the same article.

16. Mitchell, *Mean Things*, p. 146.

17. Thomas N. Bethell, "In Defense of Freedom's Victory!" *Southern Exposure* 21 (Spring/Summer 1993): 21.

18. The Executive Council was directed to organize migratory workers in 1910 and reported on its investigation in 1911; the report is summarized in AFL, *American Federation of Labor—History, Encyclopedia, Reference Book*, 3 vols. (Washington, D.C., 1919), 1:289. For an analysis of the AFL's approach to agriculture, see London and Anderson, *So Shall Ye Reap*, pp. 22–23.

19. Irving Bernstein, *The Turbulent Years: A History of the American Worker, 1933–1941* (Boston: Houghton-Mifflin, 1970), pp. 150–51.

20. London and Anderson, *So Shall Ye Reap*, pp. 128–29. Galarza, with a Ph.D. from Columbia University, had been an official of the Pan American Union. A grant from the Robert Marshall Civil Liberties Fund to examine the status of civil liberties of Mexican Americans enabled the NFLU to hire him to do research. To the NFLU, "'research' meant organizing and 'Mexican Americans' meant farm workers": Craig Jenkins, *The Politics of Insurgency: The Farm Worker Movement in the 1960s* (New York: Columbia University Press, 1988), p. 102. Galarza went on to become a notable union organizer.

21. Kirke Wilson, personal communication, August 22, 1996. Wilson writes, "The questions of how many farm workers there are in California, how many are migrant, how many Latinos (and how many are undocumented) are complex and controversial. In order to block proposals for a new bracero program, Rosenberg grants (along with Ford grants) have paid expenses of challenging the U.S. Census on these issues."

22. London and Anderson, *So Shall Ye Reap*, pp. 144–45. Collection of the United Farm Workers/Office of the President, Archives of Labor and Urban Affairs, Reuther Library, Wayne State University, Detroit; Meister and Loftus, *Long Time Coming*, pp. 114–15, 122–23; Peter Matthiessen, *Sal si Puedes: Cesar Chavez and the New American Revolution* (New York: Random House, 1968), pp. 46–49.

23. Jason De Parle, "Last of the Manongs: Aging Voice of a Farm-Labor Fight," *New York Times*, May 11, 1993.

24. Craig Jenkins, "Radical Transformation of Organizational Goals," *Administrative Science Quarterly* 22 (December 1977): 577, 579; Kirke Wilson, personal communication, August 22, 1996.

25. Matthiessen, *Sal si Puedes*, p. 28. By the late 1960s, cash contributions totaling $2 million had been received from church organizations, politicians, labor, and the Office of Economic Opportunity.

26. Jenkins, *Politics of Insurgency*, p. 141; "Reuther Opens Farm Union's Center," *New York Times*, September 15, 1969.

27. Ronald B. Taylor, *Chavez and the Farm Workers* (Boston: Beacon, 1975), pp. 117, 182.

28. Dolores Huerta, "Reflections on the UFW Experience," *Center Magazine* 18 (July/August 1985): 3.

29. Leslie Dunbar, interview with author, April 11, 1994. See also Field Foundation Archives, University of Texas, file 2S428.

30. "Grapes of Wrath," *Economist*, August 20, 1988, p. 25.

31. G. Pascal Zachary, "United Farm Workers Are Finding New Life after Chavez's Death," *Wall Street Journal,* December 19, 1995.

32. Also in 1996, the UFW ended one of its longest campaigns, winning a seventeen-year struggle with Bruce Church Inc., the nation's third-largest lettuce-growing company. The union won immediate pay raises plus extended health benefits.

33. U.S. Congress, House of Representatives, Select Committee to Investigate Tax-Exempt Foundations and Comparable Organizations (Cox Committee), *Hearings,* 81st Cong., 1st sess., 1952, p. 725.

34. Kirke Wilson, personal communication, October 1, 1992.

35. Ibid.

36. Ruth Chance, oral history, p. 15 and passim, Rosenberg Foundation Archive, San Francisco. Chance's successor, Kirke Wilson, had himself been a community organizer in the San Joaquin Valley.

37. Ibid. p. 100.

38. Mitchell Sviridoff, oral history, February 12, 1975, Ford Foundation Archive, New York City; hereafter FFA.

39. Request for Grant Action, September 28, 1970, p. 2, PA 700-0657, FFA. The service centers addressed economic, social, and legal problems faced by migrant farm workers, helping them to secure their civil rights, to collect workmen's compensation and Social Security benefits to which they were entitled, and to resist exploitation by landlords, creditors, and vendors. The major emphasis of the legal services department was on health, particularly the dangerous effects of hazardous pesticides and herbicides. At the time growers, responding to increased restrictions on the use of DDT in California, were shifting to more highly toxic chemicals. In addition, the legal department worked to obtain enforcement of state sanitation laws in the field.

40. Siobhan Oppenheimer-Nicolau to Robert L. Hunt, April 29, 1971; PA 700-0647; Nicolau to L. K. Shepard, December 8, 1971, both in FFA.

41. David Ramage Jr. to Siobhan Nicolau, memo, July 11, 1972, PA 700-0657, FFA.

42. Gary Delgado, "Beyond the Politics of Place: New Directions in Community Organizing in the 1990s" (Oakland, Calif.: Applied Research Center, 1994), pp. 60–61.

43. Ibid. Another MacArthur Fellow (for his organizational work with labor unions, citizens' groups, and religious denominations) is Ernesto J. Cortes Jr., who founded San Antonio Communities Organized for Public Service and directs the Texas Industrial Areas Foundation, which employs the strategies of Saul Alinsky. Information on MacArthur Fellows from the foundation's brochure on the program.

44. Starry Kreuger, executive director, RDLN, personal communication, May 23, 1994. The chairperson of the RDLN, Billie Jean Young, won a MacArthur Fellowship for her work as a community organizer for the Southeast Alabama Farmers Cooperative Association. She is executive director of the Southern Rural Women's Network.

45. Veatch Foundation, *Bulletin,* Spring 1993, p. 3. Since the early 1980s several foundations (e.g., Mary Reynolds Babcock, Lyndhurst, Shalan, Raskob, and Arca) have funded projects that supported migrant worker organizing, advocacy, and helped to enable small, independent farmers to embrace sophisticated scientific agriculture.

46. Ann Bastian, "Farmworkers and Environmental Funding," memorandum to National Network of Grantmakers colleagues, April 19, 1991, New World Foundation, New York.

47. Request for Grant Action, August 12, 1982, p. 5, no. USAIP 175–179, FFA. Subsequent RGAs in 1984 and 1988 follow up on program objectives and actions of the FJF.

48. D. Michael Hancock, executive director, FJF, interview with author, May 28, 1995.

49. Ibid.; Bastian, "Farmworkers."

50. Jonathan J. Higuera, "They Harvest Our Food," *Foundation News & Commentary,* May/June 1994, pp. 12–19; Bruce Goldskin, executive director, FJF, interview with author, April 15, 1998.

51. Steven Greenhouse, "U.S. Surveys Find Farm Worker Pay Down for 20 Years," *New York Times,* March 31, 1997.

Chapter 8. Education

1. Elizabeth A. Fones-Wolf, *Selling Free Enterprise: The Business Assault on Labor and Liberalism* (Urbana: University of Illinois Press, 1994), pp. 207–10.

2. AFL Executive Committee Minutes, 1907, *American Federation of Labor—History, Encyclopedia, Reference Book*, 3 vols. (Washington, D.C.: AFL, 1919) 1:159. Organized labor's sensitivity on the issue of indoctrination of youth was reflected in its suspicion of the Boy Scout movement, whose alleged emphasis on militarism raised the specter of training Scouts sub rosa as strikebreakers (ibid.).

3. George Miller, "Education and the Labor Movement," *American Federationist* 9 (October 1902): 691; cited in John P. Beck, "Highlander Folk School's Junior Union Camps," *Labor's Heritage* 5 (Spring 1993): 30. Beck discusses two later programs designed to implement these ideas: In 1924, Pioneer Youth of America was founded by a coalition of progressive educators and churchmen as well as labor leaders to counteract antiunion and open shop propaganda in the public schools through camps and city-based clubs. A similar effort—the "junior union" movement—was sponsored by the AFL in the 1930s, and the Highlander Folk School ran junior union camps in the 1940s.

4. Lawrence A. Cremin, *The Transformation of the School: Progressivism in American Education, 1876–1957* (New York: Knopf, 1961), pp. 39–40, 52–53.

5. At the same time the NAM warned of the potential appeal of unionism to underpaid teachers, "which naturally breeds sympathy" to promote labor's views in the classroom, adding force to labor's drive for power. See Fones-Wolf, *Selling Free Enterprise*, p. 201.

6. Diane Ravitch, *The Great School Wars: New York City, 1805–1973* (New York: Basic Books, 1974), pp. 210–16.

7. Ellen Condliffe Lagemann, *Private Power for the Public Good: A History of the Carnegie Foundation for the Advancement of Teaching* (Middletown, Conn.: Wesleyan University Press, 1983), pp. 188–89.

8. JoAnn Wood, "Margaret Haley and Democratic Teaching," unpublished paper, Teachers College, Columbia University, December, 1993, pp. 5, 12, 14.

9. Local, state, and national teachers' associations had been established before the Civil War, but they concerned themselves with professional training and classroom problems, rarely with questions of salaries, tenure, or controversial social issues: R. Freeman Butts and Lawrence A. Cremin, *A History of Education in American Culture* (New York: Holt, 1953), pp. 288–89, 457. Significant teacher unions per se began with the organization of the American Federation of Teachers in 1916.

10. Paul Woodring, *Investment in Innovation: An Historical Appraisal of the Fund for the Advancement of Education* (Boston: Little, Brown, 1970), pp. 148–49.

11. Ibid., p. 247.

12. The concept, with teacher union support, was a linchpin in President Clinton's second-term campaign for educational reform.

13. Frederick Mosher, interview with author, December 10, 1994.

14. The union movement was hard to ignore. It had emerged from World War II as a powerful force in American society, unprecedented in size and organizational stability. Union membership soared from 8.8 million in 1940 to 14.9 million in 1946 (just over one third of the civilian labor force). Most basic industries were 80 to 100 percent organized.

15. Among the dozens of individuals consulted were Clinton S. Golden, former steel union official, consultant to the Twentieth Century Fund, and Garland Fund board member; Steward Meacham of the Amalgamated Clothing Workers of America and director of the Sidney Hillman Foundation; and Boris Shishkin, economist with the AFL.

16. Mitchell Sviridoff, "Organized Labor and Organized Philanthropy: A Discussion Paper," n.d., Report no. 5045, Ford Foundation Archive; hereafter FFA.

17. Basil Whiting, "The Suddenly Remembered American," September 1970, Report no. 2098, FFA, p. 51.

18. Basil Whiting, interview with author, October 23, 1992.

19. Robert B. Goldmann, *A Work Experiment: Six Americans in a Swedish Plant* (New York: Ford Foundation, 1976). According to Robert Schrank, a program officer at the Ford Foundation, the term "quality of work-life" was coined at the first international conference on the subject, convened by the foundation in 1972.

20. Ravitch, *Great School Wars*, p. 357.

21. Mitchell Sviridoff, oral history interview, February 12, 1975, p. 26, FFA.

22. Ravitch, *Great School Wars*, p. 328.

23. Waldemar Nielsen, *The Big Foundations* (New York: Columbia University Press, 1972), p. 5.

24. Ravitch, *Great School Wars*, p. 350.

25. Albert Shanker, interview with author, March 2, 1993.

26. Florida School Labor Relations Service, *Statement of Purpose*, December 1, 1975, PA 760-0081, FFA.

27. Charles T. Kerchner and Julia E. Koppich, *A Union of Professionals: Labor Relations and Educational Reform* (New York: Teachers College Press, 1993).

28. Mosher interview.

29. Eugene R. Wilson, personal communication, January 19, 1993.

30. B. Stephen Toben (Hewlett Foundation), personal communication, April 23, 1993. See also Lorraine M. McDonnell and Anthony Pascal, *Teacher Unions and Educational Reform* (Santa Monica: RAND Corporation, Center for Policy Research in Education/Center for the Study of the Teaching Profession, April 1988).

31. An NEA spokesman describes this as "a propaganda line widely disseminated by opponents of public education": Vince Stehle, "The Right's Aggressive 'Battle Tank,' " *Chronicle of Philanthropy*, April 6, 1995, pp. 6–8.

32. Myron Lieberman, "Pseudo School Reform," *Weekly Standard*, March 25, 1996, pp. 15–17.

33. Sophie Sa, personal communication, June 17, 1994. *Panasonic Partnership Program Newsletter* 5 (Fall 1995): 4.

34. John T. Dunlop, *The Management of Labor Unions: Decision-Making with Historical Constraints* (Lexington, Mass.: Lexington Books, 1990), p. 134; Bennett Harrison with Marcus Weiss and Jon Gant, *Building Bridges: Community Development Corporations and the World of Employment Training* (New York: Ford Foundation, 1995), pp. 66–67.

35. National Education Association, *Stewardship Report—1985 to 1993* (Washington, D.C., 1993), p. 3.

36. Donna Rhodes, interview with author, March 10, 1993.

37. William S. McKersie, "Philanthropy's Paradox: Chicago School Reform," *Education Evaluation and Policy Analysis* 15 (Summer 1993): 109; also his "Reforming Chicago's Public Schools: Philanthropic Persistence, 1987–1993," *Advances in Educational Policy* 2 (1996): 141–57.

38. Peter Martinez, interview with author, November 17, 1994.

39. Deborah Walsh, interview with author, November 17, 1994.

40. Julia Vitullo-Martin, "Mayor Daley's Plan to Fix Chicago's Schools," *Wall Street Journal*, August 18, 1996. See also letter from Adele Simmons, the president of the MacArthur Foundation, to *Wall Street Journal*, October 31, 1995, in which she observes, "Notable in the school reform process has been the degree of participation by the teachers union. Its Quest Center is unique in the nation in work on classroom innovation." Peter Applebome, "Chicago Experiment Offers Lessons, but No Verdict on Decentralization," *New York Times*, November 8, 1995.

41. Kenneth K. Wong et al., "Integrated Governance as a Reform Strategy in the Chicago Public Schools" (Department of Education and Irving B. Harris Graduate School of Public Policy Studies, University of Chicago, January 1997), pp. 6, 12, 20. See also Penny Bender Sebring et al., "Charting Reform in Chicago: The Students Speak" (Chicago: Consortium on Chicago School Research, December 1996).

42. Sarah Mosely, "A City School Experiment That Actually Works," *New York Times Magazine*, May 28, 1995, p. 49.

43. "Unions Consider Charter Schools of Their Own," *New York Times*, September 22, 1996.
44. Cross City Campaign publications include "Reinventing Central Office," "Principles of Policy and Practice," and "Schools and Community Partnerships" (May 1994). On NCEA, see *Social Justice Unionism: A Working Draft. A Call to Education Unionists* (Rhinebeck, N.Y., 1994).

Chapter 9. Labor Education

1. *American Federation of Labor—History, Encyclopedia, Reference Book*, 3 vols. (Washington, D.C.: AFL, 1919), 1:381.
2. Ellen Condliffe Lagemann, *The Politics of Knowledge: The Carnegie Corporation, Philanthropy, and Public Policy* (Middletown, Conn.: Wesleyan University Press, 1989), p. 119; Harry Millis and Royal Montgomery, *The Economics of Labor*, vol. 3 (New York: McGraw-Hill, 1945), p. 327.
3. Steven Fraser, *Labor Will Rule: Sidney Hillman and the Rise of American Labor* (Ithaca: Cornell University Press, 1991), pp. 221–23.
4. Because of grants to the California Labor School in the 1940s, the Rosenberg Foundation was investigated over a twenty-year period for un-American activities, and charged with being "Communist dominated." See the discussion of California farm workers in Chapter 7.
5. Gloria Garrett Samson, *The American Fund for Public Service: Charles Garland and Radical Philanthropy, 1922–1941* (Westport, Conn.: Greenwood), p. 120.
6. Quoted ibid., p. 88.
7. Raymond Koch and Charlotte Koch, *The Story of Commonwealth College* (New York: Schocken, 1971), pp. 20–21.
8. Brookwood Labor College Collection, boxes 1, 22, 23, 55; Starr Personal Papers, 1920–56. Both are in the Archives of Labor History and Urban Affairs, Reuther Library, Wayne State University, Detroit.
9. Irving Bernstein, *The Lean Years: A History of the American Worker, 1920–1933* (Boston: Houghton-Mifflin, 1960), p. 106; Jonathan Bloom, "Brookwood College: The Final Years, 1933–1937," *Labor's Heritage* 2 (April 1990): 24–43.
10. Lawrence Rogin, "How Far Have We Come in Workers' Education?" in *The Labor Movement: A Reexamination*, ed. Jack Barbash (Madison: University of Wisconsin Press, 1967), pp. 121–26.
11. Among the prominent students at Highlander was Betty Friedan, pioneer of the modern women's movement, who attended a writing workshop there in 1941 and became a labor journalist. See Karen J. Winkler, "Relooking at the Roots of Feminism," *Chronicle of Higher Education*, April 12, 1996, p. A10.
12. Frank Adams and Myles Horton, *Unearthing Seeds of Fire: The Idea of Highlander* (Winston-Salem, N.C.: John F. Blair, 1975), p. 106.
13. John M. Glenn, *Highlander, No Ordinary School* (Lexington: University Press of Kentucky, 1988), pp. 71–72.
14. Quoted in Adams and Horton, *Unearthing Seeds of Fire*, pp. 87–88.
15. Dan La Boz, "Solidarity Schools Link Study and Struggle," *Labor Notes*, March 1995, p. 5.
16. Quoted in Doris Cohen Brody, "American Labor Education Service, 1927–62: An Organization in Workers' Education," diss., Cornell University, 1973, p. 1; Alfred Gilbert Belles, "The Julius Rosenwald Fund: Efforts in Race Relations, 1928–1948," diss., Vanderbilt University, 1972, pp. 78–82. Highlander's integration policies were a factor singled out by the Reece Committee, as we saw in Chapter 3.
17. Belles, "Julius Rosenwald Fund," pp. 85–94.
18. Brody, "American Labor Education Service," pp. 82–83.
19. Lagemann, *Politics of Knowledge*, p. 103. See also "Workers' Education" in *Encyclopedia of the Social Sciences* (1933), 15:484–85.
20. Lagemann, *Politics of Knowledge*, pp. 105, 107, 118–19, 121.

21. Joseph Mire, *Labor Education: A Study Report on Needs, Programs, and Approaches* (New York: Inter-University Labor Education Committee for the Fund for Adult Education, 1956), pp. 19, 20.

22. Robert Howard, "Worker Education Comes of Age," *Working Papers for a New Society* 10 (January/February 1983): 34–41.

23. The LHF carries out the most systematic labor-directed effort in the arts. Founded in 1984 as a branch of the Industrial Union Department of the AFL-CIO, it is funded mainly by unions and state and federal arts and humanities councils. The LHF sponsors music festivals, collects performing arts material, assists filmmaking on labor themes, and conducts labor arts exchanges.

24. Foundations have assisted historical aspects of the labor movement, such as the Shiffman Foundation's funding of the Detroit Labor History Project. This project produced an audio tape and brochure about the controversial Diego Rivera murals depicting Detroit labor and industry at the Detroit Institute of Arts (financed in 1932 by Edsel Ford), a 250-page labor history of Detroit, and slide shows. At the University of California, Berkeley, the Skaggs Foundation gave a grant for an oral history of the International Longshoremen's and Warehousemen's Union. The Lucius N. Littauer Foundation of New York provided $20,000 to New York University's Wagner Labor Archives to enable a Yiddish-reading archivist to process the papers of the old Jewish Labor Committee.

25. Elizabeth A. Fones-Wolf, *Selling Free Enterprise: The Business Assault on Labor and Liberalism, 1945–60* (Urbana: University of Illinois Press, 1994), pp. 195–96.

26. David Montgomery, *Workers' Control in America: Studies in the History of Work, Technology, and Labor Struggles* (New York: Cambridge University Press, 1979), p. 158.

27. Steven Schlossman et al., "The 'New Look': The Ford Foundation and the Revolution in Business Education," *Selections* (McLean, Va.: Graduate Management Admissions Council, 1987), pp. 12–27.

28. Quoted in Joseph DePlasco, "The University of Labor vs. the University of Letters," *Labor's Heritage* 1 (April 1989): 53.

29. *Trade Union Program, 83d Session* (brochure, 1994); Harvard University Trade Union Program, *Summary* (1993), Introduction, *Curriculum Summary*, 82d Session of the Harvard Trade Union Program (1993); Ken Gewertz, "Where the Real World Meets the Classroom," *Harvard Gazette*, April 5, 1991, p. 7.

30. Martin M. Wooster, "Chairs of Entrepreneurship Are Bad Business," *Wall Street Journal*, May 25, 1990.

31. Montgomery, *Workers' Control*, p. 158.

32. "Working Together: Labor-Campus Collaboration," Report from a National Survey (Washington, D.C.: Labor/Higher Education Council, American Council on Education, and the AFL-CIO, July 1991), p. 2.

Chapter 10. Health, Safety, Environment

1. Robert Kohler, "Philanthropy and Science," *Proceedings of the American Philosophical Society* 129 (1985): 9–13.

2. Harry Becker, "Organized Labor and the Problem of Medical Care," *Annals of the American Academy of Political and Social Science* 273 (January 1951): 122.

3. Quoted in David T. Beito, "The Lodge Practice Evil Reconsidered: Medical Care through Fraternal Societies, 1900–1930," *Journal of Urban History* 23 (July 1997).

4. Quoted in George Rosen, "The Stabilization of the Medical Market," in *The Structure of American Medical Practice, 1875–1941*, ed. Charles E. Rosenberg (Philadelphia: University of Pennsylvania Press, 1983), p. 104.

5. Paul Starr, *The Social Transformation of American Medicine* (New York: Basic Books, 1982), p. 28.

6. An example of such initiatives is the National Tuberculosis Association, founded in 1904, as cited in Michael Davis, *America Organizes Medicine* (New York: Harper, 1941), p. 106. The AMA opposed federal grants to states for maternal and child health introduced in 1921 under the aegis of the U.S. Children's Bureau.

7. Daniel S. Hirschfield, *The Lost Reform: The Campaign for Compulsory Health Insurance in the United States from 1932 to 1943* (Cambridge: Harvard University Press, 1970), pp. 12–17.

8. Ibid., pp. 18–23.

9. Starr, *Social Transformation,* pp. 249, 251.

10. On the role played by fear of radicalism, see especially Ronald Numbers, *Almost Persuaded: American Physicians and Compulsory Health Insurance, 1912–1920* (Baltimore: Johns Hopkins University Press, 1978), pp. 86–88.

11. Gloria Garrett Samson, *The American Fund for Public Service: Charles Garland and Radical Philanthropy, 1922–1941* (Westport, Conn.: Greenwood, 1996), pp. 88–89.

12. Angela Nugent, "Organizing Trade Unions to Combat Disease: The Workers' Health Bureau, 1921–1928," *Labor History* 26 (Summer 1985): 423–46.

13. Samson, *American Fund,* p. 89; Nugent, "Organizing Trade Unions," pp. 423–46; David Rosner and Gerald Markowitz, eds., *Dying for Work: Workers' Safety and Health in Twentieth-Century America* (Bloomington: Indiana University Press, 1987), p. 61. This book and a research study by the same authors, *Deadly Dust: Silicosis and the Politics of Occupational Disease in Twentieth-Century America* (Princeton: Princeton University Press, 1991), were both sponsored by the Milbank Memorial Fund.

14. Ray Lyman Wilbur, "The Cost of Being Ill to Be Surveyed for All," *New York Times,* September 23, 1928, section X; Michael M. Davis, "The American Approach to Health Insurance," *Milbank Memorial Fund Quarterly* 12 (April 1934): 214–15. Davis concluded, "People who are economically secure . . . against all ordinary demands, are not secure against the costs of sickness. Thus, the economic problems of medical care now implicate not merely wage-earners but the whole population, except the 5 per cent with the largest incomes." The CCMC also planned to address growing needs in preventive medicine and chronic disease among those living longer.

15. Wilbur, "Cost of Being Ill."

16. All data from Isidore Falk, C. R. Rosen, and Martha Ring, *Medical Care for the American People: The Final Report of the Committee on the Costs of Medical Care,* Publication no. 28 (1932; U.S. Department of Health, Education, and Welfare, 1970); *The Costs of Medical Care: A Summary of Investigations . . . of the Committee on the Costs of Medical Care,* Publication no. 27 (1933; U.S. Department of Health, Education, and Welfare, 1970); see also CCMH publications no. 5 and no. 18, on industrial surveys.

17. Daniel M. Fox, personal communication, October 15, 1996.

18. "Socialized Medicine Is Urged in Survey," *New York Times,* November 30, 1932. There were at least four dissenting opinions from the thirty-five CCMC supporters of the final report (see *New York Times,* November 30, 1932).

19. The *Journal* of the AMA also declaimed, "The alignment is clear—on the one side the forces representing the great foundations, public health officialdom, social theory—even socialism and communism—inciting to revolution; on the other side, the organized medical profession . . . urging an orderly evolution guided by controlled experimentation which will serve the principles that have been found through the centuries to be necessary to the sound practice of medicine." Quoted in "Medical Journal Attacks Report," *New York Times,* November 30, 1932; cited in Odin W. Anderson, "Compulsory Medical Care Insurance, 1910–1950," in *Annals of the American Academy of Political and Social Science,* 273 (January 1951): 109.

20. Hirschfield, *Lost Reform,* p. 203; Daniel M. Fox, "The New Vulnerability of Foundations in Health Affairs," paper presented at a conference at the Rockefeller Archive Center, Pocantico Hills, N.Y., April 25, 1996, p. 11. Fox notes that in response to a request from Harry Hopkins (FDR's relief administrator), Milbank funded I. S. Falk and Michael Davis to act as consultants to the Committee on Economic Security, the advisory group on Social Security legislation (1934) that framed the Social Security program.

21. Davis, *America Organizes Medicine*, p. 297; *Proceedings*, National Health Conference, Washington, D.C., July 18–20, 1938, sponsored by the Interdepartmental Committee to Coordinate Health and Welfare Activities.

22. On Kaiser's legacy, see Robert Sullivan, review of Rickey Hendricks, *A Model for National Health Care: The History of Kaiser Permanente*, in *Journal of American History*, 81 (September 1994): 781–82; Joseph Gabarino, *Health Plans and Collective Bargaining* Berkeley: University of California Press, 1960, pp. 93–95; Richard Carter, *The Doctor Business* (Garden City, N.Y.: Doubleday, 1958), pp. 161–66.

23. The 1990 figure is from Sullivan's review of Hendricks's book cited above. On the award, see Waldemar Nielsen, *The Big Foundations* (New York: Columbia University Press, 1972), pp. 245–47.

24. Starr, *Social Transformation*, pp. 310–12. Based on 140 unions with 4.3 million workers, a 1950 Department of Labor table shows 9.4 million (including dependents) covered for health and hospital care under collective bargaining; cited in T. Parran and L. Falk, "Collective Bargaining for Medical Care Benefits," *British Journal of Preventive and Social Medicine* 7 (July 1953): 88. In 1947, Carnegie Corporation granted $30,000 to the University of Wisconsin for a study of health and welfare benefits under collective bargaining, conducted jointly by the Law School and the Industrial Relations Research Center.

25. "Health Insurance Proposed for All," *New York Times*, December 5, 1944.

26. Starr, *Social Transformation*, pp. 284–88. "The Whitaker-Baxter team hardly missed a trick": James M. Perry, "In Remembrance of Fiery Battles Past, Cries of 'Socialism' Still Reverberate," *Wall Street Journal*, September 22, 1993.

27. *New York Times*, May 1, 15, 1944; January 1, 8, 1947; March 1, 1948; George Baehr, *The Health Insurance Plan of Greater New York: Ten Years of Service, 1947–1956* (New York: HIP, 1957).

28. Garbarino, *Health Plans*, p. 9; Starr, *Social Transformation*, p. 311.

29. This is not to say that unions on their own, without foundation assistance, were not responsive to members' health care needs. The United Mine Workers, the International Ladies Garment Workers Union, and the Amalgamated Clothing Workers established their own clinics and group health plans. David Rosner, "From First Person to Third Part: Financing Health Service in the Greater American Metropolis," in Proceedings of a conference, *Private Action and Social Policy: The Impact of Federations and Associations in the American Metropolis, 1900–1929* (Cleveland: Case Western Reserve University, 1989), pp. 11–12; see also Becker, "Organized Labor," p. 123.

30. Terrance Keenan, *The Promise at Hand: Prospects for Foundation Leadership in the 1990s* (Princeton: Robert Wood Johnson Foundation, 1992), p. 15. One of the nation's largest foundations, the Howard Hughes Medical Institute, devotes virtually all of its $5.6 billion endowment to university research on genetics and other aspects of cellular and molecular biology.

31. Terrance Keenan, "Health Philanthropy and Health Reform," *GrantScene/Grantmakers in Health Newsletter*, Spring 1993, pp. 7–8; Commonwealth Fund, *For the Common Good; The Commonwealth Fund, 1918–1993* (New York, 1993).

32. Terrance Keenan, personal communication, October 2, 1996. *Health Affairs*, Winter 1990 discusses and evaluates this project. CHPAC did contribute to the knowledge base about health care financing, but Robert Wood Johnson officials, on the whole, judged the effort a failure.

33. John A. Hartford Foundation, *Annual Report*, 1993, pp. 12–15, 31–33.

34. George Anders, "New Rules Press HMOs to Disclose Data," *Wall Street Journal*, July 16, 1996.

35. *Tobacco Policy Research and Evaluation Program* (Princeton: Robert Wood Johnson Foundation, 1993).

36. Glorian Sorensen and Richard Youngstrom, "Smokefree or Free to Smoke? Labor's Role in Tobacco Control: Introduction to the Conference Proceedings" (1995), a *New Solutions* preprint, Spring 1996, Dana-Farber Cancer Institute, Boston.

37. The foundation's call for proposals was issued in the form of two pamphlets: *Smokeless States: Statewide Tobacco Prevention and Control Initiatives* (1993) and *Smoke-Free Families: Innovations to Stop Smoking During and Beyond Pregnancy* (1994). See also Shari Rudavsky, "Health

Foundation Grants $10 Million to Support Local Anti-Tobacco Efforts," *Wall Street Journal*, August 15, 1994.

38. Samuel B. Bacharach, Peter Bamberger, and William J. Sonnenstuhl, *Member Assistance Programs in the Workplace: The Role of Labor in the Prevention and Treatment of Substance Abuse*, ILR Bulletin 69 (Ithaca: ILR Press, 1994).

39. John Sweeney, personal communication, September 2, 1993.

40. Anne Lowrey Bailey, "Health Care's Merger Mania," *Chronicle of Philanthropy*, November 16, 1995, pp. 1, 32–34; *States of Health Newsletter* 6 (February 1996).

41. Author interviews with Carol Regan, October 10, 1996, and Bill Roush, October 15, 1996.

42. Bailey, "Health Care's Merger Mania," p. 33; *Responsive Philanthropy Newsletter*, Fall 1996, pp. 2–3, 12.

43. Philip M. Gasel and Jay E. Gerzog, "Conversions of Not-for-Profit Organizations Proliferate," *New York Law Journal*, August 26, 1996, p. 7.

44. Susan Sherry, interview with author, October 4, 1996.

45. Domenica Marchetti, "States Urged to Postpone Hospital Sales," *Chronicle of Philanthropy* August 21, 1997, p. 27. See also "Columbia May Have Destroyed Data," *Wall Street Journal*, April 7, 1997; "Federal Agents Step Up Pressure in Columbia/HCA Investigation," *New York Times*, August 20, 1997. Columbia, managing 340 hospitals at the time, began to retrench (by giving up some assets) under new leadership. Columbia/HCA was subsequently indicted.

46. "The New Conversion Health Foundations: Preliminary Results of a GIH Survey," paper presented at the Council on Foundations, Atlanta, April 23, 1996 (Washington, D.C.: Grantmakers in Health). See also Linda Miller, "The Non-Profit Sector in Health Care," conference of the Association for Nonprofit and Voluntary Sector Research, November 8, 1996; Monica Langley and Anita Sharpe, "As Big Hospital Chains Take Over Nonprofits, a Backlash Is Growing," *The Wall Street Journal*, October 18, 1996.

47. Domenica Marchetti, "Redefining Health Philanthropy," *Chronicle of Philanthropy*, July 24, 1997, pp. 1, 12–15.

48. David Rosner and Gerald Markowitz, eds., *Dying for Work: Workers' Safety and Health in Twentieth-Century America* (Bloomington: Indiana University Press, 1987).

49. Ironically, eighty-odd years later this union boycotted a labor conference on restricting workplace smoking, as noted above.

50. Charles Levenstein, Diane Plantamura, and William Mass, "Labor and Byssinosis, 1941–1969," in Rosner and Markowitz, *Dying for Work*, p. 221.

51. William Graebner, "Hegemony through Science: Information Engineering and Lead Toxicology, 1925–1965," ibid., pp. 140–52, 162–63; quotation on p. 143.

52. Ibid., p. 155; "Environmental Protection Agency Concludes Phaseout of Lead from Gasoline," *Wall Street Journal*, January 30, 1996.

53. Basil Whiting, "Request for Supplement to Delegated-Authority Project #729-241," March 12, 1973, Ford Foundation Archive, New York City.

54. Nicholas Ashford, *Crisis in the Workplace: Occupational Disease and Injury* (Cambridge: MIT Press, 1976).

55. Karin Abarbanel, "The Youth Project: Seeding a Grass Roots Revival," *Foundation News*, November/December 1978, p. 26. The Youth Project was also involved with coal miners suffering from black lung disease. Later it assisted the White Lung Association, organized by victims of asbestos exposure at West Coast shipyards during World War II.

56. Bennett M. Judkins, *We Offer Ourselves as Evidence: Toward Workers' Control of Occupational Health* (Westport, Conn.: Greenwood, 1986), p. 114; the Campaign for Human Development began with grants of $27,500, then provided $75,000 a year for several years. The funds were funneled through the CBLA and the Southern Textile Organizing Project, which later merged into the Southern Institute for Occupational Health.

57. Ibid.; Levenstein et al., "Labor and Byssinosis," pp. 221–22.

58. Koralee M. Miller, personal communication, November 24, 1993; Charles Noble, *Lib-*

eralism at Work: The Rise and Fall of OSHA (Philadelphia: Temple University Press, 1986), pp. 133–35, 141–42.

59. *Louisiana Injured Workers Union News* 2 (1st quarter, 1996): 2; Robert Asher, "Organized Labor and the Origins of the Occupational Safety and Health Act," *Labor's Heritage* 3 (January 1991): 57–76. Asher notes the intrinsically contradictory industry approach: "stressing safety . . . while striving for a greater intensity of labor, which increased the likelihood of fatigue and accidents."

60. Hilary Marcus, staff member, Massachusetts Coalition on New Office Technology, interview with author, June 27, 1996; see also Robert Howard, *Brave New World* (New York: Viking, 1965), pp. 73–75.

61. "Jobs, the Economy and the Environment: A Grassroots Training Program for Local Trade Union and Environmental Activists" (New York: Public Health Institute, March 1992), pp. 2–3; "Labor and the Environment: Does Smoke Mean Jobs?" *American Labor*, no. 19 (Washington, D.C.: American Labor Education Center, 1982).

62. Patricia Bauman, interview with author, January 12, 1995. All textual references to the work of the Bauman Foundation are based on this interview.

63. Jack Sheehan, interview with author, March 21, 1995. See *Our Children's World: Steelworkers and the Environment*, report of the USWA Task Force . . . (Pittsburgh: USWA, 1990).

64. "The Labor/Community Strategy Center," unpublished paper, Wiltern Center, Los Angeles, n.d. (1993?).

65. Davis, *America Organizes Medicine*, p. 118.

Chapter 11. Economic Development

1. "Saving Manufacturing—Charting a New Course for Our Unions and Communites," *Labor Research Review* (Midwest Center for Labor Research, Chicago), 19 (Fall 1992), tenth anniversary issue.

2. "Special Issue on Military Conversion," *FIRR News* 4 (Fall 1992).

3. Midwest Center for Labor Research, *Annual Reports*, 1987–88, 1989–90.

4. A campaign against unwarranted tax incentives was successfully waged by the Calumet Project for Industrial Jobs in northwest Indiana, funded by the Woods Charitable Fund, Veatch, and other foundations. Under legislation permitting citizens to monitor tax incentives given to companies to retain or increase jobs, Calumet's research found that companies were given more than $15 million in tax abatements in Gary, Hammond, and East Chicago, but had delivered only a fraction of the jobs promised to these cities. The study led to a Hammond city ordinance requiring companies to demonstrate a need for tax abatement, to pay prevailing wages, and to provide health care benefits: "Give Me a Zillion Dollars, and I'll Create Some Jobs. Maybe," *Labor Notes*, January 1995, p. 11; *Neighborhood Works Newsletter*, April–May 1992, p. 14. In Silicon Valley, Santa Clara County is seeking to implement requirements (for example, health benefits for new workers) in exchange for tax breaks. See M. Person, "Rules Added to Tax Breaks," *San Jose Mercury News*, September 20, 1995.

5. Dan Swinney, Miguel Vasquez, and Howard Engelskirchen, "Towards a New Vision of Community Economic Development," paper presented at National Network of Grantmakers conference, Chicago, May 16–17, 1991, p. 1. Swinney is in close touch with Professor Joel Rogers at the University of Wisconsin Center on Wisconsin Strategy, who coined the term "CEDS" (Conventional Economic Development Strategies) to characterize failed responses to economic/community problems. Swinney's alternative approach is developed in "The New Chicago Campaign: A Proposal to the Rockefeller Foundation," Midwest Center for Labor Research, Chicago, January 12, 1995.

6. Eric Mann, interview with author, September 23, 1994; see also Eric Mann, *Taking on General Motors: A Case Study of the UAW Campaign to Keep GM–Van Nuys Open* (Los Angeles: Institute of Industrial Relations–UCLA, 1987).

7. The ICA has also worked with CWA, UAW, USWA, ACTWA, and the Bakery and Confectionery Workers. However, not all attempts have a happy ending; in New York City, several foundations assisted a union/community campaign to save the jobs of nearly five hundred bakery workers by converting a closing plant to worker ownership, but the effort failed.

8. *RERI Newsletter* (Heinz School, Carnegie Mellon University Center for Economic Development, Pittsburgh), June 1994.

9. Regional Economic Revitalization Initiative, *The Greater Pittsburgh Region: Working Together to Compete Globally* (November 1994), p. 32.

10. Ibid., p. 10.

11. Northwest Area Foundation, *Northwest Report*, April, 1996, pp. 23–24.

12. For background on the Sugars and their legacy, see the center's *Bulletin* 3 (December 1994); on the legal decisions on WARN, see Paul M. Barrett, "Unions May Sue on Behalf of Members in Plant-Closing Cases, High Court Rules," *Wall Street Journal*, May 14, 1995. In a unanimous ruling later that month, the Court said states may give unions two or more years within which to sue on violations of the WARN Act (some states had applied a six-month limit): *Wall Street Journal*, May 31, 1995.

13. Kary L. Moss, personal communication, December 2, 1994.

14. Bruce Allen, "Labor Heeds the Call," *Positive Alternatives* (Center for Economic Conversion, Mountain View, Calif.) 5 (Winter 1995). See also the center's annual reports and its *Overview Statement*, May 1995.

15. Minnesota's Jobs with Peace (MJWP), a FIRR affiliate that grew out of the peace movement, was viewed suspiciously by unions when it was organized in 1984, but it later joined with the International Brotherhood of Electrical Workers Local 2047 to explore the conversion of UNYSIS, a major defense contractor that cut more than 6,500 Minnesota jobs.

16. Peter diCicco, interview with author, March 21, 1995.

17. Gus Gugliotta, "Getting Off Welfare Is Half the Job," *Washington Post*, November 8, 1993; Rogers Worthington, "Milwaukee Project Injects 'New Hope' for Poor," *Chicago Tribune*, March 13, 1994; Nick Chiles, "Milwaukee's Job Program May Be Model," *New York Newsday*, December 29, 1993.

18. Jack Norman, "Support Jobs Initiative Remains Strong," *Milwaukee Journal Sentinel*, September 18, 1995, and "Critics Attack Bradley Foundation's Role" (foundation accused of leaking information to damage the jobs program), *Milwaukee Journal Sentinel*, August 31, 1995; Mary Van de Kamp Nobl, "Gift Horse," *Milwaukee Magazine*, December, 1995 (in which Joel Rogers is described as "the brains behind Sustainable Milwaukee"); "Activists Vow to Rebuild Milwaukee," *Labor Notes*, January 1995, p. 8; interviews by author with Janice Nittolli of the Annie Casey Foundation, April 6, 1995, and Julia Lopez of the Rockefeller Foundation, June 8, 1994.

19. "Fighting for a 'Living Wage,' " *Labor Notes*, March 1996, pp. 1, 10; Steven Greenhouse, "Minimum Wage, Maximum Debate," *New York Times*, March 31, 1996; Louis Uchitelle, "Some Cities Flexing Fiscal Muscle to Make Employers Raise Wage," *New York Times*, April 9, 1996.

20. Madeline Janis-Aparico, Steven Cancian, and Gary Phillips, "Building a Movement for a Living Wage," *Poverty & Race* 5 (January/February 1996): 5–6, 10; Jean Merl, "Riordan Grudgingly Decides Not to Veto Job Protection Law," *Los Angeles Times*, December 8, 1995; *Organizing for Economic Justice and Neighborhood Revitalization*, Tourism Industry Development Council brochure, Los Angeles, n.d.

21. "Community Groups Join with Union," *Labor Notes*, June 1995, p. 2. Marc Levine, "A Nation of Hamburger Flippers," *Baltimore Sun*, July 31, 1994; G. P. Zachary, "New York Is Expected to Push Up Pay of Some Private Low Skilled Workers," *Wall Street Journal*, July 10, 1996.

22. Quoted in David Bacon, "L.A. Labor—A New Militancy," *Nation*, February 27, 1995, p. 276.

23. David Sickler, interview with author, April 23, 1998.

24. Mission Statement, LAMAP, February 16, 1994, p. 1; David Bacon, "Putting L.A. on the Map: How California's Immigrant Workers Are Revitalizing Labor," *Village Voice*, March 19,

1996; *Manufacturing in Los Angeles: Opportunities for Organizing* (1995), a thirty-page document with data that forms the basis of LAMAP's activities.

25. Bacon, "L.A. Labor—A New Militancy," p. 274.

26. Lawler and Olney are quoted in Mary Helen Berg, "Labor Leaders Aim Efforts at Immigrants," *Los Angeles Times, City Times*, October 30, 1994.

27. Joel Ochoa, "A Labor and Latino Alliance: The Future Is Now," mimeo, LAMAP, March 25, 1996.

28. Chris Benner, "Growing Together or Drifting Apart? Working Families and Business and the New Economy: A Status Report on Social and Economic Well-Being in Silicon Valley" (San Jose: Working Partnerships USA, 1998).

29. See *Perspectives on Partnerships: Corporate and Community Leaders Speak Out on Collaborative Strategies to Revitalize America's Urban and Rural Communities* (New York: Ford Foundation, 1996); Bennett Harrison, *Building Bridges: Community Development Corporations and the World of Employment Training* (New York: Ford Foundation, 1995).

Chapter 12. Public Policy

1. "Never before had the American working class asserted itself so decisively at the polls": David Montgomery, *The Fall of the House of Labor* (New York: Cambridge University Press, 1979), p. 435.

2. J. David Greenstone, *Labor in American Politics* (Chicago: University of Chicago Press, 1977), p. 38. "The CIO espoused a modern version of social unionism in which organized labor was envisioned as a force that would lead to the raising of the living standards of an entire nation": Kim Moody, *An Injury to All: The Decline of American Unionism* (New York: Verso, 1988), p. xiv.

3. Robert Bremner, *From the Depths: The Discovery of Poverty in the United States*, (1956; New Brunswick, N.J.: Transaction Books, 1992), p. 249.

4. Elizabeth Brandes, "Organized Labor and Protective Legislation," in *Labor and the New Deal*, ed. Milton Derber and Edwin Young (Madison: University of Wisconsin Press, 1957), pp. 196–97. Founded in 1904 and still active, the NCLC has always enjoyed substantial funding from foundations (it received grants from nine foundations in the decade that ended in 1993, for example). The United Automobile Workers and the AFL-CIO gave major support for several years.

5. Reynold Levy and Waldemar Nielsen, "An Agenda for the Future," in Research Papers III, pt. B, Commission on Private Philanthropy and Public Needs (Filer), *Giving in America* (Washington D.C.: U.S. Department of the Treasury, 1977), p. 1050.

6. Murray Edelman, "New Deal Sensitivity to Labor Interests," in Derber and Young, *Labor and the New Deal*, p. 189.

7. *Wall Street Journal*, October 30, 1991, credited Project Vote with surging voter registration in several large cities.

8. Julius Rosenwald, quoted in Brian Ross, "Paternalism in Action: The Origins of Cleveland's Federation for Charity and Philanthrophy," paper presented at the conference *"Private Action and Social Policy History"* Cleveland, September 14, 1989, pp. 37–38.

9. Mary Anna Culleton Colwell, "The Foundation Connection: Links among Foundations and Recipient Organizations," in *Philanthropy and Cultural Imperialism: The Foundations at Home and Abroad*, ed. Robert Arnove (Bloomington: Indiana University Press, 1980), pp. 433–34.

10. Quoted in *Responsive Philanthropy*, Winter 1996, p. 20.

11. John M. Murawski, "Report Blasts Foundations for Sitting on the Sidelines in Fiscal Debate," *Chronicle of Philanthropy*, November 2, 1995, p. 10. Liberal opinion on this issue is not uniform, however. Murawski quotes David Cohen, co-director of the foundation-assisted Advocacy Institute, who names several major foundations that are supporting valuable work in advocacy for the homeless, campaign-finance reform, environmentalism, and other public policy issues.

12. Peter Passell, "Basics of the Accord," *New York Times*, August 22, 1993.

13. National Network of Grantmakers, *Network Newsletter*, Winter 1994, p. 2.

14. Clyde Hufbauer and Jeffrey J. Schott, *North American Free Trade: Issues and Recommendations* (Washington, D.C.: Institute for International Economics, 1992); Hufbauer and Schott also wrote *NAFTA: An Assessment* for the IIE in 1993, a response to the anti-NAFTA arguments of Ross Perot. The IIE, established in 1981 with a grant from the German Marshall Fund of the United States, has a prodigious output of books and reports. The largest category is trade and competitiveness, which includes work on NAFTA and the General Agreement on Tariffs and Trade (GATT).

15. Thomas O. Bayard to Enid C. Schoettle and Thomas Trebat, August 8, 1990, p. 2, provided by Bayard to the author.

16. Ibid., p. 10.

17. *Memorandum—Summary of SVRI Latino Leadership*, Programming on NAFTA/Economic Integration, 1992–93 (San Antonio: SVRI), June 11, 1993, Ford Foundation Archive, New York City.

18. William Spriggs, interview with author, November 18, 1994.

19. John Cavanagh and Sarah Anderson, "History Counsels 'No' on NAFTA, and Europe Offers Practical Insight," *New York Times*, November 14, 1993.

20. Funding Report to the Norman Foundation, September 1991, from the Institute for Agriculture and Trade Policy. Mark Ritchie, executive director, describes the origin of the IATP as an effort to influence GATT negotiations.

21. "1993 General Support Proposal" (Chicago: Fair Trade Campaign, 1993).

22. Gabriella Boyer, interview with author, November 19, 1994; *Public Citizen Annual Report*, 1993, p. 3.

23. Sierra Club, "The Sierra Club Declares NAFTA Environmental Side Agreements Flawed," press release, August 23, 1993.

24. Don Wiener, interview with author, October 12, 1994. Thea Lee, who headed the EPI's work on NAFTA, believes that foundations' resistance was due to their "conventionally pro–free trade stance": interview with author, October 12, 1994.

25. Jill Abramson with Steven Greenhouse, "Labor Victory on Trade Bill Reveals Power," *New York Times*, December 12, 1997.

26. Edward Miller, interview with author, October 2, 1994.

Chapter 13. Union Democracy

1. Sarah C. Carey, "Philanthropy and the Powerless," *The Filer Commission Report* II (Washington, D.C.: U.S. Department of the Treasury, 1975), p. 1139.

2. Quoted from Reuther's preface to H. W. Benson, *Democratic Rights for Union Members: A Guide to Internal Union Democracy* (New York: Association for Union Democracy, 1979), p. v; Pete Hamill, "In Defense of Honest Labor," *New York Times Magazine*, December 31, 1995, pp. 18–19.

3. For a vivid account of union corruption and authoritarian rule in the late nineteenth and the early twentieth centuries, see Philip Foner, *History of the Labor Movement in the United States*, 2d ed. (New York: International, 1975), vol. 3, chap. 6, "Business Unionism."

4. Herbert Harris, *American Labor* (New Haven: Yale University Press, 1938), pp. 175–76.

5. *Minutes of the Eighth Meeting of the Committee on Labor and the Government*, Twentieth Century Fund, New York, February 19, 1938.

6. Summer Slichter to Evans Clark, January 29, 1943, files, Twentieth Century Fund.

7. Miners for Democracy Collections, boxes 15, 20, 24, 25, 83, "funding correspondence," Archives of Labor History and Urban Affairs, Reuther Library, Wayne State University, Detroit.

8. Kenneth C. Crowe, "Linking Democracy and Civil Rights: Union Reformers and Dissidents Find They Have a Home in the AUD," *Newsday*, June 12, 1994.

9. Thomas Geoghegan, *Which Side Are You On? Trying to Be for Labor When It's Flat on Its Back* (New York: Farrar, Straus & Giroux, 1991), p. 60.

10. The eight foundations that were defendants in the United Steelworkers of America suit (1978) were Community Funds, Inc., Field, J. M. Kaplan, New World, Ottinger, Rockefeller Family Fund, Samuel Rubin, and the Youth Project. For a detailed analysis, see *Union Democracy Review*, AUD Newsletter nos. 16 (November 1979), 23 (January 1980), 90 (October 1992); the Benson quotation is in no. 90.

11. Herman Benson, personal communication, September 17, 1992.

12. Kenneth C. Crowe, *Collision: How the Rank and File Took Back the Teamsters* (New York: Scribner's, 1993), p. 98: "The information and legal arm of Teamsters for a Democratic Union— the Teamster Rank and File Education and Legal Defense Foundation—received much of its funding from foundations."

13. Phil Sparks, interview with author, May 7, 1993.

14. Solomon Barkin, *The Decline of the Labor Movement and What Can Be Done about It* (Santa Barbara: Center for the Study of Democratic Institutions, 1961).

15. Dan LaBotz, "Solidarity Schools Link Study and Struggle." *Labor Notes*, March 1995, p. 5.

Chapter 14. Organizing

1. Workplace Partnerships USA, a labor-advocacy group, found that at least a quarter of the workforce in Silicon Valley firms are temporary or other so-called contingent workers. In October 1996, a federal appeals court ruled in favor of plaintiffs alleging that Microsoft Corp. had wrongly classified them as independent consultants rather than direct employees: Charles McCoy, "Temps Win Full-Time Benefits at Microsoft in Business Setback," *Wall Street Journal*, October 14, 1996. The temporary workforce is no longer the exclusive domain of secretaries and clerical workers, but increasingly includes bankers, accountants, engineers, architects, and others who can command more: Jeffrey L. Hiday, "As Temp-Employment Sector Changes, Workers Get Higher Pay, More Benefits," *Wall Street Journal*, November 8, 1996.

2. Karin Abarbanel, "The Youth Project: Seeding a Grass Roots Revival," *Foundation News*, November/December 1978, pp. 223–38.

3. Karen Paget, interview with author, October 7, 1994.

4. Charles Biggs, *Community Organizing: A Retrospective, 1970–1984* (Washington, D.C.: Youth Project, 1985).

5. Paget, interview.

6. Margery Tabankin, interview with author, March 10, 1997.

7. Tom Blanton, "Occupational Safety and Health: A Retrospective, 1970–1984" (Washington, D.C.: Youth Project, 1985).

8. Leslie Dunbar, interview with author, April 11, 1994.

9. Blanton, "Occupational Safety," pp. 7, 8.

10. Richard Bensinger, interview with author, March 30, 1994. In 1995, Bensinger was asked to address the annual gathering of the AFL-CIO Executive Council, waited through three days of meetings, and never got called to the podium. In 1996, under the new administration, Bensinger was the featured speaker at the opening session: David Moberg, "The New Union Label," *The Nation*, April 1, 1996. See also Richard Rothstein, "Toward a More Perfect Union: New Labor's Hard Road," *American Prospect* no. 26 (May–June 1996): 51–52.

11. Kim Fellner, interview with author, March 22, 1995.

12. Fred Azcarati, interview with author, March 20, 1995. JWJ works with local religious and activist groups around such issues as plant closings, strike support, and wage and benefit cuts, using such tactics as boycotts, work site demonstrations (including a disruptive bridge blockade in Washington, D.C.), and participation in legislative hearings. See also Jeremy Smith, "'Jobs with Justice' Activists Hope for Warming Relationship with AFL-CIO," *Labor Notes*, August 1996, p. 5.

13. Jeanine Appelman, interview with author, April 16, 1996.

14. Seth Borgos, interview with author, May 2, 1996.

15. "Characteristics of Workers' Centers," in Consortium of Independent Worker Centers brochure (El Paso, Tex., n.d.). The variety of worker centers is astonishing: in Boston, the Chinese Progressive Association won agreements to retrain immigrant workers in the face of a garment factory shutdown; in New York, the Chinese Staff and Workers Association demonstrated and won employment for Asian workers at two multimillion-dollar federal construction sites; in San Antonio, Fuerza Unida organizes and provides services to Latina garment workers laid off because of a plant closure; and in Rhode Island an Economic Justice project persuaded state agencies to provide interpreters for the sizable Portuguese population who deal with social service agencies.

16. Kirke Wilson, personal communication, December 12, 1993.

17. Quoted in David Bacon, "Putting L.A. on the Map: How California's Immigrant workers Are Revitalizing Labor," *Village Voice*, March 19, 1996.

18. Henry Allen, interview with author, March 7, 1996; Susan A. Ostrander, *Money for Change: Social Movement Philanthropy at Haymarket People's Fund* (Philadelphia: Temple University Press, 1995), pp. 23–27.

19. Martin Halpern, "The Labor Movement: Leader of Social Change or Just Another Interest Group?" paper presented at the 1993 annual conference, Association for Research on Nonprofit Organizations and Voluntary Action, Toronto, October 28–30, 1993, p. 23.

20. Peter Olney, interview with author, January 23, 1996.

21. Alfred Gilbert Belles, "The Julius Rosenwald Fund: Efforts in Race Relations, 1928–1848," diss., Vanderbilt University, 1972, pp. 108–15; Charles R. Wilson and William Ferris, eds., *Encyclopedia of Southern Culture* (Chapel Hill: University of North Carolina Press, 1989), s.v. "Southern Regional Council," by Anthony Newberry.

22. Newberry, "Southern Regional Council."

23. Emory F. Via, personal communication, May 5, 1994.

24. Paul Anthony to Basil Whiting and Clifford Campbell, July 29, 1968, Southern Regional Council Archives (1965–67), series I, reel 19, Woodruff Library, Atlanta University Center.

25. Via, personal communication, May 5, 1994.

26. Robert Hall, interview with author, April 11, 1994.

27. Leah Wise, interview with author, April 12, 1994.

28. Leah Wise and Cynthia Brown, "Women Forge Economic Justice Model," *Women and Foundations/Corporate Philanthropy Newsletter*, Fall 1993, pp. S1, 8.

29. Louis Uchitelle, "Union Goal of Equality Fails the Test of Time," *New York Times*, July 9, 1995.

Chapter 15. Prospects

1. Maurice F. Neufeld, "The Historical Relationship of Liberals and Intellectuals to Organized Labor in the United States," *Annals: American Academy of Political and Social Sciences* 350 (November 1963): 116. See also Peter B. Levy, *The New Left and Labor in the 1960s* (Urbana: University of Illinois Press, 1994).

2. News release, December 4, 1995, issued by Steve Fraser, Nelson Lichtenstein, and other signers.

3. Quoted in Steven Greenhouse, "Labor and Clergy Reunite to Help Society's Underdogs," *New York Times*, August 18, 1996. Two religiously connected foundations have long supported labor-related activities—the Catholic-sponsored Campaign for Human Development and the Unitarian Universalist–sponsored Veatch Foundation. Many labor organizers cut their teeth at Saul Alinsky's Industrial Areas Foundation, a training center for community activists, to which the Chicago Archdiocese was the first major donor.

4. David Smith, interview with author, October 28, 1996. The quotation is from "Proposed

Task Force on the Future of the American Labor Movement" (New York: Twentieth Century Fund, November 1995).

5. Steven Greenhouse, "Union Leader Urges Companies to Forge Alliance with Labor," *New York Times*, October 27, 1996.

6. Janet Hotch, "Common Interests," *Neighborhood Works*, November/December 1996, pp. 16–20. See also Wade Rathke, "The Call of the Streets," and Bill Wylie-Kellerman, "Unions/Communities," in "The Future of Unions," a reprint for the Democracy Project, from the *Boston Review* 21, no. 2 (April/May 1996) and no. 3/4 (Summer 1996): 6, 8.

7. "Charity and Labor Bump Heads over a State Welfare-Overhaul Proposal," *Wall Street Journal*, December 7, 1995; Glenn Burkins, "Unions Aim to Recruit Workers Entering Job Market Because of Welfare Overhaul," ibid., February 7, 1997.

8. E. S. Savas, "Welfare Reformers vs. Public-Sector Unions," *Wall Street Journal*, November 21, 1996; Burkins, "Unions Aim to Recruit Workers"; "Welfare Recipients Taking Jobs Often Held by the Working Poor," *New York Times*, April 1, 1997; "Workfare Rights," *Newsday*, April 20, 1997; Leah Samuel, "Workfare Workers Signing Union Cards in San Francisco," *Labor Notes*, August 1997, p. 1.

9. Stephen G. Greene, "Foundations' Shareholder Activism," *Chronicle of Philanthropy*, January 25, 1996, p. 25.

10. Bill Patterson, Teamsters' director of corporate affairs, quoted in Judith H. Dobrynski, "Board Members, Too, Are Getting Investor Scrutiny," *New York Times*, March 13, 1996, p. D1. This contrasts with the awkward situation of some union pension funds that inadvertently invested in nonunion firms or racially segregated housing. See also Stephen Viederman, "Adding Value to Your Grants," *Foundation News and Commentary*, January/February 1997, pp. 65–68. In 1997, the Union Labor Life Insurance Company invested in a $4 billion West Coast construction project expected to generate more than 100,000 union jobs during its ten-to-fifteen year term. The project was expected to include a community of office and studio space and 3,200 residential units, and restoration of wetlands in West Los Angeles (AFL-CIO, *Work in Progress*, [Washington, D.C., October 20, 1997], p. 1).

11. Lance Lindblom, personal communication, October 10, 1997.

12. Rich Ferlato (director, AFL-CIO Office of Investment), interview with author, October 9, 1997.

13. Christina Duff, "Better Census Data Show Income Gap Widening Fast," *Wall Street Journal*, June 24, 1996. In 1980, average CEO pay was 41 times average worker pay; by 1993 it was 149 times more (*Business Week*, May 11, 1981, April 15, 1994). See also Barry Bluestone, "The Inequality Express," *American Prospect*, no. 20 (Winter 1995): 81–93; Thomas Geoghegan, "The State of the Worker," *New York Times*, January 15, 1996; Alan Murray, "Income Inequality Grows amid Recovery," *Wall Street Journal*, July 1, 1996. Employees who lose their jobs earn less in new jobs; those who lost jobs in 1993 and 1994 and found new ones in 1996 earned 14 percent less than they had been making: *Wall Street Journal*, April 28, 1997.

14. Carnegie Corporation, *Annual Report*, 1960, p. 18.

15. John Sweeney, personal communication, September 2, 1993.

16. Orlando Patterson, Plenary Address, Columbia University Teach-in on Labor, October 4, 1996, in *Audacious Democracy: Labor, Intellectuals, and the Reconstruction of America*, ed. Steve Fraser and Joshua Freeman (New York: Mariner Books, Houghton-Mifflin, 1997).

17. "Newswatch," *Labor Notes*, November 1996, p. 4.

18. Ferris Harvey (International Labor Rights Fund), interview with author, April 22, 1998.

19. In a 1996 survey of salaries of the heads of nonprofit organizations, eighteen foundation executives were reported to have salaries over $200,000, excluding benefits; two had paychecks over $600,000, net of benefits. Deborah Blum et al., "Top Dollar for Charity's Top Leaders," *Chronicle of Philanthropy*, September 19, 1996, p. 1.

20. Peter Frumkin, personal communication, April 25, 1995.

21. Neighborhood Funders Group, mission statement: "NFG Establishes Working Group on Organized Labor and Communities" (McLean, Va., n.d.).

22. Comment in Wieck's "Proposed Study of Changing Trade Union Structure" (1942), in Papers of Edward C. Wieck, box 11, Archives of Labor History and Urban Affairs, University Archives, Wayne State University, Detroit.

23. Peter T. Kilborn, "Feeling Devalued by Change, Doctors Seek Union Banner," *New York Times*, May 30, 1996; Glenn Burkins, "More Doctors Set to Vote on Unionization," *Wall Street Journal*, November 19, 1996. The 5,000-member Union of American Physicians and Dentists, which seeks to be "a voice for those forgotten by giant health care corporations," voted to affiliate with AFSCME. AFL-CIO, *Work in Progress*, (Washington, D.C., September 3, 1997); Steven Greenhouse, "Podiatrists to Form Nationwide Union," *New York Times*, October 25, 1996.

24. Joan E. Pynes, "The Anticipated Growth of Nonprofit Unionism," *Nonprofit Management and Leadership* 7 (Summer 1997): 355–56. See also Tom Pope, "The New Gold Rush: Nonprofits Are Latest Unionization Targets," *Nonprofit Times* 11 (October 1997): 1.

25. Reported at conference of Working Group on Organized Labor and Community, Neighborhood Funders Group, New York City, October 19, 1997.

26. Thomas Geoghegan, *American Prospect*, no. 24 (Winter 1996): 72–74.

27. Edwin R. Embree, "Timid Billions—Are the Foundations Doing Their Jobs?" *Harper's*, March 1949, pp. 28–37. The quotation is on p. 32.

28. C. Wright Mills, "The Labor Leaders and the Power Elite," in *Industrial Conflict*, ed. Arthur Kornhauser, Robert Dubin, and Arthur M. Ross (New York: McGraw-Hill, 1954).

29. Frederick Mosher, a senior program officer of Carnegie Corporation, recalls that Donahue "was . . . very statesmanlike. . . . He made no special pleading for unions, unlike some minority and women members of our board who were advancing the interests of their constituencies." Mosher, interview with author, December 20, 1995. Donahue himself recalls that the board did draw on him for his knowledge of worker retraining: "I was a voice that often doesn't get heard." Donahue, interview with author, October 22, 1992.

30. About his service on the Rockefeller Foundation board, Kirkland wrote: "I dealt with all matters coming before the board . . . in exactly the same manner of other members . . . without regard to background, occupation or previous condition of servitude. I found it worthwhile and interesting. . . . No conspiracies that I am aware of were hatched; the board members and officers were serious and well-intentioned people; and the projects undertaken and funded by the Foundation did, I believe, make a contribution to the general welfare." Personal communication, November 25, 1992.

31. "Buying a Movement: Right-wing Foundations and American Politics," *People for the American Way Bulletin*, 1996, p. 8.

Conclusion

1. Quoted in "Labor Letter," *Wall Street Journal*, August 24, 1993, p. 1, from a speech by Gompers in 1893.

2. Jane Slaughter, review of Nelson Lichtenstein, *The Most Dangerous Man in Detroit: Walter Reuther and the Fate of American Labor* (New York: Basic Books, 1995), in *Labor Notes*, March 1996, p. 7.

3. Robert H. Zieger, *American Workers, American Unions, 1920–1985* (Baltimore: Johns Hopkins University Press, 1986), p. 160.

4. Mark Elliott, "Welcome to the Global Economy," opening address, Jobs and the Economy Conference, convened by Neighborhood Funders Group, San Antonio, Tex., February 1996.

5. Address before the annual conference of Independent Sector, Boston, October 24, 1995.

6. B. R. Barber, "Public Space for a Civil Society in Eclipse," *Kettering Review*, Fall 1995, p. 24. See also R. Madsen, "Contentless Consensus: The Political Discourse of a Segmented Society," in *American at Century's End*, ed. Alan Wolfe (Berkeley: University of California Press, 1991), pp. 458–59.

Index

Names asterisked (*) are noted in text as respondents to author's surveys of union and foundation officials.

DATE DUE

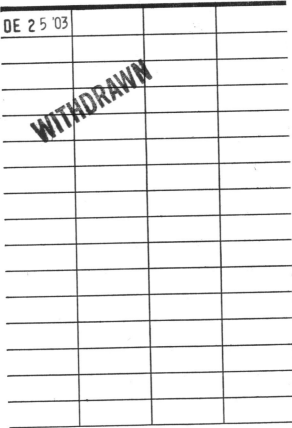

DE 25 '03			